American Men

Jordan Ritter Conn is the author of *The Road From Raqqa: A Story of Brotherhood, Borders, and Belonging*, runner-up for the 2021 Dayton Literary Peace Prize. He is a Senior Staff Writer for The Ringer and the host of the narrative podcasts "What If: The Len Bias Story" and "Sonic Boom," named by The Atlantic as one of the best podcasts of 2019.

AMERICAN MEN

JORDAN RITTER CONN

canelo
AUGUST

First published in the USA in 2026 by Hachette Book Group, Inc.

This edition published in the United Kingdom in 2026 by

August Books, an imprint of
Canelo Digital Publishing Limited,
20 Vauxhall Bridge Road,
London SW1V 2SA
United Kingdom

A Penguin Random House Company
The authorised representative in the EEA is Dorling Kindersley Verlag GmbH. Arnulfstr. 124, 80636 Munich, Germany

Copyright © Jordan Ritter Conn 2026

The moral right of Jordan Ritter Conn to be identified as the creator of this work has been asserted in accordance with the Copyright, Designs and Patents Act, 1988.

All rights reserved. No part of this publication may be reproduced or transmitted in any form or by any means, electronic or mechanical, including photocopy, recording, or any information storage and retrieval system, without permission in writing from the publisher.

No part of this book may be used or reproduced in any manner for the purpose of training artificial intelligence technologies or systems. In accordance with Article 4(3) of the DSM Directive 2019/790, Canelo expressly reserves this work from the text and data mining exception.

A CIP catalogue record for this book is available from the British Library.

ISBN 978 1 83598 562 5

Cover design by Albert Tang. Cover art by Amer Karic

Printed and bound in Great Britain by Clays Ltd, Elcograf S.p.A.

Look for more great books at
www.augustbooks.co | www.dk.com

For Noah

Introduction

Every Saturday night when I was in high school, I sat in a room with a half dozen other teenage boys, and I announced whether I'd made it through the week without masturbating. Usually, the answer was no. I was seventeen and impossibly horny. But whenever I could say yes, I felt like I was the strongest man who'd ever lived.

I understand that this ritual may seem odd, at least if you've never spent much time in conservative Christian circles. But my parents raised me to love Jesus. And what I learned, from the Christian schools I attended as a child in Atlanta and a teen in Philadelphia, the youth groups and the church camps where I spent weeks every summer, was that the best way for a teenage boy to love Jesus was to never ever lay a finger on his own penis.

There were exceptions, of course. Peeing. Showering, though you should make sure to scrub quickly and move on. But other forms of touching led inevitably to erections, and erections left you vulnerable to the siren's call of masturbation, and that, along with accepting hand jobs or blow jobs or, god forbid, sexual intercourse outside of marriage, was among the gravest of imaginable sins.

This small group of guys from my small Christian school gathered each Saturday night for "Bible Study." Rather than *studying* the *Bible*, though, we asked each other a list of questions, confessing how we'd sinned and advising each other about how to be better. I only remember a few of the questions. Did we lie? Did we gossip? Did we disrespect our parents or struggle with pride? Did we objectify or demean any girls or women? But all of those came after the first question: *So, uh, any of you guys jack off?*

I barely remember anything specific that was said. But I remember my desperate striving. I remember the torture of being left home alone with high-speed internet; the pain of beating my parents to the mailbox to grab the *Sports Illustrated* Swimsuit Issue but then heroically throwing it straight in the trash; the shivering while standing in yet another cold shower, where I waited for sinful urges to subside. And I remember how I learned to fear my own body.

That particular lesson wasn't restricted to the Bible Study. Everywhere I turned, then and for years to come, the same message: Your body is designed for destruction. I knew boys like me who were abusers. I knew boys like me who had been abused by men. In locker rooms and on bus rides to basketball games, I heard jokes about rape that sounded like they might not really be jokes. Sometimes I laughed and felt guilty. Sometimes I laughed and felt nothing at all. Puritanical theology taught me that my flesh was dangerous, and everywhere I looked, the world confirmed it. I became terrified of what I might do if I indulged the faintest desire. So I took the cold showers. I did everything I could to show up to that Bible Study each week and announce that I hadn't given in to temptation.

You'll be shocked to learn that as an adult I have spent thousands of dollars on therapy. Apparently it's difficult to spend years learning to hate and fear your teenage body, and then try to love that same body as a grown man. And yet, no matter how much I now disagree with the framework of those conversations at Bible Study, I still recall those Saturday nights as some of the best of my life. The strange thing about forcing yourself to confess your sins to your peers is that it forces you into the kinds of intimate conversations that young men so rarely have. Once we finished talking about our masturbation habits, we moved on to all the other ways we'd struggled during that week. We talked about our anger and our insecurities, our futures and our fathers. We pushed each other to treat our mothers and sisters and girlfriends with greater respect and care. Something was unlocked by the directness of these weekly conversations. We grew into a group of young men who actually cared about each other's inner lives. Perhaps more importantly, we gave each other permission to care about our own.

When I decided to become a journalist a few years later, I attended school in a place that promised the exact *opposite* cultural experience of my evangelical upbringing: Berkeley, California. On the first day of class, my tiny, terrifying professor told us to take the train into San Francisco's Mission District, interview ten people about their lives, and write a paragraph about each one by the end of the day. This presented a problem: I was afraid to talk to strangers. My entire life, I had been debilitatingly shy. I forced myself to get through the assignment, mostly by only interviewing bored-looking shopkeepers, and as months passed, things got easier. Later in the semester, I spent a day under a highway overpass, talking with the men who lived in its shadows about the traumas and addictions that had brought them there, and the ambitions they believed would lift them out. I talked with one of the city's most famous provocateurs and party hosts about his journey after a life of sex work on the streets of 1980s Manhattan. I spent months with a high school soccer team filled with children of undocumented immigrants, talking with them about their angers and their joys, the ways they feared for their families and pressured themselves to provide better lives for the loved ones who'd provided for *them*.

Journalism provided a kind of shield. I didn't need to feel social anxiety, because I wasn't there to *socialize*. I was there to ask questions unsuited for polite conversation. The kind of questions that I'd had to become comfortable with back when I'd been a teenager listening to my friends confess their sins. And what I realized, quickly, was that when you ask those questions, most people *want* to answer. They're just waiting for someone who won't recoil when they tell the truth.

In the decade and a half since then, I've built my career around asking people—the vast majority of them men—about intimate details of their lives. I've sat in a Las Vegas luxury suite with a retired NBA player, listening to his memories of childhood sexual abuse. I've stood in the pulpit of a snake-handling church in Appalachian Kentucky, talking to a pastor about why he continues to worship with the same poisonous snakes that killed his father. I've been in a tattoo parlor in West Palm Beach, where a man whose sister was murdered in a terrorist attack sat while her face was inked on his body. I've talked with soldiers left adrift by the end of their time in wars, with aging athletes facing the reality of the failure of their bodies, with men full of rage and regret, jealousy and love and desperate longing. When not writing about men themselves, I've written about women who'd suffered the effects of male violence—an activist speaking against rape culture in the years after she was gang-raped by college football players, mothers of Black children who'd been killed by police, a college athlete rebuilding her life after her father's suicide.

Nearly all of us inherit similar ideas about what it means to embody an ideal form of masculinity. Physical power over other men, sexual attractiveness, emotional steadiness, and the ability to support a family, to name a few. And all of us, at one point or another, fail to live up to that ideal. Achilles takes an arrow, Michael Jordan grows a belly, Albert Einstein watches younger minds overtake his own. For some, this failure arrives early in life. For others, not until middle age or even later. For most, it happens in fits and starts as we embody certain ideals in some moments and fall short of them in others. And our relationship to masculinity comes to be defined by how we navigate the gap between the men we think we should be and the men we actually are.

American Men is a book that explores that gap. I set out to chart how several men built their own relationship to masculinity and how they navigated that relationship over time. I wanted to tell the stories of friendships and relationships they'd built and sustained or lost; of traumas they'd suffered and how they'd tried to recover; of the ways in which they'd either inflicted or survived violence; and of their relationship to sex and to their own bodies, of what they've felt as those bodies carried them through the world.

I started reaching out to people I'd interviewed in my work, as well as to friends, and friends of friends, and friends of friends of friends. I began cold-messaging strangers on social media and bringing up the book to men and women I met on airplanes and in restaurants and bars. Every one of them could think of someone whose story felt relevant. Sometimes, that someone was themselves.

In Prince George's County, Maryland, I talked with a man who told me that every day he was afraid to go home. His grandson had been shot and was paralyzed, and the sight of that boy in a wheelchair reminded him of how he'd failed to make enough money to move their family to a safer neighborhood. In a dingy bar in a corner of Honolulu far from the lights of Waikiki Beach, I met a Korean American man who boasted of his American patriotism, even though he'd never once set foot on the mainland. He had one family on Oahu, another back in Korea, and often felt caught in between. In Youngstown, Ohio, I met a man who bragged about using his mob connections to order a prison hit on a convicted child molester. I talked with a fashion designer from Los Angeles who'd pledged a sorority in college but left it when other members helped him realize that he was not a woman, but a trans man. In Green Bay, Wisconsin, I met a man who introduced himself by asking me, "Where are the bitches at?," then alternated between hitting on me, lamenting the invisibility he felt as a bisexual man in the Midwest, and referring to his boyfriend by several antigay slurs—before he aggressively groped me when I told him I had to leave.

Some of these conversations have been thrilling and nourishing. Some have been deeply unpleasant. In all, the men I've encountered shared a hunger for someone to listen as they peered into the often-hidden corners of their lives.

During the process of speaking with men across the United States, I decided on the four whose stories are told in this book. First, there is Ryan. He grows up on the Akwesasne Mohawk territory straddling the border between upstate New York and Canada, the son of a longtime leader in his community. As a kid, Ryan endures beatings at the hands of older boys. As a man, he feels compelled to inflict that same violence on other men. All along, he struggles to reconcile his relationship to his own sexuality. He wants to love men and to brutalize them. To find a nurturing romantic partner and to exact vengeance on the kinds of men who tormented him in the past.

Next, there is Gideon, a West Point graduate and former pitcher, tall and handsome and intelligent, a paragon of white American masculinity. A man who gets whatever he wants, until one day, he doesn't. The wife he loves sleeps with another man. His fast-moving career grinds to a halt. A life so full of promise settles into stasis. A worldview is shattered, bringing him undone.

And then there is Joseph, a law student in the early days of his marriage, working to flee the lives he's left behind. In one he was an aspiring minister, preaching to young men the dangers of the flesh. In another he was a soldier, promised tuition for college in exchange for a year serving in the Iraq War. And then there's the life that most haunts him: that of a small child, growing up in a home of poverty and chaos, who's repeatedly sexually abused by a teenage boy.

Finally, there is Nate, a man whom the world once saw as a girl but who always knew he was a boy and never knew how to express it, until, as an adolescent, he discovers the existence of transgender men. Throughout his life, he fights to express his masculinity in ways the world will find acceptable, and sometimes in ways that it won't. As he struggles to seek health care for his transition, he also struggles with an even more daunting dilemma: Once you have the right beard, and the right clothes, and the right chest, and the right voice, then what, exactly, does it mean to be a man?

—

I've spent years with each of these men, talking with them and following them through their daily lives. I've been staggered by their openness and vulnerability, their ability to not only face but also to share their rawest moments. I started work on this book with the belief that every man's story is interesting enough to be told, if only he would dig deep enough into the uncomfortable parts of his own existence. These were the four men I found who were most willing to dig.

To honor their vulnerability, I've agreed to change some names and details to protect privacy. Gideon's and Joseph's names have been changed. For all four, I've changed the names of several other people in their lives, as well as a few small identifying details, to protect the privacy of those who were not a part of piecing together this book. In a departure from the rules I was taught back in journalism school, I've also allowed each of these men to read their own stories before publication. I wanted to write in a style that felt fully immersed in their individual experiences. To feel comfortable doing that, I needed to make sure they are represented in a way that feels authentic to each of them. I've spoken with other people in their lives for added insight and to confirm factual details, but this book is intended to be the story of these men's lives from *their* perspectives. No one else's.

—

I am writing this in a moment when men continue to wield enormous power across most major American institutions—government, business, academia, and religion—and a moment when that power has been wielded, in the aftermath of the Supreme Court's 2022 decision in

Dobbs v. Jackson Women's Health Organization, to strip women of their long-held right to abortion. Men also continue to commit the vast majority of violent crimes. According to 2019 FBI crime data, men commit about 88 percent of all murders in the United States in which the gender of the offender is known, and according to a 2018 analysis from the United States Sentencing Commission, men make up more than 92 percent of sexual abuse offenders.

Even as men continue to wield such (often destructive) power, this is also a moment when boys and young men lag far behind their female peers. Compared to girls and young women, boys and young men are more likely to drop out of high school and less likely to graduate from college, more likely to die by suicide and less likely to seek mental health care, more likely to abuse drugs and alcohol, and less likely to find romantic partners. It's a moment, too, when an entire ecosystem has arisen online for young men to air their grievances, a moment that has made stars out of aging men who tell younger men how to fix their broken lives. You're likely familiar with some of them: the podcaster peddling weird supplements and conspiracy theories, the YouTuber with ironclad rules for life. Or the truly vile, like the influencer who's been arrested for sex trafficking. And then their legions of imitators, all armed with ring lights and XLR mics, clamoring for space on the smartphone screen of your nearest seventeen-year-old boy.

And it's a moment when the White House is occupied by a man, Donald Trump, who once used a presidential debate stage to argue that he does not have a small penis, a man who suggested in an interview that he might date his own daughter, a man who boasted of grabbing women "by the pussy" and was found liable for sexual abuse, a man so obsessed with *winning* and afraid of being laughed at that he will pursue vengeance for even the most minor slights, and who seems to care only that the world see him as *dominant* rather than as good, or kind, or wise, or just.

For the purposes of this book, I'm not terribly interested in these men. Their misogyny is the same as the loud men with large audiences who lived years and even centuries before them. They're just using new technologies to repackage ancient resentments. I am, though, interested in what their collective rise reveals, something more deeply rooted and existential—in the inadequacies men feel but rarely speak aloud, inadequacies that travel across cultures and generations, that fuel isolation and self-loathing, violence and rage.

I am interested in the experience of my great-grandfather, a railroad machinist in Georgia around the time of the Great Depression, who used to chase his son with a stick anytime he caught him with a book, afraid of the weaknesses revealed by a love for the written word. And I'm interested in the experience of my grandfather, who survived those beatings and rejected his father's demands that he learn to work with his hands, instead becoming a preacher and author and the president of a small college, but who also became dependent on the praise of strangers. And I'm interested in the experience of my father, who as a young man rebelled against his family's dictates of masculine excellence, slipping into homelessness and addiction as a teen before returning to the family script in adulthood, and then pursuing a career in science with a kind of self-obliterating focus that pushed him until there was no new measure of success for him to chase.

I'm interested in the experience of my brother, a charismatic and heavily tatted six-foot-three man living in Brooklyn, a twentysomething whose interests include sports betting, vaping, and video games, but also a social worker who helps the most vulnerable members of New York City, and who has worked to heal his own traumas. And I'm interested in the experience of my son, a toddler now, who will come of age in a time when today's bro podcasters and YouTubers have long been forgotten, when Trump is just another ex-president, when our cultural conversation around masculinity has evolved into some altogether different form. When that time arrives, though, he will still be left trying to reconcile the same internal tensions that lived in the men from generations before he was born.

—

When I talked to men around the country about the gap—the one between our inherited masculine ideal and the men we actually are—a few of them refused to acknowledge its existence. They told me about all the *other* men they knew who clearly struggled with insecurities, but insisted that they themselves had never had any reason to think about this stuff, pointing to the businesses they'd built or the women they'd attracted as proof of their ability to float above any pressures to meet a masculine ideal.

Other men I spoke with made it clear that they lean all the way in, telling themselves that if they just work hard enough to optimize themselves, eventually they'll actually meet all of the standards, all of the time. Take a trip through a young man's social media algorithm, and you'll find purveyors of the "Alpha Mindset" and the "Warrior Mentality"; entirely new realities promised by the right formula of circuit training or supplement stacking; treatises on the hidden benefits of bulletproof coffee or semen retention or a daily breakfast of cottage cheese; advice on the right way to turn attractive women into puddles of desire who will pine for the texts you'll wait the exact right amount of time before you send. All of these messages feed the goal of amassing more wealth, more power, and more sex and say little, if anything, about why men feel the need to chase all of this in the first place, and about what they might find if they searched for the roots of these ambitions.

Some men acknowledge that the masculine ideal is beyond their reach, and so turn insular and angry, often blaming women for setting an impossible standard. In 2014, a young man in California killed six people and injured fourteen, targeting the kinds of women who'd ignored him and the kinds of men who received their affection instead, and leaving behind a manifesto attributing his personal loneliness to the structures of an unjust sexual economy. Four years later, a Florida man, who'd posted angry YouTube videos blaming women for his own isolation, walked into a yoga studio and opened fire, killing two women and injuring five other people. These examples are extreme, but they're born out of a collective male rage that's evident in the online harassment that bombards any woman with a public profile in any field.

Of course, men have used their power to dominate and subjugate women for as long as men and women have been alive. But the rate at which misogynistic rhetoric now spreads can feel shocking. Inadequacy atomized into anger, distributed instantly to pocket-sized screens, consumed by millions of boys and men who feel *still more inadequacies* that can be converted into *still more anger*, restarting the cycle, again and again and again.

When faced with that same gap, most men, of course, manage *not* to become eternally consumed by their own rage. And women, after all, have spent generations battling the impossible expectations of their own gender, all without committing acts of mass violence justified by manifestos decrying the ways they've been mistreated by society at large. Whether consciously or not, most men simply move through life constantly recalibrating how we navigate the gulf between ourselves and the standard we've inherited, picking and choosing the masculine standards that suit us while eliding those that don't. Personally, I follow the advice of gym bro influencers by guzzling pre-workout and protein powders in perhaps futile attempts to build more muscle in my early middle age. I loudly announce that I have no idea how to fix the engine in my car or the wiring in my basement, as if by owning these shortcomings, I'm declaring that they don't matter. I cry easily and tell myself that the men who don't are the *actual* weak ones, because they're supposedly afraid of the emotion I embrace. I take pride in the fact that I can confidently navigate chaotic corners of the planet, but I feel no shame in the fact that I've never fired a gun.

The thing that connects me to the men in this book, and, I hope, the men in this book to other men in this country, is that we're all trying to navigate the same gap in our own ways. Ryan tries to torment the men who remind him of the boys who tormented him. When Gideon is estranged from his wife, he tries to win her back not because their marriage is worth saving but because he can't stomach the thought of "losing" to another man. When Joseph finds himself spiraling over the shame and horror that resurface from his childhood, he tells himself that his pain doesn't matter, that he just needs to keep working his way through law school, that the ability to earn more money will free him from the terrors living inside his mind. Nate was born into a different script, one of femininity, and he had to reject those ideals first before he could navigate his relationship to masculinity as a man who is five-foot-one, trans, Black, and poor.

Over these past five years, I've been asked the same question by many of the people I've told about this book: *What's your angle?* Mostly, I've said I had none. This is largely true. I've never set out to advance any argument about what masculinity should be. This book contains no bold proclamations or grand theories. I'm not concerned with redefining or reinforcing any ancient ideas about what makes a man.

But if there's anything I've found myself thinking more and more as I've worked on this book, it's that the gap—the one between the men we've been taught we should be and the men we actually are—*matters*. It matters to who we are as sons and fathers, to how we treat our spouses and friends, shaping in imperceptible ways our relationships to each other and ourselves. It mattered to my grandfather and my father, it matters to me and my brother, and it will matter to my son.

He is nearly two years old now, obsessed with monster trucks and musicals. When he dunks on his toy basketball goal, he thumps his chest in celebration. During nap time at day care, teachers have to shush him because he won't stop singing his favorite songs. He is largely unaware of the scripts that bind him to me and his uncles and grandfathers, that separate him from his mother and the other women he so deeply loves. Neither he nor I know the ways in which he'll contend with his future feelings of inadequacy, or how he'll be impacted by my own. But someday, many years from now, I hope he'll pick up this book and read about Ryan and Gideon and Joseph and Nate, about how they struggled with the same internal tensions that he will encounter as he grows, and that maybe, as he finds pieces of himself reflected in their stories, they will help him find his way.

Ryan

The recipe was simple, amaretto with sour mix and Sprite, the perfect drink before the drinks before Ryan first bludgeoned another man's face. He mixed them in Julieta's kitchen and passed them around to all their friends, and as they clinked glasses Ryan felt so very *adult*, more sophisticated than the kids in other dorm rooms, drinking vodka cran or Busch Light. The room was bright and buzzing, full of that Friday energy, and he rocked his head and shoulders to the sounds of Daddy Yankee and Tego Calderón. His hips stayed still, not yet warm enough to move with the rest of him, and he watched his friends sway, a whir of laughter and limbs. He thought about how lucky he was, to be drinking such grown-up cocktails at the beginning of a night out with such fun and beautiful friends.

In a couple of days Ryan would get on the road back to the Akwesasne Mohawk territory for winter break. It was dark on the reservation this time of year, way up on the Canadian border, and dotted with people who'd tormented Ryan from the first moment he could remember until the last moment before he escaped. But tonight he was still here, in Buffalo, celebrating. The fall semester of their junior year of college had just ended. Ryan passed his last exam in marketing and managed to survive his final turn in front of the class in rhetoric and speech. Now they downed their drinks and piled into his Pontiac Sunfire, and he drove them off campus and toward downtown, all the way to Chippewa Street, where they tore off their coats, rushing through the snow toward the thumping invitation of La Luna, the city's biggest Latin club.

He wore a black and tan striped shirt, dark jeans that fit perfectly around the thick mass of his butt and thighs. His hair was dark and gelled with fresh blond highlights. The club felt liquid, and he let himself melt inside. A couple of Captain and Cokes got his hips moving, just a little at first, until Julieta grabbed his hand and pulled him onto the dance floor, and that's where he vanished, lost in the tangle of bodies, imprecise but still perfect, sweating to the beat of salsa and merengue. He scanned the room and saw men move with confidence and grace, all of them. Julieta liked to say that if your man can't dance he can't fuck, and Ryan wondered, in the brief moments he let his eyes linger on the men around him, if maybe that was really true.

—

He never talked to them, of course. He wouldn't dare. Not unless he was saying "Excuse me" on his way to the bathroom or the bar. He just let himself be passed from Julieta to Maria to female strangers. The mirrors around the room had been warm and flattering on arrival but turned opaque with steam as the night wound on. And then, sometime around 3 a.m., began the rituals of the night's end. A last-call announcement over the loudspeaker. A rush of people to the bar, Ryan among them, for one last Captain and Coke, and then back to the dance floor after guzzling his final drink. And then, the hard stop. Music off. Lights on. The room jarred back into focus. An announcement that the bar was closing and all present needed to leave.

He barely noticed the commotion at first, just a few shouts above the hum of voices moving outside. A few heads turned, Ryan looked up and saw the door and the cold darkness just beyond it, and then to the right he saw Julieta's friend Gloria, short and round and ferocious, and she was shouting at the man who'd been shouting at everyone else just moments before.

Who knows what they said—slurred nonsense, fuck you asshole, shut the fuck up, go home you stupid bitch. Gloria approached the man and kept spewing venom—you fucking loser, get the fuck out of here—and then Ryan stepped in front of her and put his arms around her shoulders, like come on, turn around, let's go.

They started walking back toward the car when Ryan heard him.

"If she's going to talk like a man, let her fight like a man!"

In the moment, Ryan barely understood what the guy had said. He would piece together the rest of the sentence later, but for now, only a few words stuck out.

She. Man. Fight.

He's talking about me, Ryan thought. He's saying I can't fight. He's saying I'm a *she*.

He turned back around, squared up. "The fuck did you just say to me?" He felt his skin prickle, then burn, energy shooting through his body. He took another step, propelled by a rage he'd long felt but never unleashed. He felt a push, two hands to the chest, and he staggered back and nearly fell. He stopped, found his balance. And in the moments that followed Ryan realized something: Violence could be fucking awesome. You just had to be its instrument, never its victim. Ryan had spent years taking beatings. But right now, without thinking, he did what he'd long fantasized but never imagined he'd follow through on. He punched a man in the face.

Ryan would remember that the man was tall and thick, but in Ryan's memory he would have no race, no defining features, no face at all. Just a large casing of human anger, now stumbling backward. The man grabbed Ryan's collar as he fell, pulling them both to the pavement, and then Ryan kept going, knuckles on skin and bone underneath it, one blow after another, as many punches as he could throw, until the security guards grabbed his shoulders and yanked him upright and Ryan felt his arms go limp.

"We good?" the guard asked him.

"I'm good," Ryan said.

"Then get the fuck out of here."

He turned and headed back to the car, Julieta and the others alongside him, all of them whooping with equal parts thrill and horror, Oh my god, Ryan, what did you just do?

"How did he look?" Ryan asked them as he drove back toward campus. "Was he bleeding? Did I fuck him up?"

Bad, they told him. Yes, he was bleeding. Yes, Ryan fucked him up.

Ryan laughed as he drove, dropping the women off at their apartments, and the next morning he woke up and realized that he felt no pain in his hand or body, and he wondered if the fight had been real or a dream.

Gideon

It wasn't so much that his penis was small (he swore it wasn't), or that it failed when asked to perform (really, it never had), but rather, Gideon thought, in his quieter moments, usually while drinking gin on the couch next to his pit bull, Charlie, that anyone would be right to expect something more. *More*, after all, was the promise of Gideon's body. Excess in all directions. He was six-foot-six, taller than guys who were taller than guys who women approached in bars to say, *You're so tall*. And yes, he'd measured himself at seven inches (when hard, being a true grower rather than shower, another source of internal strife), and Google had told him this was more than adequate, but he still imagined women undressing him, admiring the slope of his shoulders and definition of his abs, before their eyes traveled downward and stopped, confused. *That's it?*

Relevant: His wife was leaving him. Or maybe he was leaving her. Or maybe they were clawing their way back to each other. It was still too early to tell. Her name was Caroline, and she was blonde and wild-eyed and nearly six feet tall, with beauty and confidence that most men found obliterating. Like him, she was a West Point grad. Like him, an ex-jock. Now, like him, an officer in the United States Army. Sometimes, people called her "GI Barbie." Gideon presented as a plausible Ken. Strangers often approached, not to thank them for their service, but to tell them how gorgeous their future children would be.

At least until a couple months ago. Now she had an apartment on the other side of El Paso, where they were stationed, and he was here, in the home they still owned together, pounding Tanqueray next to the dog they'd rescued and loved, watching John Wayne movies to keep himself from staring at the spot on the wall where their wedding portrait used to hang.

And so, eventually, when the dog began to snore and the gin did its work and John Wayne's righteous murders started running together on the screen, Gideon wondered about his dick. Namely, its size, in comparison to the other guy she'd fucked. Gideon was compiling a dossier, necessary for side-by-side comparison. He knew most of the relevant facts. Gideon was taller, but the other guy, Connor, was still a respectable six-foot-three. Gideon was leaner, chiseled, but Connor was stronger, beefy. Both were more than capable of making a woman like Caroline, towering and muscular, feel willowy and small underneath them. Both had been athletes at West Point. Gideon was a starting pitcher but not the ace. Connor was the fucking quarterback. Connor was a few years older, and he outranked and outearned Gideon as a result. There was so much, though, that Gideon couldn't quantify with available evidence. Who caused in her more bursts of laughter per minute. Who gave more intense orgasms. In whose presence her most vulnerable pieces felt safe. All of these comparisons were too complicated, measurements turned meaningless by impossible math.

A simpler measurement: Who was packing a bigger hog? This could be answered. Gideon would see to it. After weeks of no contact, he'd started seeing her again. It started with a text one night. She missed Charlie. She wanted to come by and snuggle her dog. And then she was there, back on their couch, her long blonde hair pulled into a messy bun, wearing the same *ARMY WOMEN'S SOCCER* sweatshirt and shorts she'd often worn since they'd met his sophomore year. Charlie welcomed her back, licked her face, and lay her head on Caroline's thigh. Gideon and Caroline caught up, a little awkwardly at first, until slipping into their shared language and recycling familiar flirtations, and finally she told him she'd been wondering something. Did he ever think they could be together again? Like, sexually?

Gideon hated what the question did to him. Desire and revulsion, an immediate certainty of which one would prevail. He told her he had to think about it. He wished that was actually true.

—

A few weeks after they started fucking again, Gideon told Caroline he needed to know everything that had happened between her and Connor. When did it start and where? How many times? Gideon craved an accounting of every lie she'd told, revelation of the horrible truths that lay underneath. Was this the reason the passenger's seat in your car was always reclined? When I went to the beach with my friends and you said you couldn't come because of work, was this the real reason why?

She answered him, calmly, dutifully, and he believed her. It helped some, to see her stare at the grotesque shape of her own betrayal. He felt closer to her then, like they'd stepped into shared reality. None of the answers, though, gave him what he really needed.

And so he asked her who was bigger, and she said what do you mean? Come on, he said. That's so fucking stupid, she said. But of course he knew that it was so fucking stupid, had known from the moment the thought entered his mind, had known on some level even years before that, from the first time he'd walked into the group showers at West Point and had seen small, stout men possessed of truly equine dong, spectacular displays of length and girth that caused him to wonder, *What does this say about* me?

He persisted. Who's bigger, he said, and she just shook her head and laughed as if entertaining the wonderings of a child, and Gideon didn't care, because he'd sunken to a place where he found no need for pride, only for the liberating clarity he believed her answer could give him.

Tell me, he said. Who's bigger? You have to tell me. Please.

Joseph

Several months before the visions overtook him, Joseph stepped on the gas of his gold Chevy Cobalt, windows down and wind whipping past him, and wondered if soon he might die. The thought didn't linger. Death, for the moment, was one of his more faraway fears. For instance, he also feared that he might have to call someone to whom he'd never spoken, or that he might find himself driving an unfamiliar road past dark, or, if things got really dire, that he might have to seek help from his dad. He was thousands of miles from his old life and thousands more from his next, and he most feared that he'd get caught somewhere in between.

His wife, Emily, sat next to him, unafraid and enthralled.

"Look!" she said.

Joseph did not want to look.

"Do you see the bison?"

Joseph knew there were bison out there, somewhere, because bison were everywhere at Yellowstone National Park. They'd been driving the north loop of the park all day, over its bald hills and through its endless valleys, and around every bend Emily grew increasingly delighted, devouring the world with her senses.

"Look!" she said again, and so now Joseph looked, quickly, and he supposed that the bison were indeed massive and majestic, and so he said, "Wow," or something like it, but he must have said it too gruffly, or without the proper sense of wonder, because then she asked the question he'd dreaded. "Is everything okay?"

"Oh yeah," Joseph said. "Everything is fine."

Everything was not fine. Joseph returned his eyes to where they belonged: the dashboard. His vision flitted from one gauge to another, searching for meaning in numbers and blinking lights. He and Emily had a problem, even if she didn't know it. Their car, Joseph realized, was making a funny noise. Something between a rattle and a constant ping, a little metallic, a light but ominous trill. He listened for a while, and it was faint but unmistakable. After a few more minutes of driving and exclamations of "Oh, wow" to humor Emily, he finally broke his resolve.

"Hey," he said, trying on an even lighter tone. "Do you hear that noise?"

"What noise?"

Joseph explained. The rattling. The pinging. Emily said no, she didn't hear it, or perhaps she said maybe, but in a tone that indicated she didn't really, or maybe she even said yes, but her yes indicated that she didn't think the noise was a big deal.

The noise was a very big deal. But if Emily didn't think so, Joseph wouldn't tell her. Best not to worry her. He let her eyes return to the bison so he could return his to the dash, and he pushed the button that let him cycle through all the car's levels in greater detail. And then he saw it, the thing he'd feared. The engine was 230 degrees. He knew this was bad because he studied the engine's temp constantly, enough to know it typically ran between 200 and 208.

"Hey," he said to Emily, and here he took a breath to slow down his speaking, to soften his tone and sound as casual as he possibly could. "The engine's running a little hot. Can we turn the heat on and roll the windows down?"

Emily barely even shrugged. "Okay," she said.

The heater would pull heat off the engine and into the cabin where it would flow out the windows. Maybe *this* would make everything okay.

"When are we stopping to see the geysers?" she asked, and Joseph said he'd seen a sign that a few were up ahead. Emily nodded and looked pleased. He looked over at her. She had sunglasses on and her bare legs stretched out before her, pale and muscular, her brown hair waving in the wind, face serene.

For Joseph, this was simultaneously enraging and comforting. Enraging because she didn't understand that they were about to break down, that no one would help them, and that the last few dollars in their bank account wouldn't cover the cost of the engine if it blew. She didn't get that this meant he might have to call his father and ask for money, and that his father would give it to him even though he had little more than

Joseph did, but that the money would come with the message that his father had been right after all, that law school and Seattle were both too expensive, that Joseph should have settled down somewhere near them in Alabama and gotten himself a normal and stable job.

But it was comforting because she didn't care.

They reached a line of cars, and Joseph braked. They rolled to a stop. The rattle quieted. "Oh, my gosh," Emily said, and she pointed up ahead to a group of grizzly bears romping with one another in a nearby field. They were astonishing, the mass of them, the implicit threat they carried. Joseph found himself awed, and he sat there for a while, looking on in wonder, suddenly not even the slightest bit afraid.

Eventually, the bears wandered off. The cars up ahead started moving. Joseph pressed the Cobalt's gas pedal. The rattle started back up again.

―

He was going to law school. It had been a simple decision. His mind craved order; his heart craved justice; both could be found in the law. His dad had flunked out of college and only returned as he neared the age of fifty, but all Joseph's life, his father had gone on and on about the importance of education, desperate for his kids to earn what he lacked. Joseph had finished high school and wasted a few years, some of it partying and waiting tables at Applebee's, some of it leading worship at church and selling Bibles at a Christian bookstore. And then he'd joined the US Army Reserve and followed his pastor's advice by enrolling in a good Christian college, an *expensive* Christian college. He'd made his way toward a degree using the GI Bill and tens of thousands of dollars in student loans.

And now here he was, heading off to become an attorney. He was ready. Before he'd even been accepted to law school, he'd started scouring Seattle's neighborhoods. He'd found low-income housing in a nice building on Capitol Hill, an apartment close enough that he could walk to class, convenient enough that they could even buy groceries without needing their car. In the months before the move, he'd lost full afternoons to Google Maps Street View, dropping himself into the city and wandering around. He would click on the arrows like he was driving down every road, until he knew which way to turn to pick up coffee or take the dogs to the park, how to cross the downtown's busiest one-way streets, how to handle the tricky merge when I-90 connects with I-5. He liked to tell people that he never went somewhere he'd never been before, and this was what he meant.

The whole trip, he'd been ready for everything. He mapped out every day—Charlotte to Nashville to Kansas City to South Dakota and on to Montana, this quick dip into Wyoming to see Yellowstone, then on to Central Washington for their last night before they arrived at their new home. He'd studied highways and exits, planned each day's drive with the proper mix of efficiency and leisure. And Emily, he loved her, but he had to say this because it was true: She'd spent the entire trip fucking everything up.

First of all, she wanted to stop and see every possible attraction. In South Dakota alone, she had insisted that they stop at Wall Drug, a tourist shop in the style of the Old West, and at the Corn Palace, which was, as suggested, a palace made of corn. She found these places delightful. Joseph found them fine. Both stops cost them at least forty-five minutes of driving time. Second, she always had to pee. Like, at least once every four hours, which to Joseph seemed outrageous. She would make him pull off the highway and into the parking lot of a gas station or a McDonald's, and then she would disappear inside, and sometimes it would take far longer than it should ever take a person to use the bathroom. Joseph would text to make sure she was okay and he'd hear her phone ping, right next to him in the car where she'd left it, and then he would worry. What if she took so long that there was traffic when she returned, and they didn't make it back to the highway and on to their destination by the time his schedule *clearly* mandated they arrive? Or if she took a *really* long time, he'd start to think that she was in danger, that someone was attacking her, and so he'd rush out of the car and into the gas station, and there he'd see her, walking casually to the door and saying, "What? There was a line." Joseph never peed in public. The toilets were too unsanitary, and the act of pulling out his penis next to strangers left him feeling overexposed. Instead, he just avoided liquids all day and then hydrated and peed at their hotels at night. This was simpler. Emily should do it too.

Even with all of that, they'd been fine. They made it all the way to Wyoming, well past halfway. This rattling, though, represented something different. This was a problem he hadn't worked hard enough to prevent.

Emily perked up.

"Do you want me to drive?" she asked.

"That's okay," he said.

"I like to drive," Joseph added, and this was true. But he couldn't tell her that she couldn't drive because if she drove their lives would be ruined. She had driven, days ago, for a couple of hours somewhere in Kansas or South Dakota. Joseph had tried to keep his eyes on the dashboard from the passenger's seat, but he just couldn't quite see all the gauges, not even when he leaned his seat back and pretended to be napping so he could get a better angle. Her hair and shoulders blocked his view. And so then he asked, once or twice, if she would tell him what the temp gauge said, and she did, kindly and accurately. But that wasn't enough. He supposed that he could let her monitor the gauges on her own, that she could let him know if anything seemed off. Actually no. He didn't suppose that. That was preposterous.

If he asked her to monitor the gauges, then he would have to say out loud that their car might be *really* giving them problems. That it wasn't just a little casual overheating but something truly dire, something that would leave them stranded miles from nowhere, broke and hungry, stuck in a place where not even Joseph could come up with a plan. If she knew that, he was certain, then she would finally understand the truth: Joseph could not keep them safe. So no. She would not drive. She would stare out the window. And he would check gauges and map out the exits and play images of each possible disaster in his mind.

Most married people needed their spouses, but Joseph liked to think she needed him more than others. They'd first dated in high school, briefly, but then they'd broken up for a while. Later, they'd attended the same college and reconnected. She'd told him she wanted to be single, and that lasted until the first time she saw him on campus looking comfortable with another woman. That was when she decided she didn't want to be single anymore.

They fit. Both grew up poor, but she grew up poorer, the daughter of an absent father and a mother who did a lot of drugs and slept with the men who sold them. Sometimes her home was violent. Other times it barely felt like a home at all. Still, she'd emerged from poverty and neglect to become one of the world's truly special people, someone who radiated warmth and goodness, the emotional weathervane of every room.

She could have dated anyone at their college. But she'd chosen Joseph. He was handsome, pale with dark hair and darker eyes, and he was funny in the way that she was funny, direct and dry, leaving strangers unsure whether or not he was joking. She cherished independence, now rid of the town and the family that had hurt her, and she feared commitment, but still, in Joseph, she found comfort. His dad had been a minister and his mom a small business owner, and to her they seemed like the American ideal, which is to say that they seemed like they were nice (debatable) and nonviolent (false). And they were not divorced (true!).

A person like Emily should be taken care of, protected, and provided for. And so that's what he'd done, what he would continue to do. He would be the one to make sure she was always okay. He would finish at the top of his law school class so he could pay for their life and her dreams. And whether she knew she needed it or not, he would be the one to keep her safe. And that meant checking the damn gauges.

—

Joseph had to admit something a few days later. This was after they'd stopped and seen Old Faithful, which was gorgeous, and after they'd left Wyoming and driven through Montana and northern Idaho, then into Washington, and crossed the Columbia River Gorge, with the car still rattling and the engine temp nearing 240 as they finally approached Seattle late on a bright clear Tuesday morning. He had to admit that the car was fine.

Like, really, totally fine. The engine had been running hot, sure, but that's just what engines do at elevation. There had never been reason to worry. A few weeks later, when Joseph took it in for an oil change, the mechanic couldn't find a single thing wrong.

The panic, though, had lingered. All along the road toward Seattle and into their new home. Often it hid in some corner of his mind that Joseph couldn't reach. Sometimes it hid behind awe, such as on the drive through the mountains and into the city, the sun reflecting off the skyline, an entire metropolis nestled between tranquil water and jagged earth. Sometimes the panic hid behind excitement, such as on day one as a 1L student, as he sat in the orientation and heard about the subjects he would soon master, surrounded by people in whom he recognized a shared hunger. And then, here and there, the panic broke through to the surface: when the dogs got sick, and the vet bills mounted, and their savings dwindled from meager to no savings at all.

Through it all he carried that relentless churning, a buzzing and shape-shifting energy, euphoria one day and fear the next. They wandered the blocks near their home, which looked just as they had on Google Street View. Joseph delighted in giving Emily precise directions to anywhere she wanted to go. She carpooled to work; he walked to school. They were thousands of miles from anyone who truly knew and loved them, but the dangers of the open road had vanished.

Isolation sharpened them. Joseph spent twelve hours each day in class or in the library. He found joy in his textbooks' pages, a genuine thrill in every class. Every morning, Emily rode with a colleague to the hospital where she worked as a social worker, and she returned home every night with new stories, some of them devastating, others thrilling. They'd fled past lives and past pains, and had reemerged here in the Pacific Northwest to encounter new parts of each other and inhabit new versions of themselves.

—

Those were the early days, before the visions started. The first one arrived on a Friday in October. It was evening, maybe sometime around eight, after they'd both exhaled the weight of a long week. Joseph had found himself spending more time in the library as the semester wore on. He had to. No matter what people thought about the salaries of lawyers, only a fraction of graduates from his program emerged making six figures. Many started at $60,000 or $70,000 a year, huge chunks of which went back to paying off the massive debt they'd piled up to earn their degree.

Still. Emily and Joseph had their Friday date night. The routine was the same, always. A Tombstone frozen pizza. A six-pack of Dos Equis. Stories from each other's week. And then, eventually, sex. No matter how stressed, Joseph always set aside time for this ritual. No matter how broke, they found a few bucks for pizza and beer. Their weeks pulled them apart, but date night brought them back together. He couldn't imagine a life without this anchor; he felt its familiar pull as every week wound toward its end.

This night unfolded the same as always. Joseph downed the first beer on an empty stomach, quickly, and then half of the second, so that while the pizza warmed in the oven he felt a buzz. Emily shed the week's stresses, taking a few minutes for her mind to leave the hospital and arrive fully in their home. They ate and they laughed, and Joseph cracked a third beer and drank it, until he felt himself dissolving fully into the present. Soon they kissed, warm and familiar. A shirt slipped down a shoulder. A belt unbuckled. They rose and walked together to their bed, naked in the dark.

The vision arrived when he was inside her. He didn't understand it. Not then, or for many months to follow. They moved together, hips adjoined in motion, and then he saw it, right there in front of him, near the top of his field of vision, just a little off to the right. A penis.

What the fuck, Joseph thought.

His chest contracted. His breath left him. Her hair smelled good and her skin felt soft. He kissed her and he ran his hands over her body and the penis remained there. He knew it existed only in his mind but he could still somehow see it with his eyes, and so he closed them and did his best to stay in the moment.

What the fuck.

He knew this penis. Vision was memory. Part of him was here in Seattle, and part of him was in a strip mall in Florida. Part of him was thirty years old, and the other part was eight. He was clinging to his wife's body, here in their bedroom, and he was paralyzed, cornered in a dark room he hadn't seen in decades, confused and afraid.

He stayed with it, with her. They moved together, and soon he came and then rolled over onto his back. He stared at the ceiling. The vision was gone. She lay next to him, smiling. She kissed him and he kissed back. He stared at the ceiling a little longer. Everything, he told himself, was going to be just fine.

Nate

Eyes open, the world dark, a gentle tremor in his leg. This was every morning: a moment of confusion, unsure of the time, maybe four or maybe seven, deep black inside his room, the gentle patter of his Chihuahuas trotting down the hall. Nate never needed an alarm clock. His body was incapable of sleeping late. The cluster seizures arrived early most mornings, tiny convulsions in his limbs, one after another, just a few seconds each. Most days, they were gentle. Nate took an anticonvulsant to limit how much his body would shake.

He got up and opened the door and the dogs rushed in, ravenous and demanding. He walked downstairs to the kitchen, his footsteps light so as not to wake his mom or her husband, and he fed the dogs and felt a cold blast of winter Ohio air as he let them outside. He put on a pot of coffee and drank it with cream and sugar, and he lit some incense to watch it burn. The small glow soothed him. He sipped and stared, inhaling the scent and watching the ash as it fell. He put on a hoodie and a coat and walked outside into the cold. He knew that if he left the house at 6:54, he'd make it to the corner store by 7, the moment they opened their doors.

He lived in the town of Warren, Ohio, a suburb of Youngstown. Once a hub of the steel industry and organized crime, Youngstown had been in steady decline since the late 1970s. Even as Youngstown faded, though, its outlying towns remained. Nate didn't mind it here. The people were kind, the Italian food excellent. On the right night, in the right restaurant, locals would still tell old stories about the mob.

Nate didn't go downtown much, not anymore. He couldn't drive because of the seizures, couldn't Uber because it was expensive, couldn't take the bus because it rarely came. So instead he tended to stay here, walking from his home to the corner store, and sometimes to the mall about a mile farther, occasionally to buy clothes from one of the outlets, usually just to see something besides the wall of his room or the screen of his phone.

Today he bought a Pepsi at the corner store and stayed a few minutes to talk with Miss Carol, the old lady who ran it. She told him stories from her second job at the liquor store in Giant Eagle, and every now and then she referred to the "Black girl" who showed up every day to buy tiny bottles of Wild Irish Rose. Nate tried not to think about why she insisted on calling her that—"Black girl"—tried not to imagine what she said to other people when she was talking about him. Miss Carol was sweet. She always smiled, sometimes told him he looked nice. Every now and then she recommended a new kind of malt liquor they'd just gotten in stock. Nate didn't have enough money for booze right now, though. His disability check was almost gone, and he always gave his food stamps to his mother. The number in his checking account had fallen to double digits, the number in savings a clean zero. He smiled and thanked her and started walking home.

That's when he started feeling nervous. A light buzz in his belly, spreading upward and outward, stretching to his chest and his shoulders, a gentle vibration in his fingers. When he got back to his room, he looked in the mirror, inhaled, and studied himself. His beard looked good, growing full beneath the chin and nearly connecting to the mustache that framed his lips. He had a little acne on his face, but it was under control now, and besides, he'd had that long before he'd started his transition. His jawline looked sharp, his chin jagged. When he took off his coat and his hoodie, he could see the muscles in his shoulders filling out. He craved that V-shaped torso, and he was almost there, at least in lowercase. He'd come to accept that he would always exist in lowercase. Nothing would stretch him any taller than five-foot-one. Still, in the mirror he saw a man and a miracle, someone he'd always been but had still never believed could exist. He exhaled, slowly.

Every other week, the same process. Incense burning, laptop open and playing a familiar show, *The Legend of Korra* or *Avatar: The Last Airbender*, something he'd liked as a child, back when he couldn't imagine finding the courage to live as he lived now. Something soothing. He washed his hands, then disinfected the needle and his belly. He grabbed his abdomen, a finger length away from his belly button in any direction except for down or up, and then the plunger, a small cylinder that sucked in a small piece of his skin. He heard a click, and then the needle pierced his flesh and the testosterone entered into his bloodstream, slowly transforming him more fully into the man he wished to be.

—

Now what?

That was the question that inevitably arose, on testosterone day and on every other day of his life. Existence, right now, seemed an endless series of *now-whats*.

He'd spent his entire life, from a confusing childhood through a traumatic and destabilizing adolescence and on into adulthood, wrestling his own body, and then fighting for its right to exist in the world through which it moved, and the entire time, every single day was marked by the same obsession: to do whatever possible to grow into a man. These had been his prayers when he was five, begging God from the bed where he cried at night and wiped his eyes with the sleeves of pink pajamas. This was his ache as a middle schooler, watching transmasculine YouTubers who boasted of a freedom and joy he believed could never be his own. This was his methodical work, starting gender therapy and buying breast binders, getting a prescription for testosterone and scheduling top surgery, searching the sound of his voice for drops in register, the pores of his cheeks for stubble, the faces of strangers for signs that he could pass.

And after all of it: *Now what?* At age twenty-eight, his gender identity was largely settled. He encountered no hostile stares when he walked into a men's bathroom. Cashiers and servers defaulted to calling him *Sir*. But he was unemployed and hadn't had a job in more than a year. He was poor, drawing $280 a month in food stamps, about $900 in disability for his epilepsy and its attending anxiety, and nothing else. He was stuck, unable to travel beyond where his legs could take him. He was celibate, or at least had been for the past year, and not by choice. And so he was, and he could admit it: very deeply depressed. For now he crawled back into bed, pulled out his phone, and began to scroll. Endless memes and videos distracted him from the question that sat atop the growing mountain of *now-whats*.

He was a man. He knew it, and so did everyone else that mattered to him. But settling that question now felt easy. In its place had emerged another one, larger and more shapeless: What kind of man was he going to *be*?

Ryan

Once Ryan felt the first crack of his knuckles on a stranger's skull, that night outside the Latin dance bar in Buffalo, he wondered when he might feel it again. It wasn't a craving, exactly. More a curiosity. He'd beaten up one man. He wondered if he could do it again. He encountered strangers and found himself sizing up their shoulders and traps and quads, mentally measuring their height and weight and reach. Before, when he'd gone out to bars, he'd always walked away the moment he'd heard an aggressive edge in someone's voice, but now he found himself lingering, getting closer and closer, creating an opportunity for their anger to land on him.

He came, after all, from a long line of brawlers. He was born in 1981, raised on the Akwesasne Mohawk territory, on the border between New York and Canada. The day he was born, the skies opened up, new shades of blue blurring into each other to create colors no one in his family had ever seen. And so his grandmother named him Karoniatens, after a Mohawk word meaning "Deep Blue Skies." This was how it worked. A matriarch bestowed a name on a child soon after birth, a name no one else on the planet could call their own.

They had nine clans, three each representing land, air, and water. His father came from the wolf clan but his mother from the bear clan, and they passed their lineage through the women, so Karoniatens became a member of the bear clan too. Before the European colonists arrived, they had never taken surnames but were known only by their Mohawk title. Now they lived in a world dominated by their colonizers, and so some generations back his father's family had taken the last name King, and now they passed down English names along with Mohawk names. For all of his life, people would know him not as Karoniatens, not for the skies that opened up on the day of his birth, but rather, simply, as Ryan King.

He'd grown up hearing about his grandfather's bravery serving as a code talker for the US Army in World War II, about his father's mastery in the boxing ring, where he'd won multiple New York Golden Gloves championships. And here and there, he'd overheard conversations about what happened after his father hung up the boxing gloves and picked up the bottle, about the nights when he and his brothers had left the local bars with strangers' blood on their fists, laughing the next day as they reminded each other of what everyone on the reservation should have already known: You do not fuck with the King brothers.

As a boy, Ryan had seemed like exactly the kind of boy you *did* fuck with. On a progress report, his kindergarten teacher, a sweet blonde woman named Miss Kelly, once wrote, "I'm very concerned that Ryan likes to play with dolls." This was true. He loved dolls. In his classroom they kept the toys stashed in different corners, and Ryan tended to float from the dinosaurs to the dollhouse. The dolls were gorgeous, a perfect-looking Native family, and he liked to make the doll mother tend to her doll baby and imagine the contours of their perfect doll lives. Of all the dolls, he loved the baby the most. The texture of it, soft rubber between his fingers, the fine strands of her dark hair. He could take her in his palm, and he could pet her with his fingers, soothing her when he imagined her crying, delighting in her when he imagined her giggling.

He was six the first time they jumped him. Older boys from his neighborhood. Ryan barely knew them, not even their names. He stepped off the bus and that's when he felt the first impact, a fist to his face, and then he lost his vision and felt his face burning, the hot rush of tears. Another fist landed immediately after, and then still more, and he crumpled on the ground. Then they kicked him, one after another, until finally they left him there alone.

He stood. He tried to run but felt that his breath had left him, desperate gulps of air going nowhere as his legs struggled to carry him home. He approached his house, with its off-white siding, sitting just feet away from the St. Regis River, and he felt desperate to fling himself into the arms of his mother. But as he reached home, he saw, instead, his father working in the yard.

"What happened?" his dad asked.

Ryan was too lost in his own tears to get out a full sentence, but his father could see the scrapes and cuts on his skin.

"Come with me," his father said.

Ryan followed him inside the house and down to the basement. His father picked up two boxing gloves and held them out to Ryan. They swallowed his hands, but he tried to hold them upright. His father grabbed him by the shoulders and squared him up to face the heavy bag.

"Hit it," he said.

Ryan hit the bag. His father told him to hit it again, harder, and to shift his weight onto his back foot and explode forward with everything he had. To hit with his right and his left and then his right again, faster now, and harder too, until Ryan stopped—and his father told him no, he could not stop, because when he stopped hitting other boys, they would not stop hitting him.

Ryan didn't want to learn to fight. He craved comfort, not instruction. But his father told him to keep going, again and again, and in his voice Ryan heard an urgency, a desperate pleading to hit the bag harder, and he felt, then, that his father's concern came not from a fear of what might happen to his son if left unprotected, but from shame at seeing up close the utter weakness of the boy he'd tried to raise.

—

The boxing lesson didn't help. That was just the first beating. Now that he'd gotten his ass kicked once, word got out. Here was a boy ripe to be dominated, a classmate so weak he could make even the mediocre bullies feel strong. He would wilt, and that would make the beatings easier; he would cry, and that would make them funnier. He would return to school the next day with his eyes cast to the ground, trying to disappear.

One word tended to accompany the beatings, wrapped in between every third or fourth punch. *Faggot*. From older boys or same-aged boys, white or Mohawk boys, on the bus or in the park or in the hallways after school. Ryan heard it everywhere, but he didn't really know what that word even meant.

One day, a few years after the first beating, when he was nine or ten, he watched a movie with his Aunt Denise. He loved Aunt Denise. Known around the rez for her beauty and her toughness, she was the kind of woman men fawned over but whose attention few ever earned.

Her voice was loud, her laugh louder, and whenever Ryan went to her house, she let him eat and do whatever he wanted, no questions asked.

On this day, that meant watching an R-rated movie, *Revenge of the Nerds*, in which a group of college outcasts wage war on their frat-bro bullies. One character caught Ryan's attention. Lamar Latrell. He wore bright and colorful clothes and spoke with an upturned lilt, and he didn't seem to walk so much as to prance, demanding the attention of everyone in his orbit.

Ryan was curious. "Why is he like that?" he asked.

Aunt Denise laughed. "Because he's a faggot," she said.

Oh, Ryan thought. Now it made sense. That's what they meant. That's who Ryan was. As he watched, he studied Lamar Latrell, trying to figure it out: *What is it in me that makes me like him?* He thought about the tone of his voice, the movement of his hands, the way he smiled as if holding a secret. And he decided then that he would tuck those pieces of himself away and make sure they never emerged again.

Gideon

The boy in the photo was too young to smile, still just a newborn, but already he stared at the camera, joyous and serene. Those baby gray eyes, wide and searching. The curve of his mouth sloping into the soft dough of his cheeks. In the photo he wore a christening gown, all white, and anyone who picked up the oval wooden frame and studied him came away with the same reaction. Oh my god. What an angel. *Look*. Just look at this beautiful boy.

"Who's that?" Gideon asked, looking at the baby picture sitting on his parents' bookshelf. And then his parents told him. This was his older brother. His name was Jackson. He'd been born right around Father's Day, a few years earlier, and then he'd died just eleven weeks later. An accident in the crib while at home with a babysitter. They missed him, they said. They thought about him every day.

Later, Gideon's grandmother told him more of the story. After his brother's death, Gideon's parents had spiraled. Fights, drinking, drugs. Cursing God and each other and themselves. Until one day, just a few months later, when his mother's body began to swell. A doctor suggested she end the pregnancy. Whatever substances she'd ingested might have done irreparable harm. But she refused, and then a few months later, weeks before the due date, there Gideon was, brown-eyed and voracious, screaming his way into the world.

"You know," his grandmother told him, "almost every couple who loses a child ends up getting divorced."

But not Gideon's parents.

"You saved them," she said.

From then on, this was the single defining fact of Gideon's life. His birth had saved his parents' marriage. His very existence on this earth was the reason his family was whole.

When his parents signed him up for pee wee football at a park in their Atlanta suburb when he was five years old, the coach took one look at Gideon and put him on the offensive line. On the first snap of the first game, Gideon casually trampled the boy placed before him, and then on every subsequent snap he trampled that boy again. On the car ride home, he told his parents that he didn't like football. He was scared he would hurt someone. But no, they told him, this was good, this was the point.

Later, he switched to baseball. While other boys flailed pitifully in the vague direction of the small white ball, Gideon's limbs seemed to understand the game's rules before his brain did, his massive body gliding across the diamond, fluid and sure. When he turned nine, he started playing in a league that allowed children to pitch, and the moment he stepped to the mound, he realized he was better at pitching than he'd ever been at anything else in his life.

Which was saying something. He'd tested into the gifted program starting in the first grade, sang solos in his school choir, and beat his classmates in footraces at recess every single day. But pitching, this was something else. He threw harder than anyone on his team, accurately enough to get three strikes against almost any hitter he faced. Other parents asked to see his birth certificate, certain this giant couldn't be nine years old. But Gideon no longer worried about hurting anyone. Hitting their bodies would require missing the plate. Gideon rarely did.

Besides, as he got older, he became more acutely aware of the ways he damaged the pride of other boys. By the time he reached high school and started playing on a club travel team, he'd found new ways to entertain himself when simple dominance came so easily that it bored him. Sometimes he would announce to the catcher that he wanted to call the pitches for a particular at bat, and then he would signal, pitch by pitch, exactly what he was about to throw—glove down with the tip up for fastball, glove open and facing up for a curve, a pushing motion to signal a changeup. All in plain view of the batter and the crowd. And then he would proceed, calmly and methodically, to earn yet another strikeout before walking back to the dugout and staring down the batter as if to say, *I told you what was coming, and you still can't do shit with me.*

After Gideon, his parents had other children, two girls and a boy. Gideon knew that his parents loved his younger siblings, of course, but he also knew they existed in his own shadow. Large men carry their own gravity, and Gideon felt his growing by the time he reached middle school. At home, an entire family was devoted to helping him throw strikes. His dad had never played baseball, but he taught himself the fundamentals of the game and coached all of Gideon's Little League teams. Every day after school, they practiced together in the front yard. At games, his mom wore a bright blue shirt, and she told him that anytime he saw that flash of blue fabric he should inhale deeply, relax his shoulders, and remind himself that all of this was just a game.

Which was true, he supposed. Baseball is, technically speaking, a *game*. But it felt like something more when his coaches told him that in order to be great he had to make sacrifices. Vast swaths of summer vacation and spring break were swallowed up by travel tournaments, year after year. It felt like something more when he began to crave the praise he received after dominating on the mound, each swing-and-miss or scoreless inning inviting reminders that he held worth in this world. When he reached high school, Gideon moonlighted as a shot-blocking center on his high school's basketball team and the goalie for his soccer team. *Those* felt like games. Baseball felt like his entire reason for existing.

Some weekends, he and his dad piled into Gideon's decade-old Ford Escort, and they drove hours to showcases across the country, invite-only events where elite talent pitched in front of college and pro scouts. Gideon packed a bag with a glove and balls and cleats, and they stopped along the way for sunflower seeds and Big League Chew. He waited his turn and stepped to the mound to show what he could do. He had a four-seam fastball and a two-seam fastball, both of which lived in the high 80s but vacationed into the 90s from time to time. He had a decent changeup that he could mix in to throw hitters off-balance. His curveball was shit, but at least it was something. He usually threw well, but he understood that on some level, that hardly mattered. Coaches would get excited the moment they assessed the look of his body. All coaches imagined themselves masters of their craft, able to mold raw potential into something more refined. Gideon *looked* like a pitcher. That's what mattered most.

After a few of these showcases, Gideon started getting personalized letters from college recruiters. Coaches wanted to schedule phone calls and visits to Michigan, New Mexico, and Illinois State. He imagined futures on campuses in states he'd never seen. One day, he opened a letter and saw big black letters with gold trim, and in all caps, one word: *ARMY*. Gideon didn't even read it. He immediately dropped it on the kitchen table to be thrown away. His mother stopped him.

"What are you doing?"

Gideon shrugged. He did not want to join the army. He wanted to go to college and play ball.

"This isn't what you think it is," his mother told him. This was not some generic letter encouraging him to enlist. This was a recruiting letter from the United States Military Academy at West Point.

"Read it," she said.

Nate

Here is a boy. Wild and curious, six years old, skinny and shy. He has a name, but he won't keep it. He wears pigtails and dresses, but he won't keep those either. He loves basketball, even though he is short. And he loves sprinting, because he is fast. At school, he smokes the other boys in footraces. From the swing set to the fence, on your mark, get set go, and he is flying, always pulling ahead while they watch from behind. Afterward, he smiles, and he laughs as he walks back to the other kids, panting just a little, and he hears them taunting the race's loser. *Dude, you just lost to a girl!*

About that. *Girl* is how the world sees him. The ultrasound technician first, he will later imagine, when he thinks about how he was given this designation in the womb that never seemed to fit. His mom and dad next, both excited to have a daughter. His dad would call him *my baby girl*. His mom would teach him to contour his makeup, extend his lashes, and care for his nails.

Does that make this chapter of life a *girlhood*? You could call it that, he supposes. He doesn't mind. Girlhood was assigned to him based on chromosomes and anatomy. He gets it. What else were they supposed to call him? And during this chapter of childhood, he answered to a girl's name, wore the clothes his mom declared pretty. But this can't *just* be a girlhood. Because if boys are small children who grow up to be men, then doesn't he need a *boyhood* too?

This is how he'll come to see it: He was always a boy and he was once a girl. Those two truths don't have to contradict each other. One life is vast enough to hold both. Here was a boy: masculine in demeanor, desperate to run around with his shirt off in the summer, to wear tank tops and boxer briefs as training wheels for growing into the clothes of a man. But here, too, was a girl: reluctantly wearing the lacy dresses his mom bought him, responding to that feminine name. He inhabited both genders simultaneously, one in private, the other in the way he knew he must present to the world. He was fluent in *Girl* but at peace in *Boy*. It would take many years before transitioning unburdened him from performing the gender that had never really been his own.

—

He will always remember the moment he began to understand these contradictions. He was maybe five years old, playing at his grandmother's house. She watched neighborhood kids while their parents worked, all day in the summers and after school the rest of the year. He was there on a slow summer day, right around noon, the Ohio air languid and thick. His cousin Danasha was with him, and their friend Austin, who was a couple years older, chubby and loud, always smiling.

They were outside, digging in the dirt together. They looked at centipedes under magnifying glasses. They snapped sticks and used them to drum on the rocks. And then they got up and started running around the yard, chasing each other, fast and aimless, until Austin stopped, doubled over and breathing heavy. He took his shirt off, wiped off his own sweat, and started running again. And then Nate joined him, ripping off his own shirt and running wild through the yard too.

"Hey!" His grandmother yelled, and here she called him the feminine name everyone called him back in those days. Nate heard that name and he stopped. He looked in her direction, unsure what he'd done wrong. She put down her can of Milwaukee's Best, the beer she sipped on the porch from morning to evening, day after day.

"You can't do that, baby," she said, her tone not chiding but sweet.

Nate pointed at Austin.

"But he took *his* shirt off," he said.

His grandma nodded.

"I know, baby. But he's a boy. You're a girl. It's different."

Until this moment, he'd never realized that it was *different*. Yes, he understood that there was a word for some of his friends, *girls*, and a word for others, *boys*. He understood that Daddy was a man and Mommy was a woman. But these were just words for people he loved. They held no larger meaning, no attachment to any rules. Now he knew a rule: Boys could take their shirts off. Girls could not. Nate was a girl.

At night, Nate liked to pray. He'd been going to his grandma's church on Sunday mornings and Wednesday nights. They ate snacks and made art and listened to stories from the Bible. That's where Nate learned how to talk to God. And so on most nights, when he got into bed, he lay with his eyes closed, and he prayed that God would not let his mommy or his daddy or his grandma die.

On this night, he lay there in the dark on his twin bed, in sheets decorated with pastel flowers, listening to the fan as it whirred. He had a small TV on in the corner of the room, which he left playing Cartoon Network, the volume down but not mute, just enough noise and color to make him feel less alone.

"God," he said, and he pressed his eyelids together to shut out the light, "when I wake up, please make me a boy."

This became his prayer. Every single night, for years. Most nights, it felt routine. He just wanted God to keep his family safe and to please turn him from a girl to a boy. Some nights, it felt pleading. He would lie awake, staring at the ceiling, asking God what is wrong with me, why am I broken, please just fix me, please. He never heard any answer. He never felt any comfort. But he still believed he had to ask. He cried and pleaded just to hear himself cry and plead.

In between, he went about his life. His mom worked, changing jobs every few months: running a cash register at Arby's for a spell, working the floor at the furniture outlet for another. For a while, she worked as a nail tech. She loved to bring Nate in, show him how to apply polish and press on acrylics. She'd tell him that he could do this work someday if he wanted. His daddy stayed home, at least during those years when they were together, and he took care of Nate most days.

In the mornings, they sat together in the living room, and they watched Mister Rogers and *Sesame Street*. "You're gonna learn something today," his daddy told him, his voice deep and engulfing. He held close to the son he thought was a daughter, leaned into his ear, and pointed at the TV. "Just watch."

Sometimes, while they watched, his daddy would do Nate's hair. His daddy was Black, and his mommy was white, and Nate learned early on that this distinction mattered greatly when it came to his hair. Nate felt safe there, his daddy's hands working his scalp, twisting his curls together until they formed thick smooth braids. Sometimes, they went out to the garage and Nate watched his daddy work on cars. Once, his daddy turned their kitchen into a classroom, laying Tupperware on the ground to explain how the planets of the solar system orbited the sun. Nate was astounded by his father's brilliance, awed that one man could braid hair and fix carburetors and teach him lessons from the vast reaches of the universe. He hoped that someday he might be like that too.

That was before his daddy left. Around the time Nate was eight, he noticed that his father was never home anymore. As it turned out, he'd met another woman. She was blonde and skinny, and his daddy liked her better than he liked Nate's mother, who was redheaded and thick. He was going to have a baby with the blonde lady. And just like that, he was gone. Nate went to visit, but it never felt the same. Usually his dad wasn't even there. He just left Nate to watch TV with his new girlfriend and her kids. Sometimes, he was out in the garage lifting weights. Nate noticed his dad's body changing, growing thicker and stronger. He seemed like someone who could be a protector. But he wasn't very interested in protecting Nate anymore.

Now, Nate spent his days playing computer games in his room and hanging out with his mom. She was a titan of a woman, tiny and loud, a dominant presence in every room she entered. When he walked with her through the store, he noticed that men's eyes followed her. They came up with excuses to make conversation with her, and to ask if she was single, which she often enough was.

He watched his mom date a string of men. All were big and deep-voiced, often aggressive. One was violent. Jonathan. He'd been so gentle at first, a boulder of a man who giggled like a small child. Nate was in middle school when Jonathan started coming around, and they liked to smoke weed together. Nate's mom tried to make him stop, but he'd started suffering from anxiety, and he told her the weed helped. So she relented. Sometimes, he and Jonathan would smoke and play Xbox, killing bad guys on a screen, or sometimes they liked to smoke and jam, Nate on the guitar and Jonathan on the drums. On special nights they would smoke and cook together, salmon and risotto, Cajun shrimp and rice, absolute feasts served for Nate's mom and for Jonathan's younger kids who now lived in their home.

But sometimes Nate got scared. Jonathan was relaxed on pills and a little sleepy on booze, but unhinged when he took them together. He never touched Nate, but some nights Nate listened as Jonathan beat his own boys: the thump of kicks to ribs, the clunk of heads bouncing off the floor. Nate wanted to grow into the kind of man who would defend children, who would put a stop to this kind of abuse. Jonathan was massive and often enraged. Nate was tiny and afraid. So instead he just ran to his room and cried.

Once, Nate sat with his mother while she called the police. "This man is beating me," she told the dispatcher. "He's beating his children. Please help us. Please." But when the doorbell rang, they listened as Jonathan's buddy from the police force stood at their front door.

"Someone called us," he warned Jonathan. "We don't know who it was. Watch your back, though. Someone's out to get you."

Nate and his mom left Jonathan in the dead of night while he was passed out drunk and high. His mother had rushed into Nate's room and told him to pack everything in a suitcase, *now*. In the car she showed him new bruises on her neck. Before when he'd noticed the bruises, she'd lied to him, saying they were just hickeys, "love marks." Now, she told him the truth. The bruises came from the times Jonathan choked her until she thought she was going to die.

—

They moved to a town called Struthers, where Nate's mom had a place through the federal government's Section 8 housing program. Here, the lawns were tidy. The schools were sprawling. The sidewalks had no cracks. Living in Youngstown, where most of his peers had been Black, Nate had never fit in. He had watched anime and listened to metal. He'd gotten pushed around on the basketball court with the boys, but felt hesitant to play hopscotch with the girls.

Sometimes, he'd told himself this was because of his mixed race. Maybe the new, largely white school would be better. Nate was excited. For one, he no longer had to wear a uniform. Nate hated the pleated skirts and stockings his old school had required of him and all the girls. On the first day at his new school, he dressed the way he wanted.

A metal band T-shirt, baggy black jeans, Osiris skating shoes. He walked through the front door and felt he'd entered another dimension. All around him were pretty white girls, twelve-year-olds dressed as twenty-year-olds, sundresses and miniskirts, full makeup, some even with artfully placed glitter on their cheeks and around their eyes. The white boys, wearing polos and jerseys and Jordans, were running wild through the halls. Nate felt a surging panic. He searched frantically for anyone who looked more like him, whether in style or skin tone, but he found no one.

He felt a hand on his shoulder. Nate turned around and stood face-to-face with the most beautiful creature he'd ever seen.

"Hi," she said.

"Hi," he said.

"I'm Maria."

Maria wore a lavender dress and immaculate makeup. She had straight black hair and light brown skin. She smelled even better than she looked.

"Hi, Maria," Nate said. And then he introduced himself by the girls' name he'd been given at birth.

Maria looked him up and down, studied his jeans and his T-shirt, the chain connected to his wallet. She seemed perplexed but curious.

"You could be so pretty if you tried," she said.

"Oh," Nate said. "Thank you?"

"Don't worry," she said. "Come with me."

Joseph

So there was this dick, appearing in his vision, while he was in bed with Emily on that night a few months after they moved to Seattle. After that night, it kept coming back, appearing whenever they had sex. The dick, unfortunately, presented a couple of problems. First, Joseph did not enjoy seeing any dick but his own while he lay in bed with his wife. Second, and more importantly, he did not enjoy seeing this *particular* dick, which he'd recognized the first moment he saw it. And third, he *really* did not appreciate everything that came along with the dick's appearance: the increased sweating, the pounding in his chest, and the desperate need to *stop* having sex with the love of his life, because removing his body from hers seemed to be the only way to make the dick disappear.

All of it was a bit of a hassle. Incredibly annoying. But still, Joseph was fine. He had everything under control. He understood what was happening. Apparently, long ago, Joseph had suffered a trauma. He hadn't consciously realized this until recently, because, for most of his life, the memory of the trauma had been repressed. But now the memory had come back, in full force. He'd told his buddy Alex about it, and Alex, who worked as a therapist in a psych hospital, explained what was likely going on. Sometimes the brain becomes overwhelmed by traumatic memories, and it tucks those memories away someplace where the conscious mind can't access them. And then, sometimes, later in life, some kind of trigger or event brings the memory flooding back.

And here was the real bitch of it, the frustrating thing about repressed trauma: He never knew when, exactly, he'd repressed it. At some point, in the immediate moments after he'd been abused, Joseph probably remembered that it had happened. The fact of the abuse likely sat in his mind for days or weeks, maybe even years, until his mind decided that it could no longer contend with all the ways the memory wreaked havoc on his body and spirit. And so his mind had placed the memory far away, which meant that for many years, Joseph moved through the world as someone with no idea that he had been sexually abused at all.

–

Here, though, is what he'd always remembered about his childhood: He remembered how his father had beat his mother, with venom and routine. How they'd moved though their Central Florida house as if choreographed, ceramic cracking against dry wall, appliances fashioned into weapons and furniture into shields. Who knew why, maybe his mom had spent too much money or challenged his dad in public or had the gall to mention one of his many affairs. He remembered how they'd descended on him once, when he was about six, while he sat still on the bench of their piano. His dad rabid and his mom sobbing, they'd each grabbed one of his arms, let's go, we're gonna be late for church, absolutely not, you're dangerous, you're not taking my son anywhere. His dad's grip felt strong. His mom's hair felt soft. They touched him so rarely that it felt kind of nice there, in between them, each of them clinging to his body while they screamed.

He remembered the stress over money. His dad worked as a music minister, and then, after he got fired from the permanent job, as an interim music minister, and then as a bail bondsman, and then an EMT. For a while his mom ran a ceramics shop and taught ceramics classes. None of it paid much. He remembered that they couldn't afford anything Joseph asked for. Cereal, snacks, shoes, toys. When his class went on field trips, his parents couldn't manage the twenty-dollar fee. Once, Joseph's teacher asked the class where they'd gone for spring break, and their answers ranged from Los Angeles to Vail to Belgium. So when it came to Joseph, he said he'd been to the Bahamas. When his teacher called his parents to ask why they'd had enough money to go to the Bahamas but not enough to send Joseph on a field trip to Tallahassee, his parents grounded him for lying. Money, or rather, its lack, fueled most of his parents' fights. Joseph learned never to ask for anything. A request for a trip to the Space Museum could lead to a bowl flying at his mother's head. He wore his shoes until they had holes, his shirts until they showed his belly. He dribbled his basketball until it went completely flat.

In middle school Joseph turned insolent and angry. He refused to do his homework, and his parents were too oblivious to make him, so his grades plummeted, but he refused to care. Only later would he wonder if this had been a reaction to the abuse. He remembered that in those years his church became the only place he felt safe; he studied scripture with kids who liked him and adults who never hit anyone or screamed. By high school his life revolved around youth group and basketball. He was small but quick, with a decent jumper and good instincts, and even as a freshman he sometimes got to sit on the varsity bench.

He remembered moving from Florida to Alabama later that summer, after his freshman year. They rented a small house out in the country, and the kids at his school drove trucks and wore boots and spoke with an accent that Joseph struggled to understand. On the first day of school a kid asked if he wanted to fuck the girl sitting in front of him, and Joseph said no, he did not want to do that, and so then that kid and his friends started calling Joseph a faggot. They also called him a Jew, for reasons Joseph couldn't figure out. But he realized that at this school *Jew* was an insult, and so he said that he couldn't be a Jew because he hated Jews. He felt bad about that response then, and he would continue to feel bad about it for decades to come, but afterward they always called him a Jew instead of a faggot, and somehow that didn't feel quite as bad.

His father's beatings of his mother slowed down over the years, which made it all the more unnerving one day when Joseph arrived home from school and walked through the front door of the house and felt that familiar quiet, punctured only by the clacking on the family computer's keyboard, his dad playing Tetris with ferocious intensity at 3 o'clock on a Wednesday afternoon. And Joseph knew, the moment he heard the force of the keys being clacked, that that was the day the beatings had resumed.

He walked into his parents' bedroom and found his mother crying, and he felt the nausea and anger rising, each one feeding the other, as he returned to the living room and saw, in the garnet and gold Florida State Seminoles trash can sitting next to the computer, a massive clump of human hair. He asked his father what he'd done, and his father just shrugged as if nothing existed but the keyboard and the screen and the Tetris blocks before him. He hissed every time he missed clearing a row.

And then his mother walked down the hallway, and Joseph saw that the right side of her head was bald. What the hell did you do, he shouted at his father, only to be answered with more clacking and hissing, more Tetris rows clearing, and Joseph's anger erupted into its final form. He pushed his father out of his chair and told him to leave and never come back, and he remembered how his father stood wordlessly and grabbed his keys and his wallet and walked out the front door. That weekend, Joseph rode with his mom to his Mee Maw's funeral, telling her that it would all be okay, that he would get a job and take care of her, she didn't need to worry, and she told him he was sweet, thank you, and then a couple days later his father showed up at the front door. He was sorry, he said. He'd spent some time talking to the Lord. He knew he needed to change. So he moved back in. The beatings actually stopped, then, as far as Joseph could tell. No one ever spoke of them again.

Joseph floated through high school, aimless and meandering. He did fine on tests but refused to do homework. He became a leader in his youth group, preaching on Sunday nights about the dangers of lust and the necessity of daily time spent reading the Bible, and he found a spot on the outer edge of the cool clique, the kids who were disruptive during class and cursed in the halls. He got asked to prom by a girl named Amy—pretty and nice, from a turbulent home—and even one of his teachers told him you gotta go with her dude, she's *definitely* a good time if you know what I mean. But instead Joseph asked a girl named Ruth—pretty and nice, devoted to Jesus. When Ruth told him no and he asked her why, she said, "Because you're mean." Joseph wondered if she was right.

Through all of this, Joseph never knew, at least consciously, how he'd been learning to adapt to a world in which he'd been abused as a little boy. The world he understood was just the one right in front of him. In this world, he graduated from high school with a 1.8 GPA and no clue what to do next. He registered at the local community college but never showed up for a single class and forgot to withdraw, finishing the fall semester with straight Fs. He picked up a job waiting tables at Applebee's and hung out every night with the manager, an Indian immigrant named Girash who poured Joseph his very first alcoholic drink, a Miller Lite in a ten-ounce frosty mug. As Joseph drank it he prayed to God for forgiveness, begged the Lord to prevent the beer from hurting his stomach, to protect him from the consequences of his sin.

He remembered getting over that quickly. Soon he started staying after shifts several nights a week, drinking lightly, terrified of what might happen if he got drunk. Until one day Girash invited him to Tuscaloosa for the Alabama-Tennessee game, and on the way to the stadium Girash handed him a thirty-two-ounce souvenir plastic cup filled with ice and Crown Royal. Joseph finished it, and by the time they arrived he had begun to feel a little wobbly. Hours later, after Alabama won, he found himself still buzzed, screaming alongside tens of thousands of fans, and some hours after that they ended up at a house party hosted by a stranger, and Joseph did his best to help drain the keg, including a keg stand, his very first, electrified by the strangers around him all cheering. Later that night he struck up a conversation with a woman, and light conversation turned to heavy flirting, and well past midnight she stood up and announced that she was going to bed, and Joseph said I'll go with you, for he believed this was the natural and normal thing to do, but when he stood up to join her he immediately fell down face-first onto the coffee table, where he slept for several hours. It was only the next morning that Girash told him that he had never flirted with the woman in question, only mumbled incoherently in her direction, but that he had indeed smacked his head on the table and passed out.

―

All along, Joseph kept preaching and leading the youth group on Wednesday nights in worship, teaching them how to live for God's glory. He was good at it—smart, charismatic, able to draw connections between scripture and the teens' daily lives. You're gonna be a pastor someday, his pastor told him, and Joseph liked this thought, because no one had ever told him he was going to be anything before. At first, he felt no tension between the partying and the preaching. Jesus loved sinners. He had, after all, turned water into wine. Besides, Joseph had spent his entire childhood watching his father lead worship on Sunday mornings after beating up his mom on Saturday nights. Surely Joseph could show up with a mild hangover, and God wouldn't mind.

But that was before he piled up $10,000 in credit card debt, most of it on clothes and booze. And it was before he registered for another semester of classes and actually showed up for the first day, but then never went back, and before he left Applebee's for a job at Structure, the men's clothing store, but got fired for shoplifting.

And so, sometime in the spring almost a year after he graduated from high school, he remembered walking into the office of an army recruiter and saying he might like to join the reserves. The recruiter promised him money for college and the chance to shoot .50-caliber rifles and maybe even launch grenades. Joseph was sold. A few weeks later he showed up for basic training at Fort Jackson. He ran six-minute miles each morning and did push-ups under verbal assault from short men with thick necks in camouflage hats. One of his drill sergeants, Sergeant Lowe, took a special interest in Joseph, particularly in the fact that his face seemed to sprout hair within minutes after shaving, and so every day he chided him for what he deemed unlawfully long stubble. He would force Joseph to show up to formation with razor in hand, then shave Joseph's face with no cream, leaving small cuts across his neck and jawline. Sergeant Lowe would then pat him dry with rubbing alcohol while the other privates watched in amusement and horror. Joseph did his best not to wince.

He remembered how on Thanksgiving, they were given the day off. No one yelled at him. He didn't have to do push-ups or enter formations or worry that a drill sergeant might dry-shave his face. That afternoon they even got a special meal: plates with slabs of processed turkey, dinner rolls, cafeteria stuffing, and a slice of gelatinous cranberry sauce straight out of the can. Typically, they had two or three minutes to inhale their entire meal, but today, they had about fifteen, a decadence. And he remembered the private who sat down across from him, a thin blond kid with a thick southern accent. Joseph assumed he was an idiot, not because of his accent but just because he assumed everyone around him was an idiot, and the kid looked around the table at the group of privates he'd never met before this moment, and he said, just before taking his first bite, "I guess y'all are my family now," and Joseph hated him in that moment but wondered if maybe he was telling the truth.

Ryan

To minimize the number of beatings, which he'd continued to suffer both on the rez and off it, all accompanied by now-familiar antigay slurs, Ryan taught himself a few tricks. By middle school, he'd developed a sense of which pieces of himself were okay and which pieces needed to be excised. He learned what it meant to be gay, and he knew how to guard against gayness and its trappings. He became obsessed with the way he held his wrists, checking them constantly to make sure they never went limp. He did his best to throw the pitch of his voice downward, turning it from a chirp to a rumble. Mostly, though, he tried to go unnoticed, to make it to the end of each day, by barely saying anything at all.

And he played sports. First, he picked up lacrosse. The sport dated back to the twelfth century and had been played all along the St. Lawrence River Valley, with men from different nations locking in games that lasted days or weeks. In generations past, every Mohawk boy had been given a lacrosse stick on the day of his birth; it was placed with him on his first night in his crib. For men, the Mohawk people believed, the sport was a natural form of medicine. Women's medicine arrived once a month, during their "moon time," when they bled out impurities and found their bodies renewed. Nature had not blessed men with their own cycle of cleansing, and so they had to create one. The game gave order to male aggression, at times becoming a substitute for war. Men stepped onto the field with destructive impulses. They left it covered in blood, their own and that of others, and returned to their homes renewed by the violence of the game.

—

Ryan's father had been one of the greatest lacrosse players anyone in Akwesasne had ever seen, a fast and ferocious defenseman willing to break bones and lose teeth if it meant keeping his opponent away from the goal. Every time Ryan and his father went to the lacrosse field, strangers stopped by to pay their respects. They told Ryan that if he grew up to be half as good as his old man, he was guaranteed to be something special. His dad had been a local celebrity since well before Ryan was born, and his stature seemed only to grow. When Ryan was eleven, the whole family drove to Cornwall for the local premiere of the movie *The Last of the Mohicans*, the Daniel Day-Lewis film depicting tensions between Native people and European colonizers. Ryan walked the red carpet and watched strangers wait in line for their turn to talk to his dad, and then they sat and watched the movie. In the forty-seventh minute, there he was, Ryan's dad on the big screen, walking up to Daniel Day-Lewis and cutting him, gently, across the chest with a knife. When he appeared on-screen the whole theater erupted in applause, and Ryan sat there clapping and smiling, thrilled to be the son of a Hollywood star.

His dad didn't coach, at least not officially, but he was there on the sidelines for every game and most practices, collecting information for lessons he'd impart on the ride home. Ryan also played hockey, and at night his dad would call Ryan into the living room. "Rye! Come see this!" And Ryan would pause his video games in the basement to come find his dad on the couch, watching hockey on ESPN. He'd tell Ryan that he needed to study Wayne Gretzky—that he shouldn't watch the puck but only Gretzky's movements, and think about how to steal small pieces of his game. And in all of these moments, on the practice sidelines and on the car ride home, and on the couch late at night pointing at the men on TV, his dad seemed so animated and eager, almost begging his son to turn animated and eager too. Ryan looked just like his father. He had inherited that compact, wiry body, that square face with brooding eyes. Couldn't he inherit this too?

"Okay," Ryan said. "Can I go back to my room now?"

On the way to and from games, his father's advice centered largely around one word: *hustle*. Ryan needed to do it more. He had a natural quickness and strength, but he lacked the intensity or desire, his father said. He could be one of the best players on his team if he could locate his will to fight.

But Ryan didn't want to be great. He just wanted to play. Couldn't that be enough? Whatever it was that left him on the ground when punches started flying also left him flat-footed when other boys sprinted past him on the ice or the field.

Also: They *hated* him. Other boys seemed to hate him everywhere—at school, in the youth group on the rare occasions his grandmother forced him to go to church, even in the longhouse when he showed up for Mohawk ceremonies—but they *really* seemed to hate him on his lacrosse and hockey teams. They made a point not to invite him to team dinners and parties, laughed together as they went out of their way to knock him to the ground during practice.

One night, still age eleven, he showed up for hockey practice and he went into the locker room, pads and practice uniform already on. Ryan always changed at home. He hated the feeling of undressing in front of other boys. When he walked in, he saw that his teammates were all dressed, skates and pads on, helmets in hand, ready to hit the ice. He felt their eyes following him as he dropped his gym bag by the bench and sat down to wait for their coach.

"There he is," said one of the teammates, Robert. Robert was a couple years older, also Mohawk, thick and slow and strong, a goon. In a room split evenly between Native kids and white kids, Robert seemed to move seamlessly between groups. He could make the popular boys laugh at him, the smaller boys fear him, the average boys bend to his will. He took a special delight in punishing Ryan.

Now Ryan looked to the floor, pretending not to hear Robert talking, pretending not to feel every eye in the room watching as he tied his skates. "Faggot boy is here," Robert said, and Ryan heard a ripple of uncomfortable laughter.

Robert must have sensed some shift in Ryan's face, must have latched onto the overwhelming effort he was putting into ignoring everything outside of the laces on his skates, because now he said, "What's wrong, faggot?" And when Ryan still refused to look up, Robert stood and started walking out toward the ice, shrugging his shoulders. "I think he's just sad he missed us changing. I think he really wanted to see our dicks."

—

Ryan skated that night as fast as he could, head down and speeding away from other bodies, and he wondered. *Why?* Had he ever watched another boy change? He didn't think so. He felt terrified by the locker room, desperate to get in and out each day as fast as he could. He wondered why they so delighted in targeting him, what they saw in Ryan that he couldn't see in himself.

He would tell no one. If he did, his mother would tell his father, and his father would raise hell, demanding that other parents explain why their sons had mocked his boy, and demanding that Ryan explain why he hadn't stood up and punched Robert square in the face. And underneath it, he knew his father's demand would carry the whiff of a question.

Well, Rye. Was it true? Did you want to look at their dicks?

Nate

If people insisted on seeing Nate as a girl, he was going to make sure they saw him as beautiful. So when Maria told him to follow her, he did as told. Even though Maria was Mexican, at this white school, in this white town, she still existed as Queen of the White Girls. She had studied their form and perfected it. Her beauty was effortful but never ostentatious. Her intelligence evident but never shown off. At lunch, she told Nate to sit at her table, and so he did. She pointed at Nate and asked her friends if they thought the new girl could be so pretty if she tried, and they said yes, absolutely. With those eyes and that face she only needed a little bit of makeup, something natural, and she definitely needed some cuter jeans—and what was Slipknot, anyway? Couldn't she get rid of that shirt and buy some cute tops?

Nate told himself he could do this. He had long eyelashes, delicate cheekbones, a slender but angular jaw. He was fit, with smooth, clear skin. He followed Maria's advice, bought her preferred styles of jeans and tops. He even tried wearing dresses. He looked in the mirror and he vanished, no longer looking at himself but at his own experiment. He wondered how he could take the flesh he saw staring back at him and mold it into something pretty enough to have worth.

He got a middle school boyfriend, named Rodney, star of the football and basketball teams, tall and assertive and kind. When they kissed, one afternoon at the playground in their neighborhood, Nate felt awkward and ashamed and desperate for it to stop. He wanted to push Rodney and sprint in the opposite direction, but then he found instead that he could remain in this moment while slipping out of his own skin. Standing there with a boy's tongue in his mouth, his mind floated over to inhabit Rodney's body, and now he imagined that *he* was the tall, muscular one, with those rough hands and sturdy shoulders, and that *he* was caressing the face of a small and slender, unfamiliar girl.

But that only worked sometimes. Usually, he felt disgusted. Finally, he told Rodney they should just be friends. Rodney was one of the good ones. Elsewhere Nate encountered other boys, usually older, who saw in his feminine figure something to desire and to dominate. Like the boys in the bleachers at the high school football game, who watched him climb the stairs in a camisole top and his very first push-up bra, their eyes smothering him the moment he walked by, every single one staring down his shirt.

—

Nate's grandma died. His dad wasn't dead, but he was gone, so he might as well be. And Nate had never awoken one morning transformed into a boy. Grieving his grandma, and trying to reconcile his internal reality with the terrible fact of his body, he became wracked with anxiety, pummeled into depression. His mom sent him to a psychiatrist who prescribed some meds. Those helped. At least a little. But still, every day at school brought with it new panic. Every minute in those halls seemed to stretch to the ends of time.

After months of trying to follow Maria's advice, Nate finally admitted to himself that he could never be a girl. And he came to realize that he could never be white, either. With his father long gone, Nate felt little connection to his own Blackness. But at school, that didn't matter. The other kids chose his race for him. They were white. He was Black. Their cruelty would serve as a reminder.

He heard their comments. Under their breath at times, out loud for laughter at others. The first day of social studies in ninth grade, when the teacher asked the students what they might like to learn that year, a white boy said, "I want to learn about slavery!" He started laughing and looked at Nate. Another kid, standing in the risers at a choir concert the week of Martin Luther King Jr. Day, declared that killing King was the best thing America had ever done.

There were four Black kids in Nate's class of about two hundred, fewer than twenty in the entire school. Some of the Black kids were popular, such as Rodney and the other jocks. Some were nerds, and some, like Nate, floated in between. They all knew each other, but there was no *Black table* at lunch. No clique ever formed around their race. Mostly, the Black kids in his town seemed to exist in isolation, solitary vessels searching for their own niche in the social pecking order. They shared moments of connection but only briefly. Immediate eye contact after hearing some racist bullshit. Subtle nods as they passed each other in the halls.

One girl saw Nate's misery: Sweeney. A cast-off from Maria's group, Sweeney wore the right clothes but inhabited the wrong type of body. She was chubby and ginger, loud and mean. And she could see in Nate what he feared *everyone* could see. That he walked through the halls on the verge of tears and panic, every single day of every single week.

"Why don't you just cry?" she would ask him, and he said nothing.

"I know you want to cry."

"You hate yourself, don't you? You hate who you are. You wish you were someone else."

"Do you want to kill yourself? Maybe you should kill yourself."

—

Salvation arrived at the same time each afternoon: the final bell just before three, his mom in the pickup line minutes after that, the ride in near silence, and then, finally, home. He bounded upstairs, shut the door, and then shut his blackout curtains; his world would go totally dark by 3:30 each afternoon. Light reappeared in the form of his laptop, its soft glow reaching out to pull him inside.

He felt safe here, in the screen's blue light. His shoulders relaxed. His breathing slowed. As he clicked, he leaned forward. The screen held everything, possibilities beyond comprehension. He watched videos of skateboarders doing tricks. He learned about Jupiter's moons and the mating habits of stag beetles. He watched *Chopped* and Guy Fieri. He googled friends and friends' parents and his own parents' friends. He read LeBron James's Wikipedia page, learning every detail about Ohio royalty. He memorized the first thirty digits of pi. He rewatched the music video for Aaliyah's "Rock the Boat" somewhere in the neighborhood of thirteen thousand times.

But most often, he went on Gaia. He'd heard about it at school. Gaia had started as an anime site, but it soon grew into a parallel reality where kids from around the world talked to each other. He created an avatar that was Black, male, and handsome, then dressed him in baggy jeans and a *Naruto* headband. He thought up a screen name, an homage to the singer T-Pain: ~bUy_U_a_DrAnK~.

He made new friends here. He could convince himself that *this* was his real life. He walked around through digital forests and garages and grocery stores, striking up conversations with kids from London and San Francisco, Oklahoma and Singapore. They liked the same music and movies and hated the same types of people at their schools. Every time he talked to them, he felt a thrill at the knowledge that somewhere in the world existed others just like him, alone and uncomfortable outside their bedrooms, but at peace in the glow of their screens.

On Gaia, his shyness melted away. He felt confident, assertive, *known*. He was no longer the boy the world saw as a weird girl, staring into space until each school day ended. He was ~bUy_U_a_DrAnK~, a boy with confidence and swag, who talked to pretty girls and entered any room knowing he belonged.

He even got a girlfriend. Her name was Theresa. She lived in Atlanta, the daughter of Vietnamese immigrants. She was shy but funny, curious about his world. When he clicked on her avatar to see her profile picture, he felt his heartbeat quicken. When she clicked on his avatar, she saw a picture of him still deep in gender confusion. Baseball cap on but eyeliner too, hair long, stare vacant.

I've never been in a relationship with a girl before, she wrote to him. *I don't think I'm a lesbian.*

That's okay, he wrote back. *Don't think of me as a girl then.*

They talked every single day, from the moment Nate got home from school until deep into the night. They mailed each other care packages when they got sick, made matching T-shirts with both their names, physical manifestations of a relationship that seemed to exist only online. They talked about meeting in person, but they knew that was impossible. Not until they were older. For now, they contented themselves with returning to each other at the end of each day of seventh grade.

After they'd been "together" for a few months, Nate and Theresa video chatted one night.

"Hi," she said.

"Hi," he said.

They sat in silence for a few seconds, studying each other. She was as beautiful as she'd been in every picture. But as they talked, Nate found his eyes drifting to the bottom corner of the screen, watching himself—or watching this image of himself captured by the camera, an image that reflected nothing of what Nate imagined himself to be. His hair was long, straightened. He wore eyeliner and a little mascara, a cute sleeveless top, because when he wanted to look attractive, this, still, was the only script he knew to follow.

"It feels kind of weird," Theresa said, "that you're a girl."

"Yeah," Nate said. He didn't know what else to add. Of course she felt that. She'd been clear from the beginning: Theresa was straight. Nate *felt* like a boy. His online avatar was a boy. But all he had to do was look at the image in the bottom corner of the screen, watching himself watch her watching him, to know that he was nothing like they both wanted him to be.

Nate lived through seventh grade, then eighth, but just weeks into high school, he decided he couldn't do it any longer. He'd run out of the school crying one afternoon after Sweeney had called him the n-word in front of his entire biology class, and then he told his mom he was never going back.

So he didn't. He enrolled in an online program, tried to do his classwork alone every day on his laptop. Mostly, though, he ignored his assignments and returned to Gaia for hours. Late at night, when all his friends had logged off but he wasn't yet ready to go to bed, he found a YouTube video and clicked play and then let the algorithm decide what he'd watch next. And next, and next, and next. He watched comedy videos and basketball trick shot videos, dance videos and skating videos, vlogs and makeup tutorials from kids near his own age, always smiling and flashing a peace sign, asking him kindly to please like and subscribe.

And then, deep into one night, on his screen, a miracle: a teenage white guy, just a few years older than him, with an anvil jaw and deep dimples and broad shoulders, wearing plug earrings, a hemp necklace, and a confident smirk.

"Hi," the guy on the screen said. "So, it's January 21, it's like noon, and as of this morning, I'm one year old. Yay!"

Nate sat up a little, curious and confused. *One* year old? What was this dude talking about?

"All right," said the guy, named Skylar. "So here's a little comparison for you, and we'll be on our way."

And then he was gone, replaced on the screen by another version of the same person. His jaw less angular, his shoulders narrower, his dimples a little soft. "Hi," this younger, softer Skylar said. "So it's January 21, and it's late in the morning, and I went to the endocrinologist today." And then that guy was gone, replaced by another video of himself on February 18, and then March 22, and on and on and on, and in each video his body was changing, hardening and sharpening until he became the guy who had first appeared on Nate's screen.

The title of the video: "one year on testosterone comparison!"

What the hell, Nate thought. He sat all the way up and kept watching, no longer passively accepting the algorithm's directions but clicking on more of Skylar's videos to tell YouTube that whatever this was, he wanted more. And the algorithm delivered. The first video he'd seen was old, apparently. Skylar had posted many others before and since:

> "one year old—changes since I was born;]"
>
> "eight days post op"
>
> "GIRLFRIEND STORY TIME:D"
>
> "how i knew i was transgender [and some advice on coming out]"

Nate was stunned, incapable of looking away. Here, on-screen, a kind of man he didn't know existed. Here, on-screen, the kind of man he knew immediately he'd always longed to be. He'd never heard of a transgender man before. The only trans-related term he knew was a common slur, *trannies*, which he thought just referred to men who had a thing for wearing women's underwear. Dads and husbands and businessmen with some sexual fetish, which would always be found out by their wives, who would always confront them, usually on *The Jerry Springer Show*.

Now, Nate kept watching, started clicking, and watched other videos of other trans men. He learned their vocabulary. *Trans, FTM, binders, top surgery, T.* Here before him, an entire world he'd never known was within reach. And as he watched, he felt a creeping sense of doom, something terrible and suffocating. The glow of the screen held images of men describing a happiness they'd never known was possible, telling stories of how they'd come to feel at home in their bodies and started believing in the face they presented to the world. Such heartbreakingly impossible joy. *Why am I doing this to myself,* Nate wondered. *Why am I watching something I can never, ever be?*

Gideon

"You *will* think about quitting."

Those were among the first words Gideon heard spoken, minutes after he arrived at the United States Military Academy at West Point the summer before the start of his freshman year.

"*Everyone* thinks about quitting."

Coach was deeply tanned and about six feet tall, black hair and black mustache, muscles stretching the seams of a black *ARMY BASE-BALL* polo shirt. As of this moment, Coach held more power over Gideon's future than anyone on the planet. After Gideon got that first recruitment letter, Coach and his staff had been in steady contact, trying to lure him to West Point. Their case was straightforward: The Academy offered a chance to play Division I baseball and receive an elite education. And while other D-I baseball programs could only give partial scholarships to their players, West Point offered a full ride to every single student on campus. In return, Gideon had to commit to five years of service as an army officer upon graduation. But Coach had been clear: If he was drafted by a Major League team, they would work with him to fulfill his military requirements while playing pro ball.

Now Gideon was sitting in a ski lodge just outside West Point's upstate New York campus, alongside about a dozen other new baseball recruits and a few of the team's upperclassmen. In just a few minutes, he and the rest of the freshmen would begin basic training, or, as it was known at the Academy, *Beast*.

"But *when* you think about quitting," Coach continued, "I want you to ask yourself something."

He paused for a second, chomping on what Gideon imagined to be an entire fistful's worth of Big League Chew.

"Are you ready to admit that every single one of the 1,200 people here to join this class is stronger than you? Are you ready to admit that every single one of them is *tougher* than you?" His eyes blazed through the room, recruit by recruit. "If you can admit out loud that every single person here is *better* than you, then fine, go ahead and go home. You aren't really built for this place anyway. But unless you're ready to admit that, then I expect to see you at the end of Beast, dressed and ready for fall practice."

—

It was June 2003. Nearly two years earlier, Gideon had watched on the TV in his trigonometry classroom as the Twin Towers collapsed on September 11, 2001. The United States had launched a war in Afghanistan nearly a month later. But when Gideon asked his coaches about the possibility of committing to play baseball for them leading him into a war zone, they told him not to worry. "Right now, it's just CIA and special forces riding around Afghanistan killing bad guys," his pitching coach said. But then, in March 2003, just three months before Gideon was due to show up at the Academy, the United States launched Operation Iraqi Freedom, a full-blown ground invasion, requiring tens of thousands of troops. Still, everyone he'd talked to seemed to believe this would be long over by the time he graduated. The United States was looking for weapons of mass destruction. As soon as they toppled Saddam Hussein and removed his weapons, they would leave Iraq as quickly as they'd arrived.

From his first visit to West Point, the place dazzled him. On his visits to other schools, Gideon had tailgated at football games and spent Saturday nights at house parties. He drank with the baseball players who hosted him and met a smattering of college girls so beautiful they left Gideon unable to mutter much beyond his own name. At West Point, though, he sat in the barracks while his host, a freshman pitcher, spent a Friday night studying. He rose the next morning for a campus tour, walking past statues of Eisenhower and MacArthur and Patton and Washington, alongside cadets who moved with a kind of purpose that suggested they wanted their own statue erected at some future date. "Here," Coach told him, "the history we teach was made by the people we taught." Gideon sensed immediately that some version of this exact line had been used on dozens of recruits before him, and he immediately decided he did not mind.

He knew this would be hard. That was the point. Gideon understood that he glided through life with an ease unavailable to most of his peers: straight A's in high school, shutdown innings on the mound, all without an obsessive dedication to honing his mind or his body. Teachers and coaches had tended to let him do whatever he wanted, and in turn he came to loathe them. He would take naps on the floor during calculus, walk out of biology in the middle of class, telling the teacher he was going to hang out in the gym. But the real assholes—the Spanish teacher who excoriated any student who chewed gum or spoke a word of English in her classroom, the literature teacher who failed him on a paper because he didn't follow the required formatting, the basketball coach who made the whole team run suicides until they saw spots and began to heave—all of them demanded and earned his respect. West Point seemed like an entire university filled with those kinds of people. He wanted to see who he could become after four years on these grounds.

So here he was. Finishing this meeting at the ski lodge, then on his way to campus alongside the 1,400 or so other incoming students, he felt ready for what he expected to be the most brutal summer of his life. Coach tried to downplay what he was about to endure. "They cannot hit you," he said of the drill sergeants, all upperclassmen, "or they'll be in big fucking trouble. So what can they do? They'll yell at you, and they'll make you do a bunch of push-ups. You wanna tell me you can't handle that? You're a Division I athlete. If you can't handle a few push-ups, I don't know how you ended up here."

West Point's basic training differed from enlisted soldiers' basic training in critical ways. Enlistee basic was designed to turn civilians into soldiers in ten weeks. West Point was designed to turn the elite into officers over four years. Basic was just the first step. They could afford to take their time. Gideon was in a group with dozens of Eagle Scouts, hundreds of valedictorians or salutatorians, the recipients of thousands of varsity letters, all in one class.

"You can't lead," Coach explained, parroting an Academy cliché, "until you learn to follow." So for the next seven weeks, that was exactly what the new cadets had to do. Sometimes they would follow leaders who inspired in them a deep passion and will to perform. Sometimes they would follow someone they didn't like and barely respected. But all of it mattered, because all of it was part of the structure of this place, which was also, incidentally, the structure of this nation. Trusting the junior screaming in their faces meant trusting the graduate, now a lieutenant, who once screamed in his. Trusting the senators who wrote them letters of recommendation, the generals who served on the Academy's faculty, the United States president who sat atop the chain of command. Trusting all the earlier presidents who had written the documents that had given birth to this Academy, to the army it fed, and to the nation they were now swearing to protect. So when a sergeant says "About-face," you turn about-fucking-face. This was what the founders had intended.

Speaking of which: This was one of the first skills he needed to master. How to turn about face. It sounds simple enough. Step one: Listen to a drill sergeant yell at you. Step two: Using precise footwork, quickly turn 180 degrees, so you're facing in the opposite direction.

So on that morning, Gideon stood alongside a group of other new cadets, each with the same directive. One by one, they turned about face. From heels together, take the right foot and place it toe down outside the left heel, then turn on that heel in a way that rotates the right toe. The turn completed, your heels land back together. Done. Gideon watched, studying their movements, ready for his own. But if you are six-foot-six with size 13 feet, even with the agility of a Division I athlete, then turning about face in perfect form while someone yells in your ear can be difficult. When his turn came, he failed. His feet came apart. His knee buckled. His turns fell just short of 180 degrees.

Here was the most basic instruction in basic training, the very first thing on the very first day, and already, Gideon couldn't do it. He registered, out of the corner of his eye, that all his peers had moved on to the next task. Gideon had never been in a room with so many people who could do a thing he could not. All around him drill sergeants' voices were clattering into him, patience wearing thin, and he knew that soon their instruction would turn from urgent to something uglier: *The fuck is wrong with you, Big Bird? Do your legs not work, how the fuck did they let you in?*

He wondered if his other scholarship offers were still on the table. He knew he'd have to wait a year, but maybe he could move back home, work construction for a few months, then enroll somewhere else next fall. And then he saw someone walking in his direction, eyes boring into Gideon's skull, and he could tell from his black uniform that he was a senior, taking his final turn as a drill sergeant, surely ready to unload.

"What's the problem, new cadet?"

Gideon forced himself to meet the senior's eyes. "No problem, sir."

The senior laughed. "No," he said. "I'm pretty sure there's a problem. Come with me."

He pulled Gideon out of formation, away from the other new cadets, toward an open area with no one else around. He fixed his eyes on Gideon's, and Gideon imagined him choosing among the hundreds of creative insults he'd stored up for moments like these.

Instead, he said, "Take a deep breath."

Gideon took a deep breath.

"Now take another one."

Gideon took another one.

"You good?"

"Yes sir. I'm good."

"It's not as easy as they make it look, is it?"

Within seconds, Gideon was turning, perfectly on his heels rather than on his toes, just as he'd been told, about face.

—

The rest of Beast was fine. The new cadets spent their mornings running and doing push-ups, their afternoons learning to fire M16s and toss grenades. Next came a ragged week living in a ditch a few miles from campus, where Gideon fought a bout of "heat rash." Then a long march through the night back to the barracks through the woods, finishing at dawn. Delirious and barely standing, Gideon was welcomed, alongside the rest of his new classmates, with wild and exuberant applause to celebrate the fact that they were now, officially, cadets, ready to begin their first semester at West Point.

As he settled into the rhythm of the fall semester, Gideon confronted the reality of what he'd signed up for. Everything about West Point was designed to leave the cadets with no time for any life outside the Academy. They rose at 6 a.m. and assembled for breakfast formation, a massive group display of individual preparation, gathering for no purpose but to signal readiness for the day. Next came hours of classes, followed by lunch formation, and then baseball practice, which stretched into the evening until dinner. After that he had to find time to study and tend to the mundane but apparently necessary menial tasks—room tidying, uniform organizing—that were required every day. At 11:30 p.m. every weeknight, they listened as a bugler played taps. Those aching tones, stretching across campus and into the barracks, became the day's final ritual, each note a command: Now rest, so tomorrow you can work. Most nights, Gideon just heard the song as an annoyance. But some nights, it gave him chills.

—

Gideon realized, quickly, one of the great divides on this campus: athletes and nonathletes. Culturally, organizationally, and socially, the two groups seemed to move through parallel worlds. For one thing, they had all arrived here under vastly different circumstances. Most athletes had followed a path similar to Gideon's: They'd poured themselves into a sport throughout their entire childhood, until the day letters began arriving from colleges.

The nonathletes? Many had dreamed of this day since they were children. They'd grown up on *Saving Private Ryan* and *Black Hawk Down*. Some had even borrowed a few World War II books from their dads. They'd committed themselves from adolescence to becoming the smartest and bravest so that they could someday arrive here, to a place that would make them still smarter and braver, preparing them for a day when they would fly or march or ride toward danger, writing their own stories of duty and honor for future generations to study and revere.

The athletes had a name for these people. *Slugs*. The slugs' favorite word? *Hoo-ah*. This was largely an exclamation but also, with proper context, could be a noun, an adjective, a verb, even a conjunction. Finished a training run? *Hoo-ah!* Got an exam tomorrow? Just *hoo-ah* your way through an all-nighter. What was breakfast formation, if not the first daily gathering of *hoo-ah*s, to salute the flag and prepare for the day ahead?

Athletes did not say *hoo-ah*. Or they did, but only in a tone that made clear the depths of their disdain. *Hoo-ah* suggested a wholesale giving of oneself to the United States Army and all its attending missions, a ready transformation into a government-sponsored killing machine. And killing machines were, if Gideon was being honest, kind of dorks.

Not that the athletes couldn't get swept up in the Academy's grandeur, or even in the supposed rightness of its mission. But every time they heard an earnest *hoo-ah*, they heard a little boy who'd spent too much time with his GI Joes.

—

Like many first-year cadets, Gideon had a girlfriend back home. Her name was Kristen. She had red hair and blue eyes and could do somersaults from a standstill position. She'd been their high school's head cheerleader and salutatorian. He'd known her since kindergarten. In elementary school, she'd flirted by kicking him in the shins with the toe of her cowboy boots, then running away. Sophomore year, the first time she slipped her hand underneath the waist of his pants, he felt he could barely breathe.

Gideon going to West Point had never been part of their plan. The Academy was too far away, its rules too restrictive. And Kristen had zero desire to be an army wife. Or to spend years with her husband away on deployment, left alone with the kids. Or to live with the gnawing fear of the day when a uniformed soldier would arrive on her doorstep to inform her that her husband had been killed. And so she seemed to listen with great interest when, during the fall of his freshman year, Gideon began to talk at great length each evening on the phone about how much the Academy kind of sucked.

He didn't expect to feel this way. After making it through Beast, he thought the rest of his time on campus would feel easy by comparison. Basic training, though, had always felt temporary, like a sadistic obstacle course he just had to survive. Now he realized that the most obnoxious aspects of Beast—the obsession with rules and order, the reality that he existed at the bottom of a wholly constructed and seemingly meaningless hierarchy—all of that was going to remain in place for as long as he remained in the military. This meant that every day Gideon was calling minutes, delivering laundry, taking out garbage from the barracks to the dump. Upperclassmen approached him each morning to ask tedious questions—what are we eating for breakfast, when is our next formation, tell me the two stories that appear above the fold on A1 of today's *New York Times*—and Gideon was expected to answer, calmly and accurately, or to stand and listen as someone screamed in his face. The fact that there existed, on his campus, several thousand fellow cadets who could make Gideon do whatever the hell they wanted, simply by virtue of having survived this place at least one year longer than him, seemed patently absurd.

When Gideon told Kristen how tedious his daily routine was, she said oh my gosh I can't believe they make you do that. And when he explained that he wasn't sure where he stood with Coach, because he preferred not to motivate through praise but through strategically timed excoriations, she said he sounded like a jerk, how could Gideon ever play for a guy like that? And when he explained how absurd the entire ethos of the campus felt, she said that place sounds so ridiculous, why would you stay there, why not just come back home to me?

He weighed the tantalizing reality of what leaving the Academy offered: the chance that someone he loved would tell him that he made her happy. The chance, when he arrived back at the Atlanta airport and Kristen wrapped him in her arms, to be told he was doing something good. For eighteen years, praise and reassurance had become his oxygen. For the past six months, he'd been gasping for air.

—

"I need to talk to you," Gideon said, standing at the doorway to Coach's office one afternoon, and he felt himself shaking from the moment he stepped inside.

Coach nodded. "Shut the door."

Gideon did as told.

"Sit."

Gideon sat. He strained to lift his eyes, met Coach's. "I wanted to tell you," he said with as much confidence as he could feign, "that I've decided to leave the Academy."

Coach sat back in his chair, dark eyes unflinching.

"Okay," he said. "*Why?*"

Gideon gave him his rehearsed answer. "This just isn't for me." It was a great place, and he appreciated the opportunity, but this wasn't what he wanted to do with his life, et cetera and on and on. He would finish the year so he could transfer his credits—he knew he owed himself that much—but then he was gone.

Coach nodded, once, faintly, a flinch. He let Gideon finish, then sat quietly for a moment.

"You know how much effort we put into recruiting you, right?"

"Yes sir."

"You know all the hoops so many people had to jump through just to get you here, right?"

"Yes sir."

"Coaches. Cadets. Your parents. A *senator*."

"Yes sir."

"And now you're just going to turn your back on those people."

"Well, sir. I just…"

"You know how many people would give anything to be sitting where you're sitting today?"

"Sir. I just…"

"So what's the issue?"

"This place just isn't for me."

Coach sat back,shot a look at one of his assistants, who was sitting in the corner of the room, then let a smirk crawl across his face. "So. *Gideon*. Are you too much of a pussy?" His tone sounded light, almost warm, understanding. "Is that what you're telling me? Because I'll be honest, I didn't think you were a pussy when I recruited you, but I've been wrong before."

"No sir. I don't think so."

"You mean to tell me that all these thousands of people here, all these tens of thousands of people who came here before you, every single one of them is stronger than you and tougher than you? That every single one of them knew how to do what needed to be done, and you just fucking *can't*?"

"Well. Sir."

"You know there's girls here, right?"

"Um. Yes?"

"*Girls*. Girls who graduate from this place every year. You gonna tell me those girls are more *man* than you are?"

"I mean. I don't think that's…"

"Okay, fine. You're just gonna pussy out like this? You're just gonna quit? Then go ahead. Make a decision like that, and that's who you'll be for the rest of your life. A fucking quitter. So go right ahead and quit."

Gideon wanted to tell himself that Coach's speech didn't matter, that he was too sure of himself to care about the opinion of some middle-aged guy who'd never even attended this Academy. But the thought lingered. *Was* he a pussy? *Were* the other cadets all tougher and stronger than him? What did they have that he lacked?

—

That winter, his Pappo died, and his Mammo's only request of Gideon was that he arrive to the funeral in full dress, the formal West Point uniform reserved for ceremonies and parades. The uniform was hot, itchy, pointless. Gideon felt like an imposter wearing something designed for students at a school he planned to leave. But he knew that in his family, he existed as a trophy. Wearing the uniform meant showing up freshly polished, in full shine.

Pappo had served in the army during World War II, preparing to be an aviator until his plane crashed during a training exercise in the Nevada desert. Six soldiers had died. Only Pappo and one other man survived. He'd never finished flight school and had taken a year to recover from his injuries, but when he was discharged from the hospital, the army presented him with a gold ring, fixed with an insignia of the aviator wings he would have earned at the end of school. He never talked about that ring or the crash, never seemed to think of himself as a military man of any kind. But now Gideon's Mammo pulled the ring from her purse and gave it to Gideon. "He would have wanted you to have this," she said. "He was so proud."

The funeral proceeded. A prayer, a hymn, a sermon, remembrances. They moved from the church to the graveyard and began to lower Pappo's casket into the ground. And that's when he heard it, the first note of taps, not even played by a proper bugler, but on a speaker affixed to a fake bugle's nonfunctional horn. As he listened to the aching and familiar song, he felt the hair raise on his arms. Here were the simple notes that marked the end of his daily slog, now marking the end of a life. Here was the grandfather Gideon had adored as a boy, who'd regaled him with stories from his post-military career as a NASA engineer. He'd driven Gideon around the country in his Airstream trailer, including down to Cape Canaveral to watch a shuttle launch up close. And now he was laid to rest, his wife clutching the flag that the VFW reps had folded and presented to her by the grave, the notes piercing the silence of a cold and clear winter day, and Gideon began to wonder if perhaps there was some invisible line connecting the way West Point sophomores demanded that he summarize the *Times* headlines to the way these aging vets showed up at a stranger's funeral to perform reverence and care for the family of the dead.

Joseph

The deal was simple but unspoken from the moment they started dating: Joseph and Emily would save each other. Joseph had drifted without purpose through the fog of his teens. Emily had been raised by a drug-addicted mother and her rotating cast of drug-dealing boyfriends. By the time they started dating, Emily had lived a life full of ambition and vigor, but occasionally teetering on the edge of despair. Emily sharpened him; Joseph soothed her. On their own, each was broken. Together, they could be whole.

Sure, of course, there were simpler reasons for their attraction. She had dark hair and bright brown eyes, the kind of smile that made him think she'd just heard the most hilarious story, told only in her mind. Which, actually, was often true. Emily was one of the funniest people he'd ever known. She held within her both a sarcastic detachment and an effusive warmth, an ability to joke about her own suffering and ease the slightest discomfort in anyone else.

After they started dating, at their conservative Christian college, Joseph kept preaching and leading youth groups in a local church; Emily led worship in chapel and became an academic star. They had each grown up surrounded by violence committed by men who claimed to love God. Together, though, they believed they were proving how much better they were than the hypocritical Christians who'd raised them. They could push each other to levels of godliness no one around them could possibly reach.

One afternoon, they were sitting together under a pavilion on campus when a stranger walked up to them and introduced himself as Josh. He had red hair all over his head and his arms and the back of his neck. "I don't want to bother you guys," Josh said, "but I've been watching you, and I can see the way y'all love and care for each other. I just want to say, God is blessing your relationship."

They never spoke to him again, but they would forever call him "Josh the Prophet." Within a year, they were engaged.

—

Joseph had two good reasons for proposing. First, he loved Emily and wanted to spend the rest of his life with her. Second, and perhaps a little more urgently, he was about to go to war.

This was not supposed to happen. Joseph had signed up for the reserves. He was supposed to show up for his one weekend a month and his two weeks a year, collect his paychecks and his benefits and his money to pay for college, and to never even *think* about fighting a war. "You're learning all this shit," one of Joseph's drill sergeants told him during a quiet moment in basic training, "but if any of you ever actually have to use it, that means something has gone very, very wrong."

That was in July 2000. Fourteen months later, something went very, very wrong. Two planes crashed into two towers, and the United States responded by launching two wars. Now Joseph was headed to one of them. Only he didn't know which one. Joseph's unit was activated in November 2003. By January 2004, he'd withdrawn from school and moved to Fort Benning, Georgia, to begin all of the training he'd been told reservists would never actually have to face. He completed his weapons requalifications, the urban warfare training in fake Middle Eastern towns, and instruction in how to spot improvised explosive devices, or IEDs, on fake desert streets. He practiced medical evacuation requests, learned to communicate exact coordinates, and worked to calm down local actors who'd been hired to play the role of an angry mob.

At first, it felt like a kind of game. Joseph was just playing the role of a soldier, dressing up each day as someone braver and deadlier than himself. He had good reason to believe he'd never see any real action. His unit was a headquarters detachment. Their job was to handle logistics, managing the day-to-day operations of a base. They were supposed to keep up with the water supply, count the beds, and arrange the tents. They would order and sort ammo, burn garbage, and clean up shit. They were not there to fight. They were there to keep the fighters rested and fed.

They were set to deploy in mid-February. Afghanistan was the rumor, but it could still be anywhere. Joseph clung to a hope that they'd end up in Germany or Korea, filling in for some other unit that had been shipped off to war. On Super Bowl Sunday, he and a few buddies snuck off base. "Let's go to Hooters," Captain Tyler had said, and they'd responded hell yeah and piled into Captain Tyler's van. Then they drove twenty-five minutes to the Hooters in Columbus, where through the windows they could see flashes of orange and white fabric stretching around athletic female bodies as the waitresses carried pints of domestic beer to men much like themselves.

But the restaurant was full. There was a two-hour wait for a table, and not a single seat open at the bar. They kept driving, up past a few strip clubs, then an Applebee's and a Buffalo Wild Wings, all of them completely packed. They saw a Chili's with the lights on but the parking lot almost empty, and Captain Tyler said what do you think boys, let's give it a try. They walked inside and saw no one. Finally, a hostess emerged and offered a sad smile. "Our TV is out," she said. "That's why no one's here."

"What do y'all have?" Joseph's buddy, Sergeant Crompton, asked. "Cable or satellite?"

"Satellite," she said.

"Can I go up on the roof?"

Crompton and another buddy, Sergeant Byrnes, had both worked for telecom companies. They got the picture working quickly, and minutes later they were sitting at the bar watching the Super Bowl, eating whatever they wanted for free. The seats slowly started filling in all around them. Every drink Joseph finished was replaced with another before he put down the glass. The bartender was young and brunette with tanned skin and an easy smile, and she leaned over the bar and held eye contact with whoever was speaking, even placing a hand on a forearm for brief seconds, and she said oh wow when they told her they were bound for war, and she asked if they were scared and they said nah, we know what we're doing, and she said I bet you do. Joseph didn't know if she meant it this way, but it all seemed to him like the very deepest kindness, like she saw into their need and allowed herself to gently fill it, making them each feel for a moment like they were men worthy of her attention, until she smiled gently and said she had to go check on an order in the back.

Over time, the bar filled up even more. Word spread through the restaurant about the soldiers just days from deployment who had saved the Super Bowl, and this meant even more drinks arrived for them, do you want another round, I mean, we might be dead in a week so what the hell, and they toasted America and swore to kill terrorists and loudly cheered for the Carolina Panthers. Joseph may not have felt like a soldier during training exercises, but he certainly did now, deflecting praise from strangers who told him to go over to that desert and give 'em hell.

When Joseph stood to leave, he nearly collapsed. When he lay on his bed in the barracks, the ceiling spun like a top. When he woke up in the middle of the night, he rushed to the bathroom to vomit, and other soldiers followed him to laugh and take pictures, in hysterics, holy shit bro, why didn't you take us with you, looks like you had a fucking *night*. The next morning, he had to take a combat lifesaver test at 8 a.m. Most of it was written, and he stared at the words until they stopped shaking, then trusted his preparation, encircling the correct answer whenever he could. Then he had to start an IV on another soldier, and Joseph and Crompton were paired together.

You go first, Crompton said. Okay, Joseph said. And so Joseph took Crompton's forearm in one hand and held a needle in the other, and he breathed deeply and willed the arm to stop shaking, but it never quite did, so finally he knew he just had to go for it, and he punctured skin with the needle, and seconds later they were laughing, because neither of them could believe it, but that fucker went straight in the vein.

Nate

Night after night, in the glow of his laptop's screen, he kept watching more vlogs by trans men. So many that YouTube started targeting him with a very specific kind of ad. They were relentless, playing after every third or fourth video, always with the same tagline: IT GETS BETTER. On every ad, a procession of gay, lesbian, and trans people telling their stories, all following a familiar script: The confusion they'd felt as children and despair as early teens, the isolation and pain of trying to navigate a world that didn't offer them a place in it. The slow process of finding people who would love them, of finding the confidence they'd buried somewhere deep inside themselves. An awakening when they discovered that this world did, in fact, have a place for them, that they could be as worthy of love and care as anyone else. That if you give it time, if you stay true to yourself, the pain of adolescence fades.

Obviously, Nate thought, this was bullshit. The people for whom it "got better" were the kind of people for whom things always got better. They were rich, they were white, and they were in fantasyland places like California. They had TV-sitcom parents, the kind who laughed sweetly when their children came out, saying, oh, baby, we've known for a long, long time. For Nate, it would not get better. Nothing seemed more obvious.

And yet. He kept watching. He let the videos end and let the algorithm choose more. Explainers on breast binders and top surgery, chest scars and packing, bottom surgery and hysterectomies, and controversies over *PRIDE*. He googled testosterone therapy. He went on chat forums for trans people. He lurked, too afraid to create an account and ask his own questions. Surely, he thought, someone would trace the questions back to him.

So, trans men *existed*. That fact alone felt staggering. Biology did not have to determine the way he moved through life. He could never imagine finding the will to do what these men had done, but somehow just living in the same world as them gave him hope. It was possible. If he lived a thousand lives, maybe one of them would include a moment where he spoke aloud the truth of who he was.

—

One afternoon in April of the year he turned fifteen, he walked downstairs to grab a snack, pumpkin seeds and Pepsi, and on the way back up, he paused, curious about what he heard on the TV.

"What are you watching?" he asked his mom.

She explained. It was a special episode of some talk show. Maury or Ellen or Dr. Phil. They were telling the story of a transgender woman. Cameras followed her through her daily routines: to her doctor's appointments, even to her top surgery. Nate stopped, lingering just a second. What he saw on-screen looked so much like what he'd seen on so many YouTube videos, only with the genders reversed and a higher production value. He could already imagine the script.

When he reached his room he began sobbing, then shaking, and the movement of his body pushed him back down the stairs to his mom.

"What is it, baby?" she asked, and he said nothing.

"What's wrong?" she asked, and he said nothing still.

He sat down next to her. She put her arms around his shoulders, pulled him close. Her hair smelled of citrus, her skin of vanilla. He lay his head on her shoulder until he could catch his breath.

"I have to tell you something," he said finally, looking down at the floor.

"I already know, baby."

"You do?"

"Yes. You like girls."

"Um," Nate said. "I mean. Yeah. I guess."

She smiled warmly, but Nate told her there was something more.

"You know that show you were just watching?"

"Yeah."

"I'm like *that* person. Yes, I do like girls. But also, I'm transgender."

"Okay," she said, and her expression didn't change, and that nonreaction made him nervous, and so he kept speaking to fill the silence between them.

"It's called F to M," he said. "Female to male transgender. That's me."

She nodded. "Okay," she said. "Thank you for telling me."

She looked at Nate, and then at the TV, which was now off, and then down at the floor.

"No matter what," she said, and now she started to cry, just a little, "I love you. We'll get through this. We'll learn how to get through it."

At first, he felt relief. The desperation that had propelled him through so many late nights in the glow of his screen, crying his way through YouTube's algorithm, had now been spoken out loud. His mom knew. And his mom loved him. He would not lose the single most important person in his world. But after the relief, a wave of shame washed over Nate. That he had to announce to his mother that he was a boy, that he couldn't just present himself to the world in a way that everyone would know. He'd read about the hormones, knew if he started testosterone there would be injections, understood that over time, a needle puncturing his skin could mold his flesh in the ways he desired. But something about that fact—the flagrant *effort* of it all, just to be at home in his own body—felt humiliating.

—

Every month, when they had a little money left over after paying the bills, his mom would take him to Walmart to buy boys' clothes. Once again he could wear everything he'd worn as a small child—baggy T-shirts and baggier jeans, baseball caps and bandannas, all of it rendered inappropriate for a teen the world saw as a girl, but now perfectly fine for Nate, who was ready to meet the world as a boy. He wore chains on his jeans and band tees from Hot Topic—Gorillaz, Bring Me the Horizon, Killswitch Engage. He bought henleys and hoodies, a wine-colored tank top that flattened his chest, and an Ohio State snapback with a perfectly flat bill. When they got home he would run to his room and try on his new outfits, then rush to his mom's bedroom to look at himself in the full-length mirror.

"You look handsome, baby," his mom would tell him.

"Yeah," he'd answer, beaming. "I know. But thanks."

He never felt the need to "come out" to anyone else. His mother had deserved an explanation. No one else did. He just started wearing men's clothes and making plans to begin seeing a gender therapist, with hopes of eventually beginning hormone therapy. But that would come later. For now, he just continued his daily life, attending school online, and when his friends asked questions, he answered them honestly.

"Do you want us to call you *he* or something?"

"Yeah, sure. That would be good."

"Is there another name we should call you?"

"If you want to. You can call me Noah."

He'd always liked that name. It seemed gentle but brave. Like the man in the Bible who gathered every species of animal on his boat to keep them safe amid a storm. The name suited him, he thought. Plus, it began with the same letter as the name he'd been given at birth. It seemed easier to keep his initials the same.

But almost every day, his mom slipped up and called him *Nae*, a shortened version of his birth name that she'd called him since he was little. And almost every day, she stopped herself immediately and apologized.

"Noah," she said. "Noah, Noah, Noah, Noah. I'll stop doing that soon. I promise."

"It's okay," he told her. "I understand."

Until one day, he had an idea.

"What if I go by something different?" he asked.

"Like what?"

"Something that still reminds you of my old name."

"Like what?"

"What about *Nate*?"

He saw tears creeping in from the edges of her eyes. "Are you sure?" she asked.

"Yeah," he said. "I like it."

He would change his name to Nathaniel, but then go by Nate. Nate and Nae, two nicknames separated by one letter, both shortened versions of the longer names he'd held. He knew that many trans people referred to their former names as their *deadname*, and he understood why so many wanted to purge that piece of their history. But he didn't feel that way. He had grown into himself while being called that old name. Even if the world had used that name to label him as a girl, the child who'd inhabited that name was already growing into a man.

He still saw his dad sometimes, maybe once every three or four months. They were fine—cordial, though distant. His dad had been working out a lot lately, lifting weights in his garage, and he told Nate he was on a little bit of steroids, nothing serious, just some "tren." But he looked to Nate like the most muscular man who had ever lived, like one of those guys who oiled up their muscles and flexed onstage in their Speedos. When they drove around, his dad was honest, open in ways Nate had never seen from other men. He told Nate he'd been a bad husband to Nate's mother, and he was afraid he was being a bad husband to his new wife now. But what could he say, was it such a crime to love strange pussy? If so, then you could lock him up along with every other man in the world.

One afternoon they were riding around Youngstown, catching up, when his dad asked Nate if he wanted to stop by the home he shared with his new wife and their young daughters.

"Okay," Nate said, a little quietly.

"You sure?" his dad asked.

"Yeah. It's just. I haven't seen the girls in a long time. I look different now."

"Yeah. You do." His dad shrugged his shoulders and shook his head, then continued. "But, you know, everybody has their own style, right? You do you."

Nate nodded, a little relieved. "What if I want to be called *he*?" he asked. "What if I want to be a boy?"

His dad nodded, thinking for a moment. "That's cool," he said. "I respect it."

Later that afternoon, they ran into a few of his dad's friends, sitting out on the front porch of one of their homes.

"This is my son," he said, and Nate beamed as he shook their hands.

And then his dad was gone, for months again, back to lifting weights and chasing women. He would text Nate on his birthday, maybe even take him to lunch. He would call him what he wanted to be called, and embrace him as his son. But all that meant was that he would accept him from a distance. No different than before.

After he started to socially transition, suddenly Nate found that he no longer wanted to sit inside his bedroom, staring all day at his laptop. He wanted to loiter at the skate park and play pickup basketball after school, and he wanted to wander the mall for hours, sometimes with friends and sometimes alone. He wanted to talk to strangers. He wanted to talk to *girls*.

And so he did. All of those things in constant rotation, day after day after day. Who knew the physical world could be this exciting? Did any of his internet friends know how much wonder existed on the other side of their bedroom's blackout curtains? Someone needed to tell them. But it wouldn't be him. He broke up with Theresa, his internet girlfriend, and then he shut down Gaia and let his YouTube algorithm atrophy. Suddenly, the screens could offer him nothing. He wanted to bike until he smelled his own sweat and to crash and see his own blood. He wanted to walk into the barbershop and tell his boy Luca to give him a fresh fade, and to sit for half an hour listening to the buzz of shit talk and electric clippers.

He wanted to skate. He'd gotten his first pro board when he was eleven and started riding in empty parking lots with his friend Nicole. By the time he started transitioning, he'd become a regular at the skate park, the one masculine space where he felt accepted, his presence never questioned. He wasn't the *best* skater in his town, but he could hang. Grinding down railings, kick flips down the stairs, the scars on knees and elbows to show he wasn't afraid. He loved the quiet ritual of it, summer afternoons soundtracked only by rolling wheels and grinding metal. He loved seeing the gallery of spectators, most of them hot emo girls, sitting on the edge of the playground and watching while the boys skated.

He wanted to hear the stories of the older kids who'd dropped out of school to smoke weed in the mall parking lot. In fact, he wanted a hit. And then maybe another. Fuck, bro, that's good shit. He thought maybe that girl was looking at him. Was she looking at him? Should he go talk to her? Suddenly, always, he thought that he should talk to her. A new name and new clothes had given him a new aggression, the kind he'd never known he might possess. And with it, he realized, new attention from the girls in his hometown.

This wasn't what he'd expected. He'd already resigned himself to a life of relative celibacy. He would sacrifice a romantic life for the chance to comfortably inhabit his own skin. But it was now clear that had been an unnecessary concern. When he met new people, they immediately called him *he*, no questions asked. He noticed girls looking at him as he rode his board through the park, saw them smiling from across the playground, eyes lingering on him for a second too long after every conversation.

There was this one girl named Christen who grabbed his phone out of his hands and put her number in it, then walked away. She was tall and skinny, with dark hair and pale skin. She invited Nate to a party, and that night she grabbed Nate and kissed him, and here was the feeling he'd told himself he would die before he ever experienced, a girl's mouth and body pressed against his own, her scent left to linger on his neck, her eyes staring at him with still more *want* as she leaned back in for more.

He started dating and had typical high school relationships, brief and intense, one after another. He liked mean girls, erratic girls, girls with sad eyes and multicolored hair, homemade tats, and septum piercings: girls with a wildness Nate had always been afraid to access within himself. Almost every girl he dated identified as straight. None had dated a trans guy before. None had ever even *known* a trans guy before. But in Nate, they saw bashful eyes and a slicing jawline, meticulous style and a curious spirit. He was kind. He was sensitive. He asked questions and listened to answers and taught them how to do heel flips on his board. He had soft skin and good hygiene. They all seemed to agree: Nate was hot.

—

One day at the park, he was doing tricks on his skateboard while another guy was doing tricks on his bike, and soon they started talking. At first they talked about boards and bikes, and then about bands, and then about girls, and then about everything. His name was Dante. He was Nate's age, tall, Black, muscular, effortlessly handsome and confident. Every girl Nate knew had a crush on him. Before coming out as trans, Nate would have had one too. But now he realized those crushes were just envy. And that envy had softened into a simple desire to be Dante's friend.

They skated and biked and lifted weights, spotting each other on the heaviest reps. They worked on old cars in Dante's family's garage and they talked to random girls at the mall. They sat in each other's bedrooms and cranked up the music until it rattled their teeth. Occasionally, Dante asked Nate about his transition.

"How did you know?"

"How will you change?"

"Are you scared?"

In each question Nate heard genuine curiosity, an impulse to understand him.

One day, they were hanging out at the playground, smoking weed on the swings, and a few younger guys were staring at Nate from near the seesaw, poking each other and pointing in his direction.

"Yo!" one of them shouted. "What the fuck is *that*?"

The one next to him doubled over in laughter.

"I mean, I know it's not a girl. But it's not a dude either, bro."

Nate felt his insides evaporate. He thought he'd been punched, but no, he was still sitting here, swinging gently, staring at nowhere, listening to younger but bigger boys call him not a he or a she, but a *what*, an *it*, a *that*.

When he'd left home that morning, he'd felt good. He was in a black tee, with the sturdiest sports bra he owned underneath. He had on skinny jeans and Vans, a chain hanging from his pocket. Girls liked the way he looked, and he knew it. A couple had told him so earlier. But that was the difference. Girls felt confused and grew curious. Boys felt confused and grew enraged.

Except for Dante.

"Dude!" Dante yelled, and he stood up now, took a couple steps in the other kids' direction. "That's my boy, all right. *You* can see him. You know exactly who he is. Why the fuck are you saying some ignorant shit like that?"

The boys stared and said nothing. Dante walked closer and kept talking. "You got something else to say?" he asked. "Because we can handle it another way if you got some more shit you wanna say to my boy."

They shook their heads, silently, and then left.

Ryan

The road was narrow and winding, two lanes between endless forest, stretching from the reservation out through Massena and Watertown and Syracuse, leading away from one life and toward another. Ryan was going to college in the big city. *Buffalo, New York.* But as he rode in the car with his parents, he barely thought about where he was going, only about what he might finally manage to escape.

He'd always imagined that another version of his life existed somewhere, that he could find it if he looked hard enough. In middle school he'd started writing short stories about a boy named Ryan who looked and sounded and moved just the way he did, but who existed in a world where those things made him popular. By the time he'd reached eighth grade, his ass-kickings had taken on their own, inevitable momentum. He got beaten because he'd always gotten beaten. He was a fairy because he'd always been a fairy. These were laws of the universe, both in his neighborhood on the rez and in his school off it. The only way out was to invent a different, fictional universe and escape into it.

But every summer he'd gone away to a college prep program called Upward Bound, mixing with Native kids from other reservations and non-Native kids from other towns around the state, and there he found a world ungoverned by those laws. He made friends with boys and made out with girls. Even the bullies from the rez seemed to lose interest in bothering him. Maybe this, he thought, was how life might look if he went to college someplace far from home.

Growing up, his schools had been split evenly between Mohawk students and white students, with only a couple of Black students sprinkled in. But Ryan spent plenty of nights at his white friends' houses and invited them to hang out with him on the rez. Occasionally, fights broke out between white and Native kids, and Ryan heard stories of white parents who didn't want their kids to invite their Mohawk friends to their homes. But those tensions remained, for the most part, beneath the surface. Ryan endured equal bullying from everyone, regardless of race or ethnicity. No cultural difference could sever their shared belief that Ryan was a fairy and someone should kick his ass.

Most importantly, though, Ryan had always felt comfortable enough in majority-white spaces. Up in the North Country, wherever he went, people knew him. Most of the white people he encountered knew his family. Others at least knew pieces of his culture and history, or were friends with his neighbors. No one ever asked the question Ryan started hearing time and again after he arrived in Buffalo, where white and Black and Puerto Rican students all looked at him with the same confused expression.

"What *are* you?"

The first time he heard it, Ryan didn't understand the question.

"*What* am I? Don't you mean *who*?"

"No," they explained. They knew he wasn't Black. He wasn't white. *What* was he? Asian? Hispanic? Once, someone walked up to him, looked him up and down, and said, "Dude. Are you from Hawaii?"

It could be enraging, to feel erased in others' imagination. Buffalo State's campus sat just thirty miles from two separate reservations, Seneca and Tuscarora. On occasional weekends, Ryan would ride to one of them with other members of the Native American Student Organization, just to experience a few hours on a rez, any rez, to eat corn soup and fry bread with people who shared the biting sarcasm born into seemingly all members of the Six Nations people. Even if their language and traditions were different, they were still bound by history, by ancient tethers to this land.

—

Ryan made friends. Some of them were from the Native student group, some from the hall of his dorm. No one ever called him an antigay slur. He braced for it several times, at parties or on the intramural volleyball court. He had a sixth sense for the most likely offenders—they were not usually the biggest and most aggressive guys, or the most obvious assholes, but the slightly smaller and weaker ones, the ones stuck in that space between the bullies and the bullied, trying to transition from the latter to the former. In college, even those guys proved him wrong. He never heard those old familiar slurs. Not even once.

He started to open up—briefly, in select settings, with the right audience. There were times, though, when he wondered if his friends saw the same thing his bullies back home had seen, something he'd struggled to see in himself.

One night his friend Callie burst into his room, a giddy smile on her face.

"Hey," she said. "We're going out tonight."

Callie was his best friend. He'd known her since they were little kids, but they'd lost touch for a while. They'd reconnected on the first day of orientation at Buffalo State, when he walked into a seminar hall, looked for somewhere to sit, and saw her in an aisle seat near the back of the room, smiling and motioning for him to join her. They'd been inseparable since.

Now he saw her standing in his doorway, thrilled with whatever future the night held. This was fall of his sophomore year, more than a year before he would get into his first bar fight at La Luna. He was still new to college nightlife and found it all dizzying and terrifying.

"Where are we going?" he asked.

"I can't tell you," she said. "Just make sure you wear something *tight*."

And then she left. "Hurry up!" she yelled on her way out the door. He felt a rush of excitement tinged with mild panic. Did he even *have* anything tight?

A few minutes later Callie returned, this time with their friend Amir, a Palestinian American from Queens. Amir was small and loud and filled with outrageous confidence, a certainty that his presence gave life to every room he entered, that no matter the context, the people around him needed to hear whatever thought had entered his mind. Ryan loved and feared him.

Amir and Callie exchanged conspiratorial smirks as they assessed Ryan's outfit, a white button-down and the tightest pants he owned. They said it needed work but would do for the evening, and then they did the same with Ryan's roommate, Brian, a tall and quietly confident white guy from central New York.

"Let's go," Callie said.

"Okay," Ryan said. "Now where are we going?"

Amir put a hand on his shoulder. "We're going to Marcella's."

Ryan felt his pulse take flight. "Oh my god," he said. "You're not serious."

Yes, they said, of course they were serious. Amir had been inviting Ryan to come with him to Club Marcella almost every weekend, all school year. It was Buffalo's biggest gay club, a kind of wonderland, Amir promised. He returned to their dorm after weekend nights there delirious and drenched in sweat. Every time he invited Ryan, Ryan declined. He never said he was freaked out by it, and never tried to use the sentence, "I'm not gay," as an excuse. He just said that maybe he'd go some other time. Apparently, Callie and Amir had determined that time was now.

Ryan didn't argue. He felt a quiet buzz, some nervous churning in his stomach, and he made the drive downtown. He knew exactly where the club was. He'd passed it many times, often slowly, studying its clientele.

As Ryan parked, Amir bounced in the back seat. "Let's go!" he yelled.

Callie wrapped her arms around Ryan's shoulders. "Come on!"

—

He arrived to a world of bodies and color. Light fluorescent, music pounding, thighs and traps on full display. Men stretched from the entrance down a long hallway into an open dance floor, and Ryan felt his body seize with nerves as he walked past them, deathly terrified of eye contact, looking only at the back of Callie's head as she guided him in.

At first, everyone inside looked like another species to him. Short shorts, sleeveless tops, a few guys in leather harnesses and little else. Their clothing, though, seemed less foreign than their confidence. They all seemed to move through the room with an ease Ryan could hardly fathom, and he watched as Amir moved with them, his hips unlocked from the moment they entered, his hands grazing the backs and shoulders of several men as he passed them on his way to the bar.

"What do you think?" Amir asked him.

Ryan laughed, a little nervous.

"It's... interesting."

"Come on," Amir said, and he grabbed him by the arm. "Let's dance."

Amir danced. So did Callie and even Brian, who was not gay as far as Ryan could tell but seemed totally unbothered by the scene. Ryan stood on the edge of the crowd, trying to calibrate his movements, wanting to dance enough to conceal his panic, but not enough to draw attention to himself. He looked at the faces around him. Most of the people in the club were men. A few appeared to be lesbians, and a few seemed like straight women out with gay friends. Ryan scanned the crowd for any Native faces. He felt a faint terror that someone from the Seneca or Tuscarora reservations might recognize him from his visits to their territory, and that they might know other Mohawk people, and that someday they would casually mention that they had seen that guy Ryan down at the biggest gay club in Buffalo, and that all of this would lead, inevitably, to his father recoiling in horror, and to Robert, the hockey teammate who'd delighted in calling Ryan every imaginable gay slur, taking perverse delight in telling everyone around the rez that he had always been right. But he felt relief as he realized that he and Callie were the only Native people there.

—

He allowed himself to dance, just a little, when the music changed from techno to hip-hop. Missy Elliott got his hips moving; Lil' Kim kept them in motion. The movement calmed him, gave his fidgeting some purpose. And now he allowed himself to scan the room again, this time guided less by panic than curiosity. He'd only ever seen men touch each other in (firm) handshakes, (short) hugs, or, from time to time, punches to the face. Now he let his eyes linger for a few moments as men ran their fingers along each other's chests, as they danced with hips adjoined, as they pushed each other against walls and kissed each other's lips and necks.

And then he saw, standing against the opposite wall, another guy scanning the room. He looked young, maybe eighteen or nineteen, same as Ryan. He was nodding his head to the music but only just a little. The rest of his body remained perfectly still. Ryan thought he saw an aching curiosity in his eyes, perhaps a nervous rapture, as if he found the scene enthralling and terrible. He would watch the bodies on the dance floor for just a few seconds, and then his head would jerk downward, and he would stare at his own feet as if ashamed. He spoke to no one. Ryan studied his face—white and bearded and unfamiliar—and he was seized with a sudden and certain realization.

He's just like me.

Gideon

Two flashes of color appeared in the corner of Gideon's left eye, fuzzy globes shuffling in his direction, soft and bright in a place where everything else was hard and dark. Gideon wasn't sure he'd even *seen* the color pink since he'd arrived at West Point. Now he looked up to see two pink slippers moving closer, step by lazy step. His eyes kept scanning. Gray sweats, a black hoodie, a messy bun of blonde hair.

"Hey," she said.

"Hey," he said.

"You look bored," she said.

"How could you tell?"

Gideon was on Charge of Quarters duty, manning the front desk for his unit. This meant answering phones, keeping an eye on emails, and greeting anyone who arrived. At some point or another, CQ duty was required of all sophomores. Which is what Gideon now was. Weeks after Pappo's funeral, he'd put together his resignation packet to formally leave the Academy, but when it was time to submit it, he couldn't follow through. He liked this place, he realized. Even with all the tedium and the chain-of-command bullshit, he liked who he was becoming at West Point. He told Coach, and the baseball team welcomed him back. He told Kristen he was staying, and she was devastated. A few weeks later, they broke up.

And now he was here, sitting at the CQ desk, watching the clock and glancing at a history textbook. Until these pink slippers walked in.

"I have to tell you," he said, "those are the loudest fucking slippers I've ever seen."

She shrugged. "Yeah. They're comfortable though. And definitely not within regs."

Gideon laughed. "No," he said. "I would think not." He nodded toward the logo on her sweats. "You on the soccer team?"

"Yeah," she said. "Goalie. What about you? Basketball?"

Gideon smiled. "Nope," he said. "Baseball. People always assume basketball though."

"Baseball's boring. Why'd you pick a boring sport?"

"Not boring to me," he said. "I did play basketball in high school."

"Not good enough to play here?"

"Or just too good at baseball to play anything else."

"Why are you even doing this?" she asked, gesturing to the CQ desk. Athletes could often get out of tasks like CQ duty, given the extra demands on their time. "Shouldn't some slug be doing it instead?"

"Probably," he said. "But whatever. Fuckin' *hoo-ah*, right?"

She smiled, then turned to go, but as she left, she told him her room number. "Whenever you get done with this," she said, "come see me."

—

West Point wasn't exactly the kind of place you went to find romance. For Gideon, baseball, class, and "army bullshit" occupied nearly every moment of every day. Besides, this was not fertile ground for a straight man. The Academy was about 85 percent male. Of the 15 percent who were women, a significant number were lesbians. (Don't Ask, Don't Tell was still very much in effect back then, but *come on*. Gideon had heard about the softball team's road trips.)

And then there were the rules: Absolutely no public displays of affection, ever. No holding hands on the way to class, no hello or goodbye kisses, no heads on shoulders or hands on thighs. Even more confounding was the "one-to-one" rule. If ever members of the opposite sex were in the same room with the doors closed, they could not be there in equal numbers. One man and one woman, alone in the barracks? Not allowed. Same for two men and two women, or three and three, and so on until infinity. Two and one? Totally fine. Same for three and two. Finally, even if the ratios were in order, two members of the opposite sex could not share a "horizontal surface." Not a bed, not a floor, not a desk. Technically, cadets joked, this meant threesomes were okay, as long as everyone was standing up. Any other kind of sex? Not allowed.

All of this meant that many women on campus actively rejected the idea of dating another cadet. So straight male cadets started with the 15 percent of their peers who were women, then eliminated a significant number who had no interest in men, then another number whom they didn't find attractive, and then finally the group who announced loudly that they would never, under any circumstances, date a fellow cadet. After that, only a tiny fraction of the Academy's population remained.

And the guys on campus, nearly all of them, it seemed, were the kinds of guys that girls had always wanted: Fit and smart and polished. High school quarterbacks and prom kings. Valedictorians who lift. All of which meant that the vanishingly rare Hot Straight Female Cadet was treated as a celebrity, coveted and followed by hangers-on. If they were single, these women had to navigate an endless procession of men who wanted to fuck them. If they were in relationships, their boyfriends could drive themselves mad with jealousy and paranoia, aware that at any moment, somewhere on this campus was a future congressman trying to get his girlfriend to the nearest horizontal surface. And so they would hear from everyone, hey bro, I saw her talking to that soccer player after class, she was smiling a little too much if you know what I mean, just looking out for you dude, you know how these chicks can be.

The Academy often seemed to be fully powered by repressed sexual desire. When they arrived before basic training, all cadets were given a gray wool blanket that felt like sandpaper. Everyone hated it. No one slept under it. In the corner of their rooms, though, wrapped in a plastic covering, lay another blanket, one they weren't allowed to touch until they completed Beast. It was green, warm, and made of some synthetic cotton they'd been told felt like a cherub's baby fat. They called it the "Green Girl." It was a siren, just beyond reach, calling to them nightly. After Beast, they unwrapped her ceremoniously, draped her across their beds, and crawled underneath. You must cherish the Green Girl, the upperclassmen told them, give her your love and attention. She was, after all, the only girl you were going to sleep with for the next four years.

His freshman year, Gideon noticed that once every few weeks, his squad leader announced at breakfast formation that a cadet in their unit had gotten engaged, and every time, the entire squad burst into a wild conflagration of applause. This felt, to Gideon, like one of the most generous traditions among his classmates: dropping the Academy formalities to celebrate one of their own committing his life to another.

Once, one of the baseball upperclassmen was the subject of an engagement announcement, and he grinned and waved as the rest of the squad chanted his name. Later, at practice, Gideon went out of his way to offer personal congratulations.

"Huh?" the senior said, laughing. "I'm not *actually* engaged."

"You're not?"

"No, dumbass. *Engaged* means I got caught jacking off."

—

From the moment Gideon met Caroline, she seemed like a character from a movie. A model who boomed seventy-yard goal kicks and could handle an M16. On a campus obsessed with rules, she broke them all. Gideon couldn't figure out how she ended up here. This was a place for people who craved structure. And now, here, *her*. Pink slippers. Shuffling down the hall, daring someone to make her change.

United States Military Academy at West Point Code of Conduct, Section 1.4, Item G: "Affectionate physical conduct with a guest or another Cadet in public... is not permitted."

The first time they made out that same fall, on the baseball field bleachers, a little after dusk one night—no one was around to witness them. Gideon told himself that it didn't necessarily count as public, their mere presence in an open space on campus grounds, and it felt less like affection than hunger or *need*.

USMA Code of Conduct, Section 2.17: "Any jewelry worn by Cadets must be conservative."

Now, as they made out on the bleachers, he felt something cool and metallic, and he stopped.

"Is that a *tongue ring*?"

"Yeah. What else would it be?"

She wore it everywhere, to class and physical training and even on the soccer field. Gideon asked how she got away with flagrantly breaking Academy rules. "I just *wear it*," she said as if the question was absurd. The stud was clear, she explained, and she only traded it out for something more visible off campus. "It's cute. I like it. It's fine."

As the weeks passed, his life melted into hers. They stole time. An hour or two at night, in her room, talking or watching *Friends*. Walks around campus, stopping to make out in the bleachers. A constant search for any *horizontal surface* they could share without getting caught—hotel rooms just off campus; the concrete floor of the baseball stadium; occasionally, if they were feeling reckless, her bed in the barracks; and once, when they were drunk, a patch of snow-covered earth on the farthest outskirts of campus. On free weekends, they sometimes took the train to Manhattan, pooled their Academy stipend to book a hotel room neither could afford, and treated themselves to a weekend of sex and room service, staring out the window and wondering about the lives of strangers they saw below.

She pushed him. With Caroline, he found new limits to himself and new ways of seeing the world. They debated politics and religion—he'd been raised a conservative evangelical, her family was liberal Catholic—and often her arguments devoured his own, leaving him to reconsider everything he'd been taught. All his life, Gideon had chafed against rules but still followed them. He'd lived within the code of morality passed down from his parents, studied dutifully, if not obsessively, for school, done all that was required to please his coaches in every sport. And yet here was someone who'd arrived at the same place he had, a Division I athlete at the United States Military Academy, who seemed never to have attempted perfection at all. She showed up late to practice, but it didn't matter because she was nearly six feet tall with incredible instincts in goal. She skipped studying to hang out with friends, but still got good grades because her mind worked at an electric pace. She poured a fifth of vodka into a Gatorade bottle and carried it around campus like it was water, but she trusted, somehow, that she would never get caught, let alone punished. She gave him permission to forgive his own imperfections, and to release himself from the pressures of their shared world.

Gideon quickly realized what it meant to date a female cadet on an overwhelmingly male campus, particularly one as attractive as Caroline. Lots of dudes wanted to fuck Gideon's girlfriend. He would stop by her room and find a rotating cast of varsity athletes lingering in the doorway, trying to make her laugh. Most of them moved aside the moment Gideon got there, extended their hands to shake his, told Caroline it was good to see her, and then left. But a few lingered, like this one guy, a junior lacrosse player from Boston who vaguely resembled a Kennedy—about six feet tall with dark eyes and thick hair and a slicing jaw—who looked up at Gideon and said who the fuck are you? Gideon introduced himself and said I'm her boyfriend, and when the guy said nothing back, Gideon just put his hand around Caroline's waist, kissed her hello, and started asking about her day.

He knew that eventually he had to leave her there, alone in her room with guys who clearly wanted her, because soon after the lacrosse player left a football player would arrive, and a basketball player after that, all equally eager to take what Gideon had. And he knew that he could never puff out his chest or stare anyone down, could never say, "Why the fuck are you in my girl's room?" Attempting to exert physical strength would show emotional weakness. The threat he carried was not one of violence; plenty of these guys could kick his ass if they wanted. Gideon's threat was in his height and his smile, in the way her eyes ignited the moment he arrived. When he walked into a room, they ceased to exist. And yes, jealousy roiled him silently, and, of course, he looked up all their stats in their respective sports the moment he got back to his room. The lacrosse player, it turned out, had barely gotten off the bench all season. *Really stretching the definition of the term athlete*, Gideon thought. He had no business feeling threatened by a glorified *slug*.

—

In the fall, Gideon sat in the stands for nearly all of Caroline's soccer games. In the spring, she sat in those same bleachers where they'd first made out to watch him take the mound. From the very first day of practice his freshman year, Gideon had realized he had a major problem on the field: He was not the best player on the team. Not even close. He stood in the bullpen, watching other pitchers throw, and he saw immediately that a few of their fastballs had more zip; their curve balls broke with more venom; their pitches found the targets more consistently than his. Physically, he barely even stood out. A couple of other pitchers were just as tall as him. One guy, a dual recruit for the baseball and basketball teams, was *six-eleven*. Then there were outfielders who stood only five-ten or six-two but packed on 230 pounds of muscle. Gideon felt like a mannequin in his uniform. The upperclassmen looked fully enfleshed.

Gideon found a place in the pitching rotation and became an immediate contributor to a winning team. But here was the awful truth: He was not dominant. His mind fixated on the math. This was Division I, a university that boasted of attracting the best and brightest and bravest the country had to offer, but they played in a small conference filled with small schools from around the Northeast. When they played teams from the Southeastern Conference or the Atlantic Coast Conference, they got blown out. As he moved through his college baseball career, Gideon's goal remained the same as it had always been: Make the Big Leagues. But he'd begun to realize just how many athletes had similar or greater talent and the exact same goal.

—

The spring of his sophomore year, he tweaked something in his arm, a visceral pain that got worse that whole summer. It was like knives in his shoulder and something duller and heavier in his bicep, just above the elbow. Gideon felt his velocity declining, his fastball dropping from 90 to the mid-80s, and as he practiced before his junior season the hitters could pound his pitches damn near wherever they pleased.

He underwent surgery to clean up severe inflammation in his upper arm, and when he recovered, he was locked in as one of the team's top-of-the-rotation starters. But as he moved through his junior year, he saw no dramatic improvement from the pitcher he'd been earlier in his career. He was still not dominant. He had not emerged as a star. He was a good Division I athlete. But at this point, he was nothing more.

By his senior season, he'd begun to wonder if this was it. Caroline had graduated and lucked into an assignment that kept her on campus for an extra year. He spent his free weekends at her apartment, and many of his weekdays wondering about what came next if he was approaching the end of his baseball career. He told himself this was a good thing. If he let go of the dream of turning pro, he could immerse himself fully in the daily joys of his final season, at last allowing himself to fully appreciate the game he'd only ever seen as a path to his ultimate goal.

But once the season started, Gideon began to wonder if maybe that had been the secret all along, if by letting go of the dream of making the Big Leagues, he would finally play with a freedom he'd never felt, and if that freedom would push him to new levels of performance that drew the attention of Big League scouts.

He kept those thoughts to himself. Outwardly, he told friends and family he was just preparing for graduation and for his first assignment as an officer in the army. In the spring, he received his branch assignment: Air Defense Artillery, Fort Bliss, in El Paso, Texas. He would work to protect the United States and its allies from airborne missiles and bombs.

One morning his senior year, he stood at breakfast formation and listened as his company commander, a rugby player named Lieutenant Boone, made an announcement to the entire company.

Gideon, he announced, was engaged.

There was laughter, wild applause, back slaps from all those around him, and enough *hoo-ah* to power an entire brigade. Gideon smiled and shook his head, just as he'd seen so many others do over the years, and he waved with sheepish pride to the applauding throngs. It wasn't until the next formation, later that same day, when Lieutenant Berger spoke again.

"I need to make a single point of clarification," he said, adding that Gideon "did not get caught in a, um, *compromising* position. He's *actually* engaged. Getting married in June."

Now the applause returned, even wilder this time, and Gideon smiled and nodded as his company's congratulations swallowed him whole.

—

Here, finally, is how his life's dream ended: not on a baseball mound, pitching one final game, or even in a dugout, watching helplessly as his teammates failed, but rather alone, at his parents' house, staring at a computer screen. It was the summer after graduation, 2007, just weeks before his wedding. He'd gone to visit his parents. None of them knew that today was the day of the MLB draft. Hardly anyone did. The draft wasn't televised then. Only the most diehard of fans followed it. But Gideon sat in his high school bedroom, drinking a beer and clicking refresh as the picks were announced on MLB.com. He saw plenty of guys he'd pitched against get selected in the draft's early rounds. Some he'd struck out. Others had hammered him. All were now going pro.

He even saw a couple of his teammates' names, and he texted them congratulations, and he meant it. They deserved this. But really, Gideon liked to think that he did too.

He knew there was no reason to expect it. He'd had a good senior season but not a dominant one. His elbow problems lingered. The velocity on his fastball dipped. When scouts came to games, they stuck around afterward to talk to a couple of Gideon's teammates, but never to him. In order to be drafted, he was competing with everyone he'd ever played with or against, and hundreds of others from far bigger programs than West Point. And in order to make a Major League roster, he'd be competing with thousands of talented players from Venezuela, the Dominican Republic, Cuba, Japan, and so many other corners of the globe where boys grew up swinging bats and throwing balls. Gideon knew the impossible math. He told himself he accepted it.

Late his senior year, he asked Coach if he'd gotten any questions from scouts about him as a pro prospect.

"I told them you weren't interested," Coach said.

"You told them *what*?"

"It's true. You're *not* interested. Not in what they're offering. Late-round pick, tiny signing bonus, rookie ball and then Low-A ball, making basically no money with barely a prayer of ever getting to the Big Leagues." He shrugged his shoulders, then continued, "It's true, right? Scouts like your size. They like your raw tools. But you haven't shown enough to get drafted early, and you're not committed enough to make it if you get drafted late. In those later rounds, they want guys who are *desperate* to make the Big Leagues. I told them the truth. You're getting married. You're branching Air Defense. You're planning a life in the army, not in baseball."

Gideon seethed, but he knew Coach was right. West Point had been four years of slow acceptance that the life he'd planned was not the life he would live. By his junior year, he'd started imagining a different future: marrying Caroline, serving their five years together, then getting out and using his West Point degree to get a job that would pay him outrageous money while they raised their kids. That didn't seem so bad. Maybe it was even better than riding buses through rural America, making a couple hundred bucks a week, all just so he could say he played pro ball, even if he never came close to the dream of the Major Leagues.

Summer evening on the beach, her in a white dress and him in a white tux, both barefoot, toes sinking in the sand. A faint buzz as he waited for her down at the end of the long aisle, whether from nerves or from the light beers he'd been pounding since soon after the sun rose. The wait, listening to the lapping waves, for the ceremony to begin, as Gideon stood wondering when their rent-a-minister would finally arrive. Do you Gideon. Do you Caroline. Take these rings. Kiss the bride.

Dancing in a hotel ballroom in South Carolina to a DJ who called himself "Miami Steve." "Yeah!" and "Electric Slide" and "Another One Bites the Dust." Shots. Champagne. Glasses clinking, kissing again. The toasts from friends, earnest and loving, with a couple of jokes thrown in, and then one from Caroline's dad, his smile electric, in full command of the room. He made a few short and punchy remarks before he looked at Gideon and said, "I'm going to tell you the same thing my father-in-law once told me.

"She's your problem now."

Ryan

That first night at the gay club, as he watched that awkward white guy standing on the edge of the dance floor, Ryan had seen himself reflected in his unsure movements, his searching eyes. As he watched him watch the gay men dance before him, Ryan felt, for a moment, as if he could picture that man as a little boy. Ryan could imagine him being called slurs, could see the bigger and louder boys tormenting him in his own hometown. He believed he was watching the culmination of a stranger's story, the moment he found the ability to set foot in a place he hoped would welcome him when much of the world had cast him aside.

Now his eyes took in the room again. He saw the tall men, the handsome men, the leather-clad men who seemed so confident on the dance floor, and he let himself wonder what they'd had to go through to get here. The club was neon and leather and flesh but also courage, a place for leaping into a terrifying new reality, unsure of what you might find.

—

Callie finally asked him a few months later. They were driving back to school from winter break their sophomore year. They'd always ridden together on these trips, usually gossiping about high school classmates and talking about the strange comfort of returning home. But now, as soon as they got on the highway heading west, Callie said with a strange formality, "Ryan, I have a question I want to ask you."

Ryan knew the question immediately, but he did his best to feign surprise.

"Okay," he said. "What is it?"

"Are you gay?"

He inhaled, a quick pinprick of nerves, something hot and dangerous shooting through his body. No one had ever asked him this.

They had *declared* him gay, of course, but Callie was the first person to raise the idea out of curiosity.

It had been three months since that night at Club Marcella. Ryan hadn't gone back. But something about that moment had sent his imagination in new directions, had let him find comfort in his own curiosities, given him a willingness to linger, if briefly, inside his own desire.

Was he gay?

"Um," he said. "I think I might be."

"Okay," Callie said. "That's cool."

Immediately, Ryan felt the buzzing in his stomach settle into something less afraid and more hopeful. *Okay. That's cool.* There was something calming about the nonchalance of those words, some restorative power in the shrugging of her shoulders. They settled into an easy quiet for a few seconds, and then Ryan saw a smile grab ahold of Callie's face.

"Oh my god," she said. "I have a gay best friend!"

Ryan laughed. He knew that, for Callie, this was something of a dream. She'd been joined at the hip with Amir all year, had become friends with the bartenders down at Marcella's. But this was different. This was Ryan, whom she'd known since they were toddlers. They'd recently realized that their grandfathers were cousins. They knew each other's families, shared the traditions of their home.

"Oh my god," she said. "We have to find you a *man!*"

No, Ryan said. He was not ready to find a man. He told her that he'd never spoken those words aloud to anyone. "Give me five fucking minutes to adjust to this before you try to set me up!" he said, laughing.

For now, he was terrified of what it meant to live in a world where those words had been spoken aloud. She had the power to destroy him.

"Please," he said, "you can't tell anyone."

"I won't," she said. "I swear."

—

A few weeks later he was sitting in the living room of their dorm suite in Buffalo when Amir, draped lazily across their couch and casually eating a snack, sat up and looked at Ryan.

"So," he said. "Callie tells me you're considering sucking a dick."

Ryan felt his breath leave him, blood rushing to his face. Before he could even respond, Callie walked into the room.

"What the fuck," he said, and he listened as Amir cackled.

"I'm sorry!" Callie told him.

"Don't worry," Amir said. "We're going to find you a dick to suck."

Callie and Amir felt safe. No one else did. Ryan went back to Marcella's a few times later that spring, in the final weeks before Amir's graduation, but he stayed on the periphery, watching the dance floor like he was peering through a window into another life. That spring Amir moved back to the city. Callie dropped out and moved back to the rez. Now the only people who knew Ryan was gay had left Buffalo. That fall, he dated a woman for a few months, told himself the gay thing had just been a brief curiosity. The next time he touched a man's body—*really* touched a man's body, not just a handshake or a bro hug—was that night at the end of the fall semester of his junior year, the one that started with amaretto sours and progressed to salsa dancing. He next touched a man's body when he punched a stranger's face.

He let himself imagine, though. One night he went to a townie dive with Julieta and her friend Grace, whom he barely knew. He walked up to the bar for a Captain and Coke and stood nodding his head to a wail of rock music while he waited, and then, when he moved to pay, a voice to his left told the bartender, "That one's on me."

The voice came from an older man, perhaps in his thirties, who now looked down at Ryan, taking him in. He wore a dark denim jacket and a red T-shirt, his dark hair shaved close to the skull. When he smiled, Ryan felt he'd been devoured. Ryan thanked him and rushed back to his friends.

"Oh my god!" said Grace. "Did that guy just buy you a drink?"

"Yeah."

"He's hitting on you!"

Ryan shook his head. To Grace's knowledge, he was completely straight.

"He's just a nice guy," Ryan said.

"Ryan!" she said, and tilted her head to the bar. "*Look!*"

He turned, and now he saw the man staring, a smile stretching across his face. He raised his glass, and Ryan raised his own in return.

"Ryan, he wants to sleep with you!" Grace shouted.

Of course, Ryan had seen movies where men bought drinks for women, and those drinks led to flirtation that led to sex. But no stranger had ever bought Ryan a drink before. Even on those nights at Marcella's, Ryan clung to the wall and watched Amir accept strangers' advances, never imagining himself the object of that kind of desire.

"*Noooo*," Ryan said.

"Yes!" they all said together.

"Oh my god. What the hell."

"Go talk to him! Maybe you can get us free drinks too!"

Ryan felt his face go hot, his eyes dart back to the man and again to his friends. "He's a grown man! What am I even gonna talk to him about?"

He wondered, later, in the quiet of his dorm room, what it might have been like: To stand next to a handsome stranger and gulp down his drink and listen to that man name all the parts of Ryan's body he might have admired. To feel his hand on Ryan's shoulder and then running down his arm and back. To laugh and lean closer as the man told his jokes, to finish that first rum and Coke and consider another one, to hear the man ask him to stay and drink and dance. To allow himself the proximity of this body. And he wondered, even further, what would have happened if he had finished that drink and taken another, had run his own fingers up the man's neck and over his tightly buzzed hair. What would have happened if the man asked if Ryan wanted to leave and Ryan said, with ease and comfort, sure, let's go. If he'd let the man take his hand and they'd walked out the door past all the others who'd come to the bar in search of this very experience, to find a body that compelled your own body, to leave interconnected with strange fingers and arms. He wondered what would have happened if they'd gotten in that man's car, which was probably expensive and smelled like pine, not because it had an air freshener but because it was regularly cleaned, all the way to his home, which Ryan thought must be spacious and tastefully decorated. And he wondered what it would have been like to wander inside and have the man grab and kiss him, and then that was it, the moment where Ryan could no longer let his mind wander, the place he forced his imagination to stop.

Nate

Three months before his eighteenth birthday, Nate rode home from the pharmacy with his mom, packaged hormones in his hands, shaking in the passenger's seat of her car. Ever since he'd been a small child, he'd been afraid of needles. The mere thought of metal puncturing flesh left him weak and woozy. And now, all that stood between him and the next steps of his transition was the sharp object he most feared delivering testosterone into his body, once every other week, for the rest of his days.

"I feel sick," he told his mom during the ride.

"I know, baby," she said.

"But also excited."

"I know, baby."

And then he reached his hand for her hand and she held it.

"I'll be right there with you," she said.

Beneath the needle panic, another, deeper fear. *Would he regret this?* He knew all the ways testosterone would change his body: Loss of fertility, increased acne and hair. Weight gain. His body would harden, his features sharpen. What would he think when he saw himself in the mirror? He hated what he saw now, but how did he know this new version of himself would feel any better? A new hormone would change his body. But what would he do if, even in a new body, he still felt the same ache inside?

He wanted to find out. At home, his mother drew an X on his thigh, just as the doctor had taught them. Then a circle around the X. And then she injected him, the needle directly into the skin at the top right quadrant of the circle.

"That's it," she told him as she put a small Band-Aid on his leg. "Done."

And now he started shaking again, not from fear, but elation. He'd done it. Or at least he'd taken the first step.

No matter how butch he dressed or acted, Nate knew he had three tells. First, his height, which would never change. He would forever introduce himself as a five-foot-one man. Second, his muscle tone, which he knew he could work on. He would continue working out, and the heavier he lifted and the longer he stayed on T, the more he could trust his muscles to grow. And third, finally, his voice. He had "a Minnie Mouse voice," he'd always said. Even compared to girls, he sounded high-pitched. When he sang, his voice opened up into something beautiful and soaring. This was the one gift he'd received from that second X chromosome, the ability to hit every note of any Paramore or Evanescence song with power and precision. Nate loved singing but hated speaking. When a friend saw him in skater jeans and tank tops, hair cut short, and then asked if he wanted to be called *he*, Nate hated the way he sounded when he squeaked back at them, "Yeah man, that would be cool."

His shoulders filled in first, muscle replacing fat. Then his chest, his forearms, his back. All of this was noticeable within months. Once-invisible veins started to run like rivers down his forearms. He was still thin, but his torso took on a rigidity, solid angles where once there had been a soft slope. After two months on T, his voice began to crack. First he just noticed momentary breaks in tone as if his vocal cords couldn't decide which register felt like home. Every time he heard it, he felt both embarrassed and thrilled. *It's working*, he thought.

By three months, his mom noticed. By four, so did his friends. By five, he'd dropped from a soprano to a tenor. After about six months, he looked in the mirror one morning and saw peach fuzz, just a little bit of hair growing above his lip. He ran to his mom's room to show her.

"I don't see anything," she told him.

"I do!" he said. "Right here!"

"Ohhhh, right *there*!" she said, grinning now, and he couldn't tell if she meant it or was just trying to placate him, but he didn't care.

—

He turned eighteen, got his own place in a trailer park just outside town, and found a job stocking shelves overnight at Walmart. He kept lifting until he saw mass accumulate around his shoulders. Testosterone continued to transform him, even in ways he'd never imagined. When his levels got too high, he lost the ability to cry and turned aggressive and demanding. Feelings of anger found the surface while feelings of sadness remained buried underneath.

Also, his dick got bigger: the organ most people called a "clitoris." On testosterone, it grew into something altogether new, even more sensitive and fully capable of penetration. He used it to sleep with a healthy rotation of women, who only seemed more attracted to him the longer he stayed on T. This wasn't just about the physical changes. Along with body hair and muscle definition, every shot seemed to deliver a new infusion of confidence. He liked feeling the rumble in his chest when he spoke, loved shaping the patches of hair on his face with a razor. He attracted women because he knew he could attract women. They liked him because he knew they should.

Even as he grew more assertive, he still preferred to let women make the first move. This seemed easier, since he knew that plenty of them weren't attracted to trans people. That was okay. Nate wasn't either. He tried dating them a few times but never felt the same spark.

As he got older, into his early twenties, he sometimes dated men. He was shocked the first time it happened, when he got a message on Facebook from a chubby white guy with sandy blond hair, green eyes, and a blazing smile.

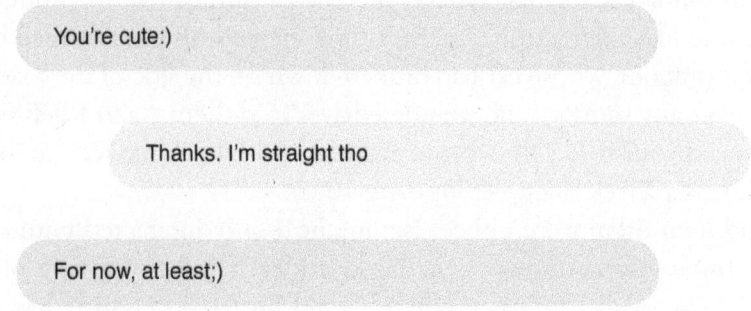

His name was Jordan. He was a firefighter, proudly out of the closet, even at work. He bought Nate gifts, showered him with compliments, told him he was one of the most beautiful men he'd ever seen. He acted more masculine when he was alone with Nate or around his firefighter friends, then more flamboyant when they went to Cleveland to dance in the gay clubs. Sometime after Jordan there was Ty, a tall Jamaican dude who was bisexual and only out to a few close friends. Ty cared for his ailing mother during the day and worked the forklift at Sam's Club overnight, and he and Nate lay on the couch together watching movies and fooling around during the hours in between.

Just as dating feminine women reinforced his sense of his own manhood, so did dating masculine men. In each of them he saw a mirror, men drawn to the same parts of himself that he most loved. If the boy-crushes he'd had as a child had felt like jealousy, these attractions felt more like self-exploration. He was drawn to the pieces of their body that his lacked, and those that he shared.

–

It's impossible to say when, exactly, he started to "pass." Once, the world looked at him and saw a pretty Black girl who liked to dress in boys' clothes. But at some point—maybe it was soon before he started T, or maybe it wasn't until he'd been on hormones for a couple years—the world began to see a young Black man. Some women expected him to hold doors open. Others politely called him *sir*. Sometimes, though, his presence inspired fear. He saw white women quicken their pace when he walked behind them. Occasionally, he heard the locks on car doors click when he was nearby. Once, he offered to help an elderly white woman unload her groceries and she waved him off, almost shouting for him to leave her alone. Another time, he and his mom pulled over to help someone whose car had broken down on the side of the road. "I don't have any money," the stranded driver told them, "and I definitely don't need your help." Presenting as a Black girl, he could feel invisible. Existing as a Black man, he felt dangerous.

And then there were police. Before, he'd only interacted with cops a few times—sometimes when they'd gotten a call about one of his mom's boyfriends, and once when he and his friend Destiny had run home from a party after a fight broke out in the front yard. Every time he'd encountered police before his transition, they'd been watchful but restrained. But now, after a couple years on T, he noticed those interactions taking on a new edge.

For example, there was the evening when he and his mom went out to pick up dinner from McDonald's, and police lights flashed behind them. He was twenty now, out of high school, more than two years on testosterone. His mustache was slowly creeping toward his goatee, his voice had already descended a few registers, and the muscles in his shoulders and back were rounding into shape. When the police looked into his mother's car, they saw a middle-aged white woman riding with a young Black man.

The cops, tall and beefy and white, had approached the car on both sides. They said a taillight was out, and Nate's mother promised she would get it fixed. They wrote her a citation; she accepted it and said, "Thank you." Then they looked at Nate.

"Do you have any drugs in the car?"

"No, sir," Nate said. He liked to smoke, of course, but whenever he bought marijuana, he took it straight home and left it there, so he'd never have to give the wrong answer to that exact question.

"What about any weapons?"

"No, sir," he said. Nate then paused for a second, before he continued. "I do have a pocketknife, though." He'd gotten the knife from his friend Ray, the only other trans man he knew in Youngstown. Ray had told him that a pocketknife was an essential tool for being a man. Nate had used it to cut boxes and open bottles, and to dig holes in trees to anchor a hammock in his backyard. He knew the law. In Ohio, a knife like his was perfectly legal. But still, this seemed wise to tell them. He didn't want them to search him, find the knife, and then declare that he'd been lying to police.

"Get out of the car," the officer said.

Nate did as told. His mom had long ago taught him that to resist a cop was to invite violence. He put his hands on the vehicle, spread his legs, and felt the police pat him from his ankles up to his calves, and then his thighs, reaching into his pocket to pull out the knife, then continuing to pat him, all the way up until stopping at his chest.

"What's this?" he said, pulling the straps of Nate's breast binder. He'd bought the binder after seeing one advertised on YouTube. It functioned exactly as advertised, giving Nate the appearance of a totally flat chest. The straps cut into his skin, but it was worth it. Nate was still hoping to get top surgery, but until then, the binder let him wear what he wanted without drawing attention to his chest. But now he felt the cop's hands on the straps, and he heard the confusion in his voice.

"It's a binder," he said. "I'm trans. Female to male."

"Oh," the cop said, pulling his hands away. "Okay, ma'am. You can get back in the car."

Joseph

They left on Valentine's Day at dusk, walking single file through a Fort Benning hangar to the plane that would take them to Afghanistan. He carried his M16, listened to the engine roaring at the end of the hangar, felt the darkness of the night folding in all around him. The plane stopped once in New York to pick up another unit, then again in Italy to refuel, and there they let soldiers out on the stairs to smoke cigarettes and stare for a few minutes at the sky, long enough to tell women they'd been to Italy once, assuming they made it back home. Some number of hours later, the captain came over the intercom and announced their impending arrival on a steep descent, diving toward the runway to limit exposure to enemy fire. When Joseph looked out the window he saw a few lights in the distance, planes and trucks and buses, but mostly, he only saw darkness. They rolled to a stop, and no one moved. Five minutes passed, then ten and then thirty and then an hour, and Joseph saw his commander up front, barking something he couldn't understand into a phone, until finally word filtered back to his row.

They were not in Afghanistan. They were in Kuwait. Their unit had shown up to the wrong war.

Who knew what had actually happened, who had been the one to mess it up. Maybe it was someone on this plane, or maybe someone in DC or Kabul. But they were here now, so they might as well stay. No sense wasting a good unit just because it's stranded a few thousand miles from its assigned post. They took a bus to Camp Victory, right on the Iraq–Kuwait border. At this point in the war, in February 2004, every single American soldier passed through Camp Victory on the way to Iraq. It was massive, a small city of twenty thousand to thirty thousand people, its population changing every single day as about a thousand soldiers filtered in and out. Joseph's unit was called the "Mayor Cell," part of the two hundred or so soldiers who stayed at Camp Victory more permanently, running it. Officers were assigned to oversee food and maintenance, personnel and armor, and anything else needed to run a base and equip the soldiers who passed through. This was small-town bureaucracy, transported to the edge of a war.

Once they got settled in, he started to think the next ten and a half months might not be so bad. The biggest reason: Joseph had, by his estimation, the very best job in the camp. He served as chaplain's assistant. Essentially, the chaplain's bodyguard. Under the Geneva Conventions, military chaplains could not be considered combatants, and therefore could not carry weapons. Which meant their assistants carried weapons instead. Most of the time, though, the chaplain was not actually facing any imminent threat, so Joseph just scheduled meetings and handled the logistics of the chapel and sat outside the chaplain's office watching Fox News.

About ten days after he arrived, Joseph was asleep in his cot when he felt someone shaking his shoulders. He woke to see a guy he vaguely recognized, a sergeant first class from another unit.

"They need you in the chapel," he said.

Joseph unzipped his sleeping bag and walked out of the tent into the early morning darkness, fumbling around to find the sink station so he could brush his teeth.

"Sergeant!"

He looked up to see another body running toward him, out of focus. "Get to the chapel! Now!"

It was about 4:30 a.m., maybe 5. The air was cold and the desert wind strong. A sliver of orange curled around the horizon, swallowing the darkness inch by inch. Joseph ran until he reached the chapel, where he saw medics rushing in and out, quiet and purposeful. Men in polo shirts and khakis took notes and spoke to each other in calm tones. Various uniformed men approached Joseph with different versions of the same questions: When did you last leave the chapel, who was the last person you saw, did you close the door and lock it, do you know who else might have come in?

The truth was that they kept the chapel open all night. Camp Victory was a place you passed through on your way into battle, where you might die, and passed through again on your way back home, when your friends were dead. In either direction, you stopped for a while at this makeshift city and you started asking questions about the meaning of it all. So here, in a tent on the edge of the camp, was a place to come and to cry or scream in the general direction of whatever deity might listen. This was a place that should be left open, Joseph and the chaplain believed, every moment of every day.

Right now the room filled with moving bodies. Some were taking photos and walking with purpose, others standing and staring with none. He moved toward the cluster until it parted, ever so briefly, and he saw another body, the one around which all the others had orbited, and he realized that this was the reason everyone else was here: this body, young and male and prone on the ground, the top of his head blown off.

Only after Joseph saw him did he smell him—nauseatingly pungent—and only after he smelled him did he see his detritus—skull fragments scattered on the floor like shavings of ice, matted hair stuck on the tent's ceiling, and the blood, more than Joseph ever imagined a human body could hold, most of it pooled around his head but some streaked along the ceiling.

A contractor got started on cutting out a section of the tent's roof to sew in new fabric. Medics collected the body, which belonged to a Marine, and drove him away. Joseph and a few others grabbed a bucket of bleach and another of water and scrubbed the floor. While they scrubbed, he learned the Marine's name, which he would soon forget, and he learned a few pieces of his story, most of which he would not.

The Marine was eighteen years old. He was from Minnesota but had been stationed at Camp Pendleton in California. He'd enlisted immediately after high school. He'd likely been on his way to Fallujah, where violence was growing by the day. But instead of proceeding to Fallujah, his life had ended here, on the floor with an M4 in his lap, skull fragments scattered all around. A Bible sat nearby, open right next to him. Joseph wondered what he had been reading, whether he had been praying, and what would have happened if he'd shown up during working hours instead, hey Sergeant, I'm here to talk to Chaps, I'm headed into the shit and I'm really fucking scared.

—

So. This was war: Days of staggering boredom punctured by moments of horror. Most of the time, Joseph and the rest of the members of his unit felt like they were watching the opening montage of the same movie, on repeat, every single day. They saw infantry units roll through camp in M1 tanks and Stryker vehicles, motoring into the desert on their way to fight for freedom. But in the movies, those soldiers looked like gods. Here, they looked like anyone else—they were just the ones who got to ride into battle while Joseph's buddies spent their days counting porta-johns and doing laundry. "This is bullshit," Sergeant Byrnes said one day while they sat around watching Fox News in the chaplain's tent. "I joined the army to blow shit up. We should be out there killing *hajjis*." Joseph just nodded, choosing not to argue that killing people actually sounded quite unpleasant, or to remind Byrnes that they both had joined the *reserves*, and that they'd done so for the exact same reason: because they had no clue what else to do with their lives. For months, the camp was packed, with hundreds or thousands of troops rotating in and out every day. By the summer of 2004, though, rotations had slowed to a trickle. The war was elsewhere. Suddenly a camp built for thirty thousand troops had a population of less than a thousand. Most days, Joseph filled his time with softball, flag football, and hours lifting weights in the gym.

A few times during that long and languidly hot summer, he was asked to fill out the security detail for a convoy of fuel trucks that filled up at Camp Victory and then traveled north, deep into Iraq, to a base just south of Najaf. They would drive twenty minutes from camp to the Iraq border, then deeper into the Iraqi desert, passing through nowhere towns, sun-bleached buildings and cars, everything tan and brown. In the town of Um Qasr they saw a Baskin Robbins, and they knew that on the way back they would stop to try one or two of the thirty-one flavors, served to them by a Pakistani expat who told them to call him James. Good guy that James. He loved America, supported the war, and always seemed to give Joseph a generous scoop of mint chocolate chip.

These trips were largely uneventful. They just sped through the desert, never stopping at lights or signs, then dropped off the fuel and sped back home: until one day, when they'd just passed through Um Qasr, and Joseph heard a voice over the radio, faint under the sound of the Humvee engine.

"We have an issue."

Joseph was in the lead Humvee, technically in charge of the whole expedition. He was the senior ranking soldier, an E-5 Sergeant, which basically just meant he'd enlisted a few months earlier than anyone else, long enough to take a Platoon Leadership Development Course that elevated his rank. The voice was coming from someone in a truck farther back in the convoy.

"Our truck is having problems. We have to stop."

This had never happened before. But still, they always traveled with mechanics in the convoy just in case. Joseph's truck pulled across the two lanes at a ninety-degree angle, shutting down traffic in the front, and the rear truck did the same on the other end. "Set up a perimeter," Joseph told his guys over the radio, and by the time he said it they'd already begun. The soldiers in the front vehicles sealed off traffic one way, the soldiers in the back sealed it off in the other, and the soldiers from the middle fanned out into the desert with their weapons, ready to call out the approach of any oncoming people or camels or cars. Joseph called the Tactical Operations Center back at the camp and told the major we're stopped, we've got an issue with a truck, no sir we don't know what it is yet, no sir we don't know if we need any extra parts, yes sir we'll keep you posted as soon as we learn more. He grabbed a few water bottles and started to walk down the line, passing out water to whoever needed it, asking if anyone wanted snacks or anything else, no that's all right, we're okay, I know it, dude, I was looking forward to that ice cream too.

On the front and back ends, a few drivers turned off their ignition and got out of their cars, talking to the others around them. From afar, they seemed to feel the exact way the soldiers did, bored and vaguely annoyed. An hour passed. Then two. Joseph kept making the rounds, checked in with the mechanics, who were talking about a water pump or something, we think we've got it figured out, just give us a few more minutes and we'll be back on the road.

Another voice came over the radio, saying, "We've got a lot of civilians lining up back here." The voice sound calm, but urgent. "They look like they want to start coming toward us." Surely, Joseph thought, no one stuck in traffic was dumb enough to approach a fully armed convoy from the most powerful army in the world. But what could they want? He started jogging to the back. He realized the convoy didn't have a translator with them. How would they even tell these people to stay the hell away?

He reached the back and he saw them, still so far away they remained blurry in his vision. They were moving, though. That was clear. They were taking one slow step after another, shouting in Arabic as they walked. Joseph called back to the base, explained the situation to the major.

"These people aren't stopping."

"So *stop* them. That's your job."

The soldiers started shouting one of the only Arabic words they knew.

"*Qaf! Qaf! Qaf!*"

Stop. Stop. Stop.

Joseph stayed on the phone with the major, asked if they should fire warning shots.

"I can't tell you that. I'm not on the ground. Just trust your people. Trust your training."

A new energy crackled up and down the convoy. They were miles from the camp's daily tedium. There were no porta-johns or laundry tents or makeshift chapels in sight. Joseph caught a glimpse of his reflection in a Humvee window, fatigues and helmet on, body armor covering his torso, and an M16 slung around his shoulder, and he registered, briefly, that no matter how he spent his daily life, no matter whether he ever imagined he might end up here, right now he *looked* like a fucking warrior. They all did. The men who carried the weapons would dictate what happened next.

This was the job. A car breaks down. A convoy stops. Soldiers pull security. They fan out in every direction and carry rifles by their sides but only raise them if a threat approaches. And now a threat was approaching. Maybe. Kind of. How were *they* supposed to know? The truth was, this region of Iraq barely saw any action. Here in the South, American troops were greeted just like the Bush administration's fantasy, as "liberators" who had come to free them from Saddam Hussein's tyrannical rule. Occasionally, they heard about a couple of rounds of mortar fire somewhere in their general vicinity, but that could have just been dumb kids trying their hand at playing war. This region held no organized threat.

And yet. Here were these people, coming toward them and refusing to stop. "Yo, what the fuck are they *doing*?" said one of the gunners atop the Humvee, Sergeant Richards. Joseph liked Sergeant Richards—kid from Wisconsin who seemed, most of the time, like kind of an idiot. But he trusted him here, knew he'd do his job. "Something bad's gonna happen if they don't stop."

They didn't stop. Now soldiers started raising their guns to the sky. Do not be stupid, people. Do not make us show you what these weapons can do. The crowd was a hundred yards away. Then ninety. Then eighty. And now they could definitely hear the shouting: "*Qaf! Qaf! Qaf!*" Joseph was certain they could see the raised weapons, because with every few steps a couple members of the group peeled off, shook their heads, and turned around to go back to their cars.

They would take two steps, then stop, blurry figures taking shape, and then they'd take two steps more. A few stopped, turned around. Others lifted their hands in the air, but kept coming. Even if this region had been quiet, Joseph had heard plenty of stories of ambushes across Iraq—civilians who appeared in need but carried bombs strapped to their chests. Some of them didn't even have a choice. They were kidnapped by insurgents, forced to sacrifice themselves as suicide bombers, or else their entire families would be slaughtered instead.

Seventy yards. Sixty. "*Qaf! Qaf!*" Enough people had peeled off that it was no longer a crowd, just a small group of four or five people. If this was a threat, it had arrived in the form of a few middle-aged men and a lone slender woman in a *hijab*. Joseph shouted at them to stop and they took more steps. He waved his gun and they kept their arms to the sky. He heard his heart beat in his skull. Fifty yards. They need to fucking stop, someone said. Forty. What the fuck goddammit what the fuck.

Sergeant Richards was the first to say it. "If they don't stop, I'm gonna shoot."

And now guns were raised not to warn but to fire, and suddenly Joseph's was raised to fire too—no thought, no conscious decision, just words in his ears and movement in his muscles, and he was staring at human flesh through iron sights. He fixed his sights for five seconds or five minutes, who could tell how long, and he knew that time had now split open, that his life had two chapters, before and after. But here he was, finger against hot metal, caught in between.

They teach you to keep both eyes open when looking down iron sights, to maintain your peripheral vision, but now the world collapsed around him, and all Joseph could see was two images, one blurry and the other a little less so. He felt his stomach twist, a surging sickness. They were unknown humans in a place where Joseph had learned that any unknown humans could carry death. They were slow-shuffling civilians, with pot bellies and flip-flops and frantically waving arms. They needed something, clearly, but Joseph feared that what they needed was to blow up his convoy. And now they were bodies lying across his sights, and he and they both knew that with one flinch of his finger their lives would end. Joseph felt omnipotent and grotesque.

"I'll shoot," Sergeant Richards said, and they kept taking steps closer, and Sergeant Richards kept saying it, I'll shoot if they don't stop, I'll shoot if they don't stop, *Qaf Qaf Qaf!* What are you doing, goddammit *QAF!* And yet they kept coming, even slower now, and soon Joseph could see that there were not two of them, but actually there were three: the potbellied man, and the small, slender woman, and there, cradled against her, head barely visible and resting on her chest, calm and trusting, a young child.

"Hold your fire!"

Joseph would never quite know exactly when he said it. Maybe right when he saw the child. Maybe seconds before or seconds after. He never *thought* the words, did not make a conscious decision to speak them aloud, only opened his mouth and heard them pouring out. He held no clarity of purpose, had no idea if what he was doing was wrong or right. He said it because he was brave. He said it because he was chickenshit. Who cared. He just said it.

The potbellied man stopped. The woman kept walking. All guns remained raised. Only now he could understand the English word the Iraqis had all been shouting for minutes now, their monosyllabic response when the soldiers had told them to *qaf*.

"Sick."

She was still walking directly toward the soldiers, pointing to the child. "Sick. Sick. Sick."

No soldier said anything in response. They did not approach her, never addressed her directly. She just continued walking, closer and closer, repeating sick, and soon she entered the convoy, and she continued, quicker now, sick sick sick sick, all the way through the perimeter and past every Humvee, to the other side of the perimeter, where another long line of cars was waiting with another group of Iraqi civilians, and she walked among them, speaking in Arabic, until Joseph got distracted. By the time he looked back in her direction she was gone.

Gideon

Every Friday during lunch, they went to see the dogs. The pound sat right off post, just a quick drive, a warehouse in a strip mall baked in West Texas sun. He and Caroline were both now graduates of West Point, second lieutenants in an army several years deep into two concurrent wars. But the fighting was elsewhere. For now, they were here at Fort Bliss in El Paso, and visiting the pound had become their weekly ritual, a moment midday to reconnect with each other and imagine what creatures they might welcome into their new family.

"Oh, my god," Caroline said. "Look!"

Gideon looked. He saw a brown mutt, floppy ears and long face.

"Cute," Gideon said. "But I don't think that's the one."

They already had one dog, Caroline's terrier Sunday, whom she'd bought after graduation. But now they were married homeowners: not yet ready for kids, but eager to fill their home with more life.

"Babe," Gideon said, and he pulled her toward the corner of the room, "I think this might be the one."

Ivory fur with big brown patches, muscled and rowdy, ravenous for attention. Gorgeous. A pit mix of some kind. The moment Gideon reached to pet her, she jumped on him and begged for more.

"Oh, my god," Caroline said, as the dog started licking her face the moment she leaned down. "Not today," she said, "but if she's still here next time, we'll get her then."

This had become their practice. Show up, find a dog, fall in love, and then declare that if it was still there next time, it was meant to be. So far, every dog that had captured their attention had been gone by the time they returned.

"Um," said the volunteer on duty, a teenage girl with big glasses and a quiet voice, "she definitely won't be here next time you guys come."

"Why not?" Gideon asked.

"Well," the volunteer said, "she's on the list to be euthanized tomorrow."

They named her Charlie. She woke them up every morning, begging for breakfast and affection, and she followed Gideon around the house as he showered and shaved and guzzled coffee on his way out the door. He and Caroline rode to post together before dawn, arriving for physical training (PT) at 6 a.m. After working out with their respective units, showering, and eating a quick breakfast together, they were off again, ready to serve.

He'd branched Air Defense Artillery, managing the operation of Patriot and THAAD (Terminal High Altitude Area Defense) weapons systems, some of the most sophisticated military technologies in the world. Every single day was dedicated to one simple task: preparing to shoot an enemy's missile out of the sky.

This was the job Gideon had wanted. He'd had no interest in following his classmates into more *hoo-ah* branches, like Armor (Gideon didn't fit inside a tank) or Infantry (he had this nagging desire *not* to die). Air Defense was critical to the nation's safety, but its duties were carried out far from the front lines in Iraq or Afghanistan. These weapons systems were vital. Their mere existence saved untold numbers of lives. So many missiles would never be fired because of the knowledge that they'd be shot down if they were. *Someone* had to know how to operate the things. Even if he was deployed overseas, he'd be serving from bases in Qatar or Korea, places with shopping malls and swimming pools and not a single insurgent in sight.

This was a good life. Mid-to-high five-figure salary straight out of college, middle-management set of responsibilities, with promises of upward mobility as far as the chain of command could stretch. Blacking out with friends on Fridays, recovering at home with Caroline and the dogs on Saturdays, doing home renovation projects with football playing in the background on lazy Sunday afternoons. Sex at least five times a week.

And yet, in everything, a glaring absence: baseball. The single task to which Gideon had dedicated his life no longer held any purpose. Without baseball, Gideon didn't know what, exactly, he was *for*. Nothing else could give him that sharpened focus, the demand of excellence paired with tangible evidence of whether he'd met the required standard. He tried to find it in his work: mastering the weaponry he'd been assigned to learn, effectively leading the soldiers under his authority, communicating clearly and directly with higher brass. That worked fine. As the months passed, he was praised by commanders and handpicked for promotions. He played the role of army officer just as well as he looked it. He could climb the ladder as high as he wanted.

He also tried to find that commitment to excellence in his home. Marriage, Gideon decided, was something he could excel at, just as he'd excelled at everything else. He woke up to make the coffee in the morning, worked to install new light fixtures and doggy doors on the weekends, committed himself to regular and enthusiastic cunnilingus, and kept an internal count to make sure her orgasms per week roughly matched his own. Old insecurities lingered, but he worked to hide them. He showed no jealousy when they went out and she danced with one of the ex-lacrosse guys who'd also gone from West Point to Fort Bliss; he knew that even if he was still surrounded by guys who wanted his wife, Gideon was the only one who'd proven he deserved her.

—

Baseball was a sport built on monotony but punctured by moments of ecstasy or devastation. Most innings passed without incident. But all held the potential for something extraordinary. Even as Gideon had followed the same routine, day after day, at the Academy, he had known that every pitch held infinite possibility.

Now, the script of his days appeared to be prewritten. He would lead his soldiers and master his weapons systems and run through the same exercises day after day in PT. He would crush a few dingers in beer league softball, and on weekends he'd go drinking with buddies from school. Someday, he'd get notice of a deployment. And then he would follow the same routine, or one much like it, on some other similarly bland base in some other corner of the world.

He knew one person, though, who expanded his sense of what might be possible. His commander, Connor, seemed to imbue the mundane rhythms of their everyday with new potential. Connor was about thirty, a rising star in the army whose name was known by generals and congressmen. He'd been a quarterback at West Point, but now he seemed nothing like the other ex-jocks Gideon hung out with. He played guitar in a rock band that booked venues all over Texas and New Mexico. His arms were covered in tattoos—none of the clichéd pieces Gideon saw on soldiers every day, but intricate and well-considered works of art. Politically, he leaned left. He rode a Harley and drove a Mustang. He'd already commanded one unit and had been handpicked to command another. He was given his choice of second lieutenants to help him lead. Connor had noticed Gideon when Gideon became a star pupil in the weapons system course that all new Air Defense officers took upon arriving at Fort Bliss. When he asked Gideon to join him, Gideon barely had to give it a second's thought.

In the months since they'd started working together, Gideon had been trying to study what made Connor such a great leader. He held a complete mastery of any and all weapons systems they might encounter, an obsessive attention to the details that made THAAD such an effective military tool. This was nerd shit, technical engineering knowledge, and Connor not only commanded it but could *explain* it to even the dumbest grunt who'd just finished basic training. He floated, effortlessly, between rooms filled with those kids, fresh out of high school in Stockton or Teaneck or Wichita or wherever, and the generals who stopped by post just back from Baghdad.

Connor remembered names. Sometimes, even birthdays. He shook hands firmly but kindly, and he always made direct eye contact. He slapped backs and asses and always knew which to slap when. He busted balls in ways that made soldiers feel included, not insulted. He talked about fantasy football and political theory and the dual engine capacity of the Harley he'd just started riding to base. Gideon understood that all of this mattered, every bit as much as his ability to shoot enemies' missiles out of the sky. Connor was a leader, not only by example, but also by effort and instinct. He'd built himself into a man others wanted to follow, and then he showed them exactly where they all needed to go. He was the kind of man this country's safety had been built on. And he seemed to believe that Gideon could become one too.

—

On weekends, they drank. Gideon, Connor, a few other officers from the unit. There was Santos, whose first name Gideon only half remembered, a little guy with big shoulders and zero impulse control, the kind of short guy Gideon had long ago learned not to fuck with, one who seemed always in search of an excuse to fight. Then there was Matt, another West Point ex-jock, but in handball or something, one of those Olympic sports that rich parents signed their kids up for with the explicit purpose of getting them into an elite school. There was also Brad, a warrant officer about fifteen years older than the rest of them, thrice-divorced, extremely competent, and wildly profane. Another second lieutenant or two, a few senior noncommissioned officers, even a first sergeant who'd been in the army longer than Gideon had been alive. Sometimes, Caroline or one of the other officers' wives or girlfriends joined them. Mostly, though, these nights were reserved for the guys.

They usually ended up at Mulligan's, a biker bar tucked in the corner of a strip mall in East El Paso. The sign was green, the decor Irish, the crowd a mix of Mexican and white. The drinks were cheap and the wait for a round of pool or darts was never long. Most Friday nights, they'd head there right after work, drink and talk shit, maybe inhale a burger and fries, then head back to someone's house to keep drinking. Gideon never had a drop of alcohol during the week. The moment a beer met his lips was the moment he guaranteed the night would end with a blackout. It had been that way from the first time he'd snuck his mom's wine coolers in high school, and had continued when he'd guzzled vodka on weekends away from West Point. He saw no reason to stop the pattern now. Friday nights were reserved for annihilation.

None of this, Gideon understood, was permitted by army regulations. The blackouts *themselves* were fine—almost expected of any soldier. But officers were not supposed to go out drinking with their subordinates. Especially not weekend after weekend, closing down the bars and heading to someone's place for afters, then finally taking a cab home sloppy sometime after 3 a.m. But Gideon didn't care. For one thing, *he* wasn't the one who would be getting into trouble. He was the youngest and lowest-ranking officer there. He'd face no discipline for saying yes to an invitation from a superior. *They* would be the ones getting written up for going out and getting ripped with the same people they spent all week working to lead.

So he went. He drank. He played a few rounds of pool (he was average) and darts (he was excellent) and he listened to their war stories and soaked up as much as he could. Now that he was no longer playing baseball, this was his team. With the dream of the Big Leagues now gone, climbing this ladder became his new goal. Every shot downed and dart thrown, he felt himself inching higher. Senior leadership had picked Gideon to be one of them. He was just walking through the door they'd opened for him.

Occasionally, deep into the night, with most of the rest of the group floating around the bar or the pool table, Gideon and Connor would find themselves sitting together, alone. Gideon felt a small thrill in these moments. Connor dissolved the barriers of rank and command. He led with technical mastery and quiet confidence. But there were moments, like these, when he slipped out of that role and into another, this paragon of ruthless efficiency now just a red-faced and happy drunk. You know, he would tell Gideon, fixing his gaze on him from just across the wooden table, you're already on your way in this world. Gideon would nod, listening, and wondering if he had what it took to grow into someone like Connor over these next few years. Both were towering and strong, both with minds that held tight to technical knowledge without giving it much effort, both with the West Point degree and easy smiles that rocketed men up these ranks. Connor was handsome, like Gideon hoped *he* was handsome, and he was competent, like Gideon *knew* he was competent, and he had an ease in command that Gideon believed he could learn. When they sat together in this dusty El Paso biker bar, Gideon felt warmed by the force of Connor's full attention, a soft and vibrant glow.

The end arrived quickly, one night the next spring, when Gideon found himself on the side of the highway, running to Connor, a still and bloody heap. They'd all left the bar late, headed someplace for afters, and Gideon had gotten a call—come back, we've got a huge problem, Connor wrecked his bike. Gideon got there five minutes later and found Connor, not moving, but conscious and alive. Gideon took off his shirt and wrapped it around Connor's head as a bandanna, trying to slow the bleeding, and told him I'm here, we're all here, we'll get you fixed up real soon, you're gonna be okay.

Which, he knew even then, was not entirely true. An officer had been riding a motorcycle, drunk, with no helmet—because he never wore a helmet, because they were all too cool for helmets—and this had come at the end of a long night out drinking with soldiers under his command. Paramedics would arrive. Police reports would be filed. An internal army investigation would be launched. Minutes ago, Connor had been untouchable, the kind of guy who looks in the mirror and sees a future senator, or at the very least, a general. Now, he was on his way to the hospital, clinging to life. As for his military career, he wouldn't be discharged, but his rapid rise would immediately stall. The crash happened on a Friday. By Monday morning, Gideon had a new commander, an older hard-ass, not the kind of guy Gideon could ever imagine inviting him out for one beer, let alone fifteen.

—

One afternoon that June, Gideon got home from work and Caroline was gone. This was unusual. Caroline typically beat him home. Thirty minutes passed, then an hour. He figured she must have gotten caught up with some administrative bullshit, the kind of mindless paperwork that landed on a lieutenant's desk at the end of the day. Still, he tried calling. No answer. He sent a text:

> Hey babe. You okay?

Minutes later she walked through the door.

"Sorry I'm late!" she said, and she kissed him hello.

"Where were you?" he asked.

"I just stopped by Connor's place," she said, "to check on him."

That felt strange. Caroline didn't know Connor the way Gideon did. She'd come out to Mulligan's plenty of times, sure, and she and Connor seemed to get along fine, but Caroline got along fine with everyone.

"Okay," Gideon said. "That's pretty fucking weird."

"Why is that *weird*?" she said. "I feel bad for him!"

It would take months before Gideon would find out when, exactly, Caroline and Connor started fucking. It started like this, she would later say. Just a few conversations when she checked in to see how he was doing. And then she started to pick him up and give him rides to base, because he was no longer allowed to drive on post, and they would linger in the car and talk for a long while before heading into work. And when Gideon would ask why the seat in her car was leaned back and she would say she'd given Connor a ride, that it was no big deal,

Gideon would try to believe her, because he knew that to show jealousy was to show weakness. But he reached a point where he couldn't take it anymore and just said, "Let someone besides my wife give him a fucking ride."

And then there was a conversation, later that summer, when Caroline told Gideon, out of nowhere, that she felt guilty that Gideon had never had the chance to sleep with anyone besides her. His high school girlfriend had said she wanted to wait for marriage, and Gideon had been content with blow jobs and hand stuff. And then he'd met Caroline, and now they were committed for life. "If you want to," she offered, "just to see what it's like, then maybe you should."

"I should... ?"

"Sleep with someone."

"I should sleep with someone."

"Yeah."

"You want me to cheat on you."

"It wouldn't be cheating. Just a one-time thing. But if you ever do, just don't tell me about it. I don't want to know."

A few weeks after that, Caroline bailed on a trip to the beach with Gideon's childhood friends, and he came home to see that she'd put sheets on the pull-out couch. She told him that she'd just been lonely one night, and that she didn't want to sleep in their bed without him, so she slept on the pull-out with the dogs. And later, when Gideon was overseas for a training exercise in the Netherlands, his buddy Matt said, "You really don't know, do you?"

"Know what?"

Matt winced. "I'm not sure I should tell you."

"What the fuck, Matt. Cut the shit."

Finally, after literally hours of this conversation, Matt said he would flip a coin, and if it was heads he would tell him and if it was tails he wouldn't. Then he tossed it in the air, let it land in his palm, and flipped it over onto the back of his left hand. Heads.

He looked Gideon in the eye and said it.

"Caroline and Connor are fucking."

Gideon refused to believe it. Or refused to admit that he believed it, to himself or to anyone else. But then, finally, back at the house one Saturday afternoon, they were folding laundry in the bedroom and her phone lit up on the nightstand with a text, and Gideon looked down and saw the words, something about tasting you or fucking you or watching you ride my cock. The name was one he didn't recognize, something preposterous—Ron Silverstreet or something—and he knew then that they had inside jokes, Caroline and Connor, that they sat in bed and they laughed about the ridiculous names they would give each other in their phones, just their little secret, and Gideon grabbed the phone and held it up to her face and said, what the fuck is this?

—

For a second, maybe less, he saw a look of guilt and shock on Caroline's face. But that was it. The two minutes it took for her to admit everything seemed a mere formality, both of them waiting for her to say the words she would soon say, it's Connor, and for Gideon to say the words he would then say, are you fucking him, and her response, which he had to give her a little credit for, direct and finally honest, yes, we've been hooking up, yes, it's been going on for months.

Gideon waited for her to say something else. It meant nothing. I'm so sorry. I don't know what's wrong with me. It will never happen again. But instead she stayed quiet, tending only to the laundry, so many gray T-shirts and black shorts, the silence between them growing fat and foreboding, until finally, Gideon began to fill that silence with rage.

He screamed. Why the fuck would you do this, get the fuck out of here, fucking leave fucking leave I can't even look at you just fucking leave. The screaming was the only way he knew how to keep breathing. His body held no function but to expel anger. Him? *HIM!* him. Of all fucking people you fucked him.

She said nothing. She did not apologize or try to reason with him. She grabbed her toothbrush. She packed T-shirts and bras. Gideon couldn't bear the silence, so he filled the air with more angry nothings, until finally she took her bag and walked outside. Gideon followed behind her, carrying Sunday, the little dog she'd gotten back at West Point. Charlie wasn't going anywhere, Charlie was *his*, but Sunday could get the fuck out. Caroline threw her bag in the car and Gideon handed her Sunday, and then finally, briefly, she cried. A soft whimper, nothing more. It was summer in El Paso, the sun bright and malevolent. He watched her drive through the West Texas desolation, and he turned around and went back inside.

Immediately, the house was haunted. Everything in his field of vision became a reminder of the life he'd thought they were going to have. They would fill this house with animals and memories, then follow each other to another corner of the world. Someday they would have children, maybe after one or both of them had left the army. They had forever to share.

A few years ago, Gideon had gone to a party for his grandparents' fiftieth wedding anniversary, and he'd been staggered by the level of commitment that number represented. So many little lives folded into one great love. He'd imagined what that day might be like for him and Caroline. Now he grabbed the wedding portrait that hung above their fireplace and he threw it across the room.

His wife was cheating on him. This seemed like an impossible sentence. This was the sort of thing he saw in movies, the kind of fact he heard about some friend's pathetic uncle. Caroline was not the kind of woman who would cheat, because Caroline was married to Gideon, and Gideon was not the kind of man who would ever be cheated *on*. Gideon was the guy who made the woman feel safe, her friends feel jealous, her father proud. And yet here he was, alone, with her words replaying in his mind. *Yes, it's Connor. Yes, we've been sleeping together. Yes, it's been going on for a few months.*

Gideon decided to make himself a drink. He grabbed a handle of Tanqueray from the fridge. He'd always been a vodka guy, but this gin had a higher proof, and even if he didn't love the piney taste, he knew it was more up for the specific job he required. He poured it over ice, filling a pint glass, then topped it with a splash of orange juice. Just enough to add a little color, so he could tell himself that he wasn't guzzling straight gin. The first glass went down quick, so easy that he decided to pour himself another, and that one went down quick and easy too.

He paced the house, took down any picture of her he could find, tried sitting on every piece of furniture, searching for any place where he might feel okay. Quickly, he realized that place didn't exist. As he got deeper into the bottle, his anger lost its shape but gained heft. He was teetering on the edge of sobbing, but crying felt weak, and weakness felt grotesque, and so he tried to steer himself back toward righteous anger. Fuck her and fuck him and fuck the people who knew they were fucking and fuck the people who didn't. All of them had contributed to building the world in which he now existed. All of them had pushed him deeper into this bottle of Tanqueray.

Speaking of which. The bottle was almost gone. Fuck. He started pacing again, now looking for anything that might help. And that's when he saw, right there on the kitchen counter, a bottle of pills. Ibuprofen or aspirin or something—who cared, he figured all pills worked the same if you took enough at once. A couple of fistfuls, chased by whatever beer he could find in the fridge, and all of this would vanish forever. He just needed relief. Temporary relief, permanent relief, either fucking way. He needed the world to no longer be a place where these feelings existed, or he needed himself to no longer exist in this world.

He paced around the house, pills in one hand and the remaining gin in the other, mumbling to Charlie, I might have to do this girl, I know you probably don't want me to, but don't worry, you'll be fine. Taking the pills felt like taking action, the only way he could exert a shred of control.

But maybe not just yet. Let's not get crazy here. Perhaps he needed to think this through. He might as well pour himself the last bit of gin while he weighed the pros and cons.

Pro: He would not feel the way he felt right now.
Con: Life would be over, and life, until the last hour or so, had been something he enjoyed.
Pro: Well, he guessed he didn't have any more pros, but here it felt important to reemphasize the first one. This feeling, whatever it was, would end.
Con: Suicide, in the army, is a bitch. His friends and colleagues would all have to deal with a ton of paperwork. That made Gideon feel like an asshole.

Speaking of his friends, he decided to check in with them, see what they thought. He texted Matt. He told him he'd been right about Caroline and Connor. Gideon was an idiot. Connor was a piece of shit. Matt told Gideon he was sorry, then asked how he was doing.

"I got some pills right here," Gideon wrote. "Let me just take a bunch of these with some gin and I'll be good to go."

Gideon kept stumbling around the house, throwing things that reminded him of Caroline onto the floor. Charlie watched from the couch, looking a little confused. The whole time, Gideon felt his phone vibrating. Matt, he assumed, texting him again and again and again.

"No," Matt wrote.

"Jesus," he wrote again.

"What the fuck," he continued when he still got no response.

> Don't do that Gideon.

> Gid.

> I'm coming over.

> Wait.

> Wait.

> Wait for me Gid please.

Joseph

He got back from war on a November afternoon, stumbling off the bus at Fort Benning and into the crisp Georgia air, and from the moment Emily rushed to embrace him, she wouldn't stop talking about his *neck*. Apparently, it had grown. Joseph hadn't really noticed this, but he supposed it had something to do with the hours he'd spent every day lifting weights in Kuwait, alongside Crompton and Byrnes, in their daily meetings of the "Get Swole Club," whose mission was, simply, to help its members get swole. When they'd started meeting, Joseph could only bench press the forty-five-pound bar. But every day, Crompton came by his bed and said let's go, dude, just give me one set, and then forty sets later they were done. Six days a week, two hours a lift, chest twice a week, back twice a week, bis and tris once, legs once, abs and post-workout protein and creatine every single day. And now his neck looked like a bourbon barrel. And something about this, even more than the lats and pecs and traps he'd worked to build, made Emily desperate to get him home to their bed.

They were both still in college. She had a year left to go, and he had two, and after they both finished she decided she wanted to go to graduate school in Charlotte. He followed her there and decided he wanted to go to seminary, maybe so he could become a pastor, but definitely so he could try to work out the questions that had been rattling around in his head ever since the day he'd held that Iraqi woman in his rifle's sights. He had questions that he couldn't quite name, not exactly, but all of them swirled around how a war he'd seen as just and righteous could leave him feeling like he'd briefly held evil in his hands.

—

The image of the penis didn't arrive until later, well after he'd started piling up debt for a seminary degree he'd never use, and soon after he'd started piling up even more debt in law school. But in truth, if Joseph had to pick a moment when things started to take a small but perceptible downturn, he would have pointed, oddly enough, to the November of his third and final year of seminary, when he had one of the greatest nights of his life.

They called it "Joe-a-palooza." His thirtieth birthday party was held at a friend's house in Charlotte. Dozens of people gathered into a small house to dance to prime Lady Gaga and early Kanye West and to toast Joseph with plastic cups filled from a keg of Amstel Light. The message written on the cake in icing said, "Happy Birthday Joseph. You're Old as Fuck."

It was true. *Thirty.* He was older than almost all of them. Their lives seemed to have all followed the same script. They'd grown up as good little Christians, leaders of their respective youth groups, making excellent grades. They'd gone straight from high school to college, where some liberal professor had planted a seed that led to their faith's deconstruction, plunging them into brief dalliances with atheism. And now they were at a liberal seminary, paying an exorbitant amount of money to figure out if they could still be Christians without believing gay people went to hell. They would cycle their way through this process by age twenty-five before going off to careers in ministry or counseling or academia, or, in some cases, sales. None of them had taken Joseph's years-long detours. Even though he was so much older, he still felt he was trying to catch up. But still. The cake was funny. Joseph blew out the candles and took a few bites.

He pounded some Amstel Lights, took a few turns on the dance floor. He would think, later, about how easy this night was, how the things that would terrify him a few months later in Seattle thrilled him here. Bodies touched his own and inspired warmth or arousal or nothing. Beer spilled on the cake and he laughed. He needed no exit plan, never grasped to exert control. This could be his life, he realized. He could be a person surrounded by people who liked him.

-

A while later, after Joseph had worked up a sweat dancing, he drifted to the side of the living room, where a few of his friends were sitting. The party was peaking now, the late arrivals were all here, and the early departures had not yet gone. One of those late arrivals sat on a couch with a group of Joseph's friends: his pastor, Mitch.

Joseph loved Mitch, who insisted that everyone call him by his first name. Hilarious and brilliant, he drank beer and voted for Democrats. Joseph had never before known a pastor who did either. Mitch was about fifty, white with salt-and-pepper hair, his potholed highway of a voice electric in the pulpit. He was everything to everyone, equally eloquent when discussing the Carolina Panthers' secondary, the problems with the doctrine of substitutionary atonement, and the glowing arrangement he'd just seen performed of Mozart's Symphony No. 41.

Mitch also liked, in the particular parlance of their time and place, to "thump nads." Thumping nads was a simple activity. A man walks up to another man. He then thumps him, with the back of his hand, in the gonads. A thump must be hard enough to hurt but not hard enough to injure. Once the thump has been completed, the thumper and everyone around him laughs. It's safe because the casual violence removes the sexual charge. Many boys played in middle school, some in high school, and a few even in college. Mitch was the first man Joseph had ever met who proved you could continue thumping nads until age fifty. He thumped nads in people's homes, he thumped them in church, and he thumped them in front of his wife and kids.

Now Mitch sat on the couch, next to Ted and Bobby and a few others, all of them talking or nodding their heads to the music, until a brief moment of quiet when Bobby took a sip of his beer and said, "*Fuck*, Jojo. *Thirty?* I can't even imagine being that old."

Joseph laughed. "I know," he said, shaking his head. "I'm practically a dead man walking."

Now Mitch interjected. "Pretty soon," he said, grinning, "your dick's not gonna work anymore."

And then Mitch thumped him. Joseph understood the logic. He had to, right? Joseph was standing right there, and Mitch was sitting right by him, and they'd just finished joking about the functionality of Joseph's dick. In Mitch's world, a dick that gets mentioned is a dick that gets thumped. And so Mitch reached around Joseph's leg and delivered a quick thump to the nads, and Joseph doubled over in laughter and pain. But Mitch wasn't done, not fully satisfied with just a perfunctory thump: He let his hand linger there, turning it so that his palm cupped Joseph's crotch, and he left it there until Joseph squirmed and fell backward into somebody's lap—Ted's or Bobby's—and around him Joseph heard laughter. Damn, Joseph, didn't know you were into that, what can I say dude, I'm trying new things in my old age. Joseph smiled and felt his face flush, and he tried to stand, but when he did he only moved into the pressure of Mitch's now wide-open palm, and as he squirmed backward again, he only moved against the anonymous lap in which he now sat. Joseph laughed. That's just Mitch, Mitch's wife Alice always said, anytime her husband smacked asses or thumped nads, you just have to let him be *him*. Finally, Joseph slithered away and stood up, still grinning, you got me good that time, *shit*. The whole thing lasted maybe ninety seconds. This was nothing this was funny this was fine. Joseph needed another beer.

—

Joseph stepped outside. He stopped by the keg, then wandered over to the fire, listening to the faint hum of traffic and the idle chatter of scattered friends. Then he felt a slap on the back.

"Happy birthday, motherfucker!"

He turned and saw Alex. Like Mitch, Alex was tall and loud and at times overwhelming, the gravitational center of every room. Joseph liked him. He was funny, smart, and more devoted to fantasy football than anyone Joseph had ever known.

"There you are," Joseph said. He raised his beer and toasted Alex's. "Man, we gotta hang out more."

"I know," Alex said. "We really do."

Things were busy. Alex worked long hours as a therapist in the psych hospital. Joseph asked how it was going, and Alex told him, "Good but *intense*." He saw people with violent tendencies and suicidal ideation, one crisis after another, day after day. "They've all been through hell," he said. "Almost every single one of them was sexually abused as a little kid."

Joseph took a sip of his beer. "Huh," he said.

"Yeah," Alex said. "Fucked-up shit."

Joseph stood for a second, a little wobbly, and then suddenly his mouth was moving, and out was coming a sentence he'd never spoken in his life. "You know," Joseph said, and it wasn't just that he'd never said this to anyone, but that he'd never even *thought* it. A memory had just arrived there, standing in that backyard on this night of his thirtieth birthday, minutes after getting his nads thumped, while he sipped his beer. But the moment the memory arrived it settled immediately into shape, fully formed. Like it had been tucked away somewhere for decades, waiting to emerge.

"I was sexually abused as a kid too."

Alex took another sip of his beer. "Oh really," he said, and in his voice Joseph heard no shock or pity, only light curiosity.

"Yeah," Joseph said.

"Man," Alex said. "That had to have been really awful."

Joseph told him that yeah, he supposed it was pretty bad, not because he felt that was true but because he knew that was what you were supposed to say. And then he went quiet for a moment and said, "This is actually really weird right now."

"Why?"

"Because it's like I just remembered this happened. Just now. But it feels like, 'Oh yeah, of course that happened. Of course I remember that.'"

Alex nodded and started telling Joseph about repressed trauma.

"Yeah," Joseph said. "It's like I just remembered, but I always remembered."

A few minutes later, Alex had to go back home, and they hugged goodbye. Joseph stood there for a moment, thinking about the stories Alex had told from the hospital. Patients who'd been abused and now turned violent. Joseph thought to himself that he was so lucky. He'd suffered something that left so many others' lives ruined, but his was intact. He took one last pull of the keg, which felt lighter now, surely the beer was almost gone, and then he heard someone yell, "Joseph! Get your old ass back in here!" He smiled and stepped out of the cold, back inside to his friends.

Ryan

He would never remember exactly how or when he ended up on Gay.com. Probably late at night, googling his way through loneliness and boredom until, on his screen, a whole new world opened up. This was the app before there were apps, the bar for people too nervous for the bar. The site was filled with profiles from cities around the world, endless bios and torsos, jawlines and thighs. By the time he finally went to bed that first night, hours had vanished, lost to his efforts to decode a new language, Masc and Bear and Twink and Daddy and Dom. Four years had passed since that first night at Marcella's, three since he told Callie he "might be" gay. Now out of college, still living in Buffalo, his routine was going to work and coming home and logging on each night to explore, a stranger in a new land.

One night, after hours of browsing, he found that his mouse was clicking on text that said "Create Profile," and he told himself that this was just a portal to a part of the site he'd never seen. And then he was entering a username, just because he might as well since the form on the screen was asking for one, and then it seemed rude not to continue answering the form's questions, so he went ahead and gave a roughly accurate accounting of his height, weight, ethnicity, and age. All of this was just out of curiosity, not really a solid declaration of anything. Surely straight men made mock profiles on Gay.com all the time, right? Besides, when the form asked him to describe the kind of man he was looking for, he left it blank. Would an *actual* gay man leave that blank?

He didn't include a photo. On Gay.com, this was common enough. Some of these men were like him, curious but not out. Many of them posted photos but hid their faces. They were torsos and dicks and thighs. There was something comforting about these anonymous bodies, their faces' absence hinting at the fact that, just like Ryan, they were sitting alone and staring at their screens, wondering who might be looking, imagining how news of their presence on this site might complicate their lives.

One problem: Guys with pics got all the attention. And unless you were built like a well-endowed version of Michelangelo's *David*, that pic better show your face. Ryan was built more like an NFL fullback—not fat, but carrying some extra padding, with layers of muscle underneath. If he opted for a body shot, he knew he had to be ready to initiate with the profiles that had contained face pics. And Ryan could not, under any circumstances, *initiate* flirting with another man. But he had to admit, it might be nice to talk to someone like the stranger at the bar who'd bought his Captain and Coke. Someone to make him an object of desire. So one night he fixed his webcam, angled it downward, and stared up with a blank expression. He clicked.

The messages arrived faster now, one after another.

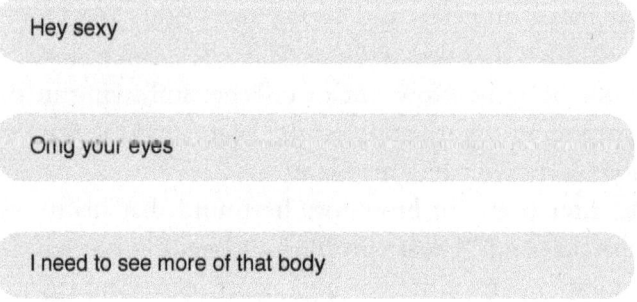

Also: A great many photos of context-free, zoomed-in and highly pixelated, veiny and fully erect dicks.

—

There was nothing special about the first man Ryan said yes to. His name was Michael, the most common name in America among men around Ryan's age. He was tall-ish and white, muscular but not ripped. He was persistent but no more persistent than the other guys who messaged Ryan. He shared Ryan's taste in movies—action flicks and comedies and, best of all, action-comedies. But that wasn't really it, either. In truth, the first man Ryan invited into his home was chosen only because Ryan was ready, Michael was eager, and, most important of all, Ryan's roommate was out of town.

After messaging for a few days, Michael asked Ryan out on a proper date.

What Ryan said: *I'm not into that whole scene.*

What Ryan meant: *I'm utterly terrified of who might see us together.*

What Ryan suggested: *Why don't you just come over to my place.*

Ryan felt a faint buzzing in his gut that started that afternoon and threatened to overwhelm him by the time the doorbell rang. The figure who appeared when Ryan opened it was no more remarkable than the one in the images Ryan had seen online. But he was flesh, and he was male, and he was here. Ryan smiled and welcomed him in.

Surely, Ryan would think later, some light small talk must have happened next. Maybe Ryan asked how Michael's week was, and maybe he responded with a few funny anecdotes from work, and maybe Ryan laughed, either too eagerly or not eagerly enough. Then, maybe they started talking through Ryan's DVD collection, which at that point was enormous, and maybe they strained to emphasize the things they had in common and to skirt past the things they did not—except in those moments when their differences opened up some kind of playful tension, in which case they made their best attempts to flirt.

All of that might have happened. But all Ryan would remember about those early, awkward moments were the thoughts running through his mind:

Does he know he's my first?

How does my mouth fit with another man's mouth?

He can't know he's my first.

Will he initiate this or do I have to?

He definitely knows he's my first.

I like how he smells. I like the size of his arms and hands. Why is he my first? I should have been doing this the whole time.

—

They sat down. On the couch, Michael looked more handsome than his pictures online, more relaxed than when he'd first walked through the door. Michael seemed to feel the same way about Ryan. "If I had known you were this hot in person," he said, "I would have made sure to come over here a long time ago." Ryan felt his face flush, tried to push down the sudden rise of a shy giggle. This was new. This was not just a stranger buying him a drink, or even a set of typed words attached to a profile pic. This was another man looking directly at Ryan and using the word *hot*.

Ryan didn't know how to respond. He'd never considered the possibility that he might be, in a stranger's imagination, *hot*. He was five-six and thick, for one. And Ryan had learned over his years in Buffalo that Indigenous men rarely fit into white Americans' popular imagination of desirability. Often, he felt invisible. But he knew he had a muscular ass and thighs, and he thought, sometimes, that in the right moment his eyes could sparkle, holding within them the hint of adventure.

There were only a few inches between them on the couch. Michael wore cologne, something musky and overpowering, and Ryan couldn't decide if he wanted to escape its reach or move closer and inhale it. Ryan drummed his fingers on the couch, watched as his left foot tapped the floor, outside his voluntary control. They turned on whatever mildly popular action movie Michael had picked from Ryan's collection, and they watched it as Michael's hand migrated, slowly, across the couch and onto Ryan's arm, and Ryan let it linger there, something hot shooting through him. Michael began running his fingers up and down the side of Ryan's hand, and when the movie ended, that's when Michael moved, as if finally uncaged, across the couch until his body was pressed against the side of Ryan's body, and Ryan felt himself tighten, immobile but wanting.

The mass, the scruff, the strength. At first it felt strange, like navigating a new city with only the faintest sense of direction, but his body learned Michael's quickly, and before long it felt that he'd always known it. Here, finally, was the thing he'd so long denied himself permission to want. Here, moving against him, was a body so much like his own.

–

Then Michael grabbed him. Back of the neck at first, pulling him so close that Ryan felt he couldn't breathe. Ryan put his hand on Michael's chest, pushed him away. "Hey," Ryan said, firmly. "I don't feel comfortable with that." Ryan was ready to make out with a man but not to have sex with one. He'd told Michael he wanted to take things slow when they'd chatted online.

"Okay," Michael said. "I'll slow down."

He grabbed Ryan gently by the shirt collar, pulled him toward his chest, and that felt better to Ryan. They kissed. Ryan began to settle into the thrill of new discovery.

But that lasted only a few seconds. Because now Michael was moving his hand back around Ryan's neck, grabbing with hunger and force. The kind of touch Ryan desired became the kind of touch he feared. Ryan pushed back against him, and Michael moved his right hand up Ryan's thigh, reaching for the button of his pants. Ryan grabbed Michael's hand and moved it to the side. His arousal remained, but alongside it there was now panic and rising fear.

"Hey," Ryan said. "I think I'm getting tired."

Michael grinned. "Well," he said, "we can go back to your bedroom."

Ryan laughed, flattered, nervous, racked with the sudden and desperate desire to be left alone.

"No," he said. "We can't do that."

Michael ran his fingers along Ryan's arm, up toward his face, and pulled Ryan close. They kissed again, and Ryan tried to melt back into that sensation. But then he felt that alien hand on his thigh again, and he pushed Michael away, on the chest, more forceful this time. Now he looked at Michael and began running internal calculations. Michael was taller, and he clearly worked out. But Ryan had a thicker base, stronger thighs. He could take him if he had to. If Michael reached for his dick again, Ryan would respond with force.

For now, though, he just said, "I think you should leave."

—

The moment Michael walked out the door, Ryan closed it and locked it behind him. He watched him leave through the peephole, only relaxing when he saw his car drive away. He turned out the lights, poured himself a glass of water, and climbed into bed. He stared at his ceiling, replaying the night in his mind. He felt thrilled by the initial contact, disturbed by the ensuing aggression, and proud of himself for knowing when to push away, to say stop, he didn't like what was happening, please leave. He found himself imagining that this must be how straight women often felt, drawn to male bodies but wary of male hunger, calibrating their response to creatures who could bring them pleasure or leave them feeling overtaken and used. *I could have taken him*, Ryan thought. *It never would have gotten bad. Two punches to the face, and he'd be done.*

As he lay there, though, he decided two things. First, it would be months before he would invite another man into his home. He could not imagine giving a male stranger that kind of proximity to his body. Second, even if he'd been overwhelmed by so much of their encounter, someday he would try it again, because he was, without question now, *definitely* gay.

Gideon

He heard a knock at the door, loud and demanding, then saw a body before him, stout, the shape of a small bear. Matt looked up at Gideon, red-cheeked and serious. "Please," Matt said as he grabbed the bottle of pills from Gideon's hand. "Tell me you didn't take these fucking things."

Gideon struggled to keep his head upright. "Eh," he managed to say, "not yet."

"Good." Matt walked into the bathroom, poured the pills in the toilet and flushed it, then went into Gideon's bedroom where he grabbed a few clothes and threw them into a bag. "Come on," he said. "You're sleeping on my couch tonight."

Gideon woke up there sometime late the next morning. The room was gently swaying, his head throbbing. He needed water. Breakfast. Maybe a shower. Definitely some aspirin. And to sit, for a few minutes, with the reality that his wife was fucking his mentor.

"Get your shit together," Matt said when Gideon emerged from the bathroom. "We've got plans."

Around noon, they went over to their buddy Brad's house, Matt driving. Brad was older, maybe fifty, white and tall and thin, balding with a comb-over. Brad was brilliant but not particularly fit, the kind of soldier the army never glamorized but desperately needed in order to keep winning wars. Already on his fourth marriage, he often seemed like an uncle with questionable wisdom and infinite confidence in his own opinions, a profane teller of unreliable truths. On their nights out at Mulligan's, he would hold court at the table telling the younger officers how to fix their lives.

"Fucking hell," Brad said, the moment Gideon showed up outside his door. "Come in. Let's get you a beer." Their buddy John was also there, and he handed Gideon a Bud Light and invited him outside to sit on the patio by the pool. The world before him still blurred on the edges, but Gideon felt the fast-rising heat of the sun overhead, and he saw a desert lizard scurrying away from the pool and out into the yard as he listened to Brad spewing profane condolences, you gotta be fucking livid man, what are you gonna do? You gonna fuck some shit up? I would be fucking *everything* up. Gideon nodded, barely meeting Brad's eyes, and took a sip of his beer. "Pound that shit, brother," Brad said. "It'll help."

"Cheers," said a guy sitting across the table. Gideon had never seen him before.

Gideon nodded back in his direction. "Cheers," he said.

"Gideon," Brad said, "this is Carlos. Carlos, Gideon."

Carlos nodded again and offered his own condolences, making clear he already knew why Gideon was here—super fucked-up, bro, same shit happened to me once, you gotta be so fucking pissed.

"Yeah," Gideon said. "It's fucked."

Carlos was thickly muscled and heavily tatted, wearing a large chain and a tank top. He crushed one beer in a few gulps and obliged when Brad offered another. Otherwise, he didn't say another word. They all just sat there while Matt and Brad went around in circles, repeating different versions of the same sentences, what the fuck, so messed up, I can't believe this shit, someone better face some fucking consequences.

Gideon stared into the distance, barely saying anything. His hangover was easing with each sip of the beer. The desire to wash down a handful of pills had vanished completely though. Suicide, in the light of day, seemed overdramatic. Even his initial rush of anger had begun to slip away. Instead, he felt a comfortable nothing. Matt and John and Brad batted around expletives, allowing Gideon to outsource his rage. John and Brad told stories from their own divorces, a psycho ex here, a cheating second wife there, and Gideon laughed as he listened to them recount their misery. They offered no real vulnerability, and they invited none from Gideon, and yet, as they spoke, he felt a growing sense of calm.

"You're gonna be fine," Brad said. "I've been divorced three times and been to war four times. Life has a lot of shit to it. You just gotta wait it out, and it gets better."

Gideon nodded. He tried to imagine his life at some future date. In the army or out, remarried or *still* married, here in El Paso or in Atlanta or Germany or Japan. All of these flashes of the future had one thing in common: They required Gideon to remain alive. That seemed nice, he thought. To live long enough to see what comes next.

Once the pep talk had run its course, Matt and Brad and John returned to the other matter at hand.

"They can't just get away with this shit."

It wasn't just that Gideon's wife had cheated on him. Caroline had violated the vows of their marriage, and sure, that was bad. Even more than that, though, adultery violated official army law. She could face internal discipline. And Connor? Not only had he committed adultery, but he had done so with the wife of one of his direct reports, an officer he was personally mentoring. And this was after he'd already faced discipline for fraternizing with subordinates on the night he crashed his bike. This time, his career really could be over.

"There have to be some fucking consequences."

The army often blurred lines between private conduct and professional punishment. This wasn't just a *job*. If you can't trust your commanding officer to keep from fucking your wife, then how can you trust him to protect you when an enemy's missile is headed straight at your base? The personal was *always* professional, because the profession was to keep yourself and your fellow citizens alive. Connor hadn't just wronged Gideon. As their squad commander, he had betrayed every officer and soldier under his command. Matt, Brad, and John included.

"Bro. If it was me? I would fuck him up."

Gideon nodded along, but the words floated by him. Matt and Brad kept egging each other on, that motherfucker has to pay, we can't just shrug our shoulders and let this shit go, and the whole time, Carlos sat on the other end of the table nodding, mostly in silence, except to occasionally say, "Yup, yup, yup." To Gideon, all of this was just chatter, the sort of things men tell each other when one among their ranks has been wronged. A few weeks later, though, he was hanging out with Matt when he felt himself pulled down into another rage spiral.

"Dude," Gideon said. "It's taking everything in me not to just *Tonya Harding* that motherfucker. Just show up at his house with a bat and fucking kneecap him."

"Hell yeah," Matt said. "It's about time you started thinking that way." And then he laughed. "Why do you think we invited Carlos that day at Brad's house?"

"Carlos?" Gideon asked.

"Fuck yeah, Carlos," Matt said. "*Muscle*. Brad had him on retainer. We were just waiting for you to say the word."

"Holy shit," Gideon said, and he shook his head and laughed. "You guys are fucking psychos." And he laughed some more. Later that day on his ride home he found himself smiling, thinking that he would never actually pay someone to beat the shit out of Connor or anyone else. But just knowing that he had the *option*, that his friends had gone out of their way to make vengeance available to him, he felt something like love.

—

Weeks passed. Gideon told his new commander about what happened, and the army launched an investigation. The investigators asked Gideon for evidence of the affair, and this seemed like a new humiliation, trying to prove the truth of his life's greatest betrayal. Connor accepted a rush deployment and got shipped off to the Middle East. Caroline texted occasionally, first to express her anger over the investigation, later to check on Charlie, finally to check on Gideon. She did not apologize. They did not discuss whatever might happen next.

On occasion, he entertained another humiliating thought: What if they could fix this? What if she wanted to come back? What if he *wanted* her back? Could she change? For him, maybe, she would change.

The first time she asked if she could come over, months after he kicked her out, Gideon knew he was supposed to say no. Only one script seemed to tell a story of justice. Man gets cheated on. Man divorces woman, finds happiness. Woman feels shamed, finds misery. The end. He shouldn't open the door to the possibility of them getting back together. But maybe she just wanted to see Charlie? That's what she said when she texted him. And Charlie had belonged to them both. Caroline had broken her vows to *Gideon* but not to the dog.

Gideon made some drinks. They hugged, because what else were they supposed to do when she walked through the door? Charlie bounded over to her and licked her face, and Caroline laughed. It was fall by now. They asked each other about their jobs, their new commanders, and rumors of future deployments. It was fine. A little awkward, but light, familiar, pleasant. Then she finished her drink and looked him in the eye and asked if he wanted to have sex. She asked it like she was asking if she could grab Gideon something from the kitchen or offer him a ride to work. A polite query over a logistical matter. A mutual favor, perhaps.

Gideon laughed, then said nothing. Caroline continued.

"I mean, feel free to say no. I was just curious."

They talked it through. What would this mean? It didn't have to mean they were back together. Gideon was still too hurt to imagine repairing their marriage, and even though Connor had been deployed, Caroline admitted that she was still in touch with him. Divorce remained an option for their future. In the meantime, they could date other people. It was just, you're here, I'm here. You're hot, I'm hot. I know that thing you like with my tongue, you know my preferred rhythm and pace, how to get me where I need to go. Why *wouldn't* we?

The bed was right there. She'd be gone minutes after. A body was just a body.

"Okay," Gideon said. "Fuck it. Let's go."

—

After they started having sex again, and after that sex led inevitably to the resurfacing of old feelings, and after those feelings pushed them toward uncomfortable conversations, and after Gideon had said he needed to know everything Caroline and Connor had done and Caroline had told him, and after he had demanded that she declare whose dick was bigger and she had told him that it was Gideon's (which he knew might be a lie but didn't care), and after they started to say that maybe we could do this, maybe we're really still in love, maybe someday we'll be sitting with our grandkids at our fiftieth anniversary party, and all of this will be a blip, washed away alongside so many of our shared struggles, then, finally, they decided to see a therapist.

The therapist was dark-haired and slim, with a Mediterranean complexion, an East Coast accent, and no trouble getting straight to the point. His manner reminded Gideon of Coach. He listened intently as Gideon and Caroline both spoke, nodding with something like empathy, but he made it clear: "Most relationships do not survive this. So you need to ask yourselves, do you even *want* your marriage to survive this?" They both said they wanted to try, that they believed in the promises they'd made to each other. But when he asked how they planned to do it, they told him they needed time to figure that part out.

When Gideon came back for a one-on-one session, Dr. Coach's tone grew even more direct.

First: "The person who loves the least has all the power. And she will always love you the least."

Then: "There is nothing in this relationship that you can't find somewhere else. You have no kids. No long history. If this is the kind of relationship you want, you will find it again. But really, you should want more than this."

And finally: "This is not a marriage. You're just drinking buddies who fuck."

Well, Gideon thought, *that* seemed excessive. But it wasn't what he said about their marriage that bothered Gideon the most. It was what he said about Gideon himself.

"You're scared to be alone," he said. "Your entire sense of yourself is bound up in this relationship. You have zero confidence in who you actually are."

All right, now that was ridiculous. Of course Gideon was confident! Look at everything he'd done. Division I athlete, degree from an elite institution, officer in the army and rising star in his unit, married to a beautiful woman, homeowner before age twenty-five. Dr. Coach seemed unmoved. "No one is asking you to give your resume," he said. "And if that's what you're relying on to tell me how you feel about yourself, then you're not in a good place."

Gideon sat quiet, unsure of what to say.

"How many times in your life," Dr. Coach asked him, "have you ever been alone?"

Before Gideon could answer, he continued. "Because the way I see it, you had three siblings and two parents and a household that revolved entirely around *you*. And then you went to West Point, where every moment of every day was planned, and you were with your roommate or your teammates or your girlfriend every second of every day. You met your wife weeks after you broke up with your high school girlfriend. You've *never* been alone. And if I had to take a guess, I'd say the reason is simple. You're scared to find out who you really are."

Fuck that guy. Gideon could be alone. *Of course* he could be alone! He would prove it. He would find comfort in solitude, day after day. He started by sitting at home on the couch, Charlie by his side, wondering what he should do. What did people do by themselves? He would figure it out.

Gideon knew that he was smart and capable, curious and energetic. But he soon realized that Caroline had always been the one who made sure they *did stuff*. Her friends were his friends. She planned dinners and home renovation projects. He usually went out to Mulligan's when she'd made other plans. Otherwise, he went out to whichever parties or bars she wanted. When they'd moved together to El Paso, she'd built herself a life, and Gideon had happily melted into it. Once, they fought because Gideon always wanted to rush home after his weekly softball games, instead of hanging out with the other guys. *"Please,"* she said, "go do *something* without me."

Now an hour had passed. He was still stuck on the couch. Who knew that days contained so much *time*? After every single minute, up marched another, demanding that he fill it somehow. Staring at the wall and drinking gin could only fill so much. Did he need a hobby? How did people find hobbies? Gideon had never had one. Baseball was not a *hobby*. Baseball had been *everything*. But now, crushing dingers and playing shortstop in his softball league didn't fill the same void. What else was there? Gideon had never been into video games. Definitely not board games. Poker nights with the guys were fun but intermittent. He'd had an immediate knack for home renovation projects, but those only mattered because Caroline thought they mattered. He'd never tried woodworking or cycling, piano or writing.

Connor played guitar. Caroline seemed to like that. Maybe *Gideon* should play guitar. He went to Guitar Center and bought one, something cheap, and he looked up a few lessons on YouTube. That's when he ran into his first problem: Gideon was bad at guitar. What the hell. This seemed absurd and unjust. *Why wasn't he good at guitar?*

Okay, fuck that. What about golf? Matt loved golf. Gideon should *definitely* be good at golf. But, sadly, Gideon was terrible at golf. He swung the club the way he swung a bat. He kept his elbow too high, shifted his weight too recklessly, sent the ball spraying all over the course.

The only thing he liked about golf was the fact that he could drink while he played.

Speaking of which. What if instead of drinking on the couch and staring at the walls, he drank on the couch and watched movies? No, that wasn't the right way to put it. What if he became a *connoisseur of film*? He'd watch the classics. He would have opinions on directors. Maybe he would even read Wikipedia pages of the movies he'd just watched. This was good. This was how to become cultured.

He decided to start with westerns. Not only were westerns *true cinema*, but they were full of righteous violence and often set in Texas. It could be a way to study men who'd felt the things Gideon was feeling, in the same place where he was feeling them. Perfect.

He went out and bought a sound system for the house, seven speakers, full surround, heavy bass, so loud you could hear every single twang of the score and shot of the pistols from the backyard. He started with a few Clint Eastwood flicks but quickly moved to John Wayne, realizing that the older the movie, the more likely it counted as *art*. He rented *True Grit*, *The Man Who Shot Liberty Valance*, *The Good, the Bad, and the Ugly*, and then more and more, many films that Gideon had never even heard of until he began this quest. After a couple of weeks, though, of pounding gin and telling Charlie to watch John Wayne kill those fuckers on the screen, Gideon realized something: He *hated* westerns. Westerns were *boring*. How many times was he supposed to watch the same actor pull out the same pistol and shoot a different bad guy from the same hip? He didn't get it.

So one night he stopped a movie halfway through, and he decided he was done. Maybe he could just pass his nights sitting here in silence, occasionally narrating his thoughts to Charlie and sipping his gin, first from a glass, later from the bottle, until, with Charlie curled up and pressed against his chest, both of them breathing together, never alone, her weight his only comfort, he could drift, finally, to sleep.

Joseph

Twenty-three years before he moved to Seattle and twenty-two years before Joe-a-palooza, the summer before he entered third grade, Joseph woke up every morning and ran outside with no shirt on into the Central Florida heat, and he shot jumpers in the driveway until his mom said it was time for them to go. Sometimes he told her no he didn't want to, but that was really kind of a lie, because his mom was going to the strip mall, and the strip mall was the most magical place in Joseph's world. He rode with her in the minivan and then went inside her shop, which sold ceramics, bowls and mugs and vases, and until the shop opened he helped her clean the molds and straighten the tables and put away anything that had been left out the night before.

Around 10 a.m. the strip mall came to life, dead bolts unlocking and signs flipping from closed to open and A-frames dragged out to sidewalks announcing sales. Joseph wandered up and down the sidewalk and waved to all the shop owners, Betsy at the salon and Pat at the wedding shop and Bob at the golf pro shop, and they all waved back, because they were all his grown-up friends, and he thought they understood what Joseph understood, that this whole strip mall could barely function without him, that he was the only person who knew everybody and could even run the register at like half the stores.

After saying hi to his friends, Joseph went and sat in the back room at his mom's store to watch cartoons. For lunch he ate a peanut butter and jelly sandwich, and in the afternoon he went to find Rachel, who was Bev the salon lady's daughter and who had the most beautiful curly blonde hair. If Rachel was there, then they ran off to dig for treasure in the sand by the sidewalks, or sometimes they went to the office building next door to play elevators, which was a game where they pressed all the buttons on the elevators and rode them up and down and up and down. Then sometime in the afternoon the thunderstorms would start, and they were always short but always heavy, rain fat and sideways, and Joseph and Rachel would run as fast as they could back to their mothers' stores.

When it stopped raining Joseph might go over to the golf pro shop, where Bob and Randy let him practice his driving on the simulator and his putting on the green, and when customers came in sometimes Joseph would tell them what kind of club they needed to improve their game. Listen to the kid, Bob would say, he's gonna be richer than all of us when he's on the tour someday, and Joseph smiled and thought that yeah who knows maybe that was true.

And then, finally, Joseph would go down to the baseball card shop, which was his very favorite place on earth. They had everything, signed cards, first edition cards, a Cal Ripken Jr. rookie card, and even a mint-condition Hank Aaron. Whenever Joseph had any money he would buy a pack of Topps and get the free piece of gum, and he chewed it while he flipped through the pack. He flipped right past the relief pitchers and the utility infielders and he hoped desperately that the next card he pulled out would be the card belonging to a star, maybe a Tony Gwynn or a Doc Gooden or even a Dale Murphy, any of them would be worth more than the whole rest of the pack combined. Jack would be working at the shop and would ask him if he'd found anything good, and Joseph would tell him yes or no, and then Jack would come over and look at all the cards he'd gotten in the pack, and they would look them up in *Beckett Baseball Card Monthly*, and sometimes Jack would buy a card back from Joseph right there on the spot.

Joseph didn't know what Jack did to make his hat look so perfect, but he had a curve in the bill that was so much better than any curve Joseph had ever seen. Maybe he put it in a coffee mug or wrapped it around a baseball with a rubber band, but Joseph had done those things with his hats too, and none of them ever looked as good as Jack's. The hat had the name of their local high school, Saint Mary's, where Jack played shortstop for the varsity team.

Jack was sixteen. Joseph was eight. They were best friends.

Jack's mom ran the shop during the school year, but Jack took over all summer long. Joseph thought Jack had the greatest job in the world. Until a customer bought them, Jack owned every card, every trophy, every copy of *Beckett Monthly*. A Mickey Mantle card sat in a display case on the shelf, and technically, if Jack wanted to, he could just pull it out of the case and take it home, and this seemed to Joseph like the most amazing kind of power, to have access to a room full of treasures and the willpower not to keep them all for yourself.

Jack treated Joseph like an employee, so sometimes Joseph thought *he* had the greatest job in the world too. He sorted cards in the back and found them for customers in the front. He even negotiated with people who came by looking to sell their most valuable cards. A lot of times Jack's friends came by, and they were almost as cool as Jack but not quite. Their hats didn't have the same curve and their jobs weren't as awesome and instead of shortstop they played something kind of lame like second base or right field. But like Jack they all had mullets and wore blue jean shorts and had dips of tobacco in their mouths, and every few minutes they pretended to swing a baseball bat they weren't even holding, fists cutting through empty air. They talked about girls and baseball, parties and baseball cards. They invited Joseph into every conversation, asking if he had a girlfriend (he did), if he'd ever smoked weed (he hadn't—again, he was eight), and if he thought the Mets were going to win the World Series (yes, duh). Every time they asked a question, they seemed to really want the answer, like whatever Joseph had to say actually mattered.

Every now and then, Jack pulled out his dick. (This was, by now, the word Joseph used for it. The older boys had convinced him. *Peepee* and *wiener* and even *penis* were little kid words and Joseph was no longer a little kid.) Jack's dick was massive, at least to Joseph, as massive as the one he'd seen that time he walked in on the babysitter showing Joseph's big sister porn. Sometimes Jack walked out of the back room and into the storefront with his shorts pulled down and his dick in hand. Dude, the older boys all said, that's so fucking gross, what the hell are you doing, and Jack would just stand there grinning, like what's wrong guys, it's hot in here, my balls just needed some air. Then they would all laugh together because Jack was crazy, seriously, who does that, just walking around with his dick hanging out? He would leave it out for a few minutes at a time, forcing the room to ignore him and go back to talking about whatever they were talking about before. Or someone would ask about a card, and Jack would walk over to the case and say here it is, then point to the card with his dick. Sometimes it seemed that he most liked springing his dick on Joseph, telling him he needed to show him something behind the counter, and then Joseph would look down and there it was.

All of this, to Joseph and the other older boys who hung out in the store, was so funny. Jack wasn't a bully, he wasn't mean. Everyone else had a dick, but none of them had the guts to whip it out. Maybe this was what it was like to be a teenage boy, Joseph thought. Maybe someday he, too, would have the confidence to pull out his dick in the middle of a store.

The first time Jack's dick scared him was late on a slow weekday afternoon, a day when none of Jack's friends came by and barely any customers trickled in. It was just the two of them there, Jack counting inventory while Joseph sat by the register studying cards, when Jack said, hey dude run to the back and get me a sheet of plastic sleeves. Joseph jumped up immediately, he knew exactly where those sleeves were, was probably the only person besides Jack who knew the store well enough to find them.

Joseph darted through the door and went straight to the shelf where they kept them, then rummaged through the boxes until he found the sleeves, and then when he turned around that's when he saw him, Jack standing in the doorway and smiling under his perfectly curved baseball cap and holding his dick, which seemed to be getting bigger and bigger in his hand.

Joseph did not like the look of Jack's penis and he did not like the smile on Jack's face, but he told himself Jack was just being funny, and he shouted *gross!* Then Jack laughed and so Joseph laughed too. Overhead the fluorescent lights were buzzing like angry bees and all around Joseph were white walls and brown boxes, and there was not a single window in the whole entire room. Jack kept laughing and so Joseph kept laughing too, so gross dude what's wrong with you you're crazy, and then Jack took a couple of steps toward Joseph and he said something he'd never said before.

"Touch it."

Joseph barely heard the words before he started running as fast as he could in his flip-flops and basketball shorts, standing about four feet tall and weighing about sixty pounds. He yelled that Jack was so disgusting and shot past him and ran back out to the storefront and then straight out the front door and into the summer heat, across the strip mall to his mother's shop, where he sat and watched cartoons in silence until it was time to go home.

Okay, Joseph understood how this worked. If he didn't want to touch Jack's dick he just needed to stay out of the back room. That was the only problem. The shop wasn't dangerous. The shop was wonderful. Not even *Jack* was dangerous. Jack was Joseph's older and cooler best friend. He was just kind of gross and one time he wanted Joseph to touch his dick, but he only asked Joseph to touch his dick when he went to the back room, and so as long as Joseph stayed up front, he would be fine.

And so for a while he did. He hung out with Jack and the older boys and he negotiated with customers and he sold the shop some of his old cards and used the money to buy new ones and then one day Jack sent Joseph to the back and Joseph decided to try it and it was fine, and then another day he did it again and it was still fine, and then another day Jack said hey Joseph will you run to the back and get one of those new boxes of Fleers, and Joseph said okay sure. He walked through the door to look for the cards and heard the buzzing of the lights and saw the white walls and the brown shelves and he knew, immediately, that he was stupid, because the back room looked different now, with a massive stack of boxes in the middle of the room, closing off space, and Joseph knew that if Jack trapped him he wouldn't be able to escape like last time, but he grabbed the cards and the moment he turned around there was Jack, standing at the door and holding his dick, and Joseph thought oh no oh no oh no.

He yelled no, I'm not touching it, that's gross, and then he started to run like last time, but now he saw Jack charging toward him, knocking down the boxes in the middle of the room, and the stacks were too high and too many for Joseph to jump over them without tripping, so he couldn't get past Jack and back to the front door. There was still a back door, and so Joseph ran to it and tried to get it open, but a piece of plywood was bolted against the frame, keeping it shut, and so he banged and he screamed, let me out let me out someone please help me please let me out. His mom was just two stores away but he guessed she couldn't hear him, and as he kept screaming Jack just stood there, right behind him, and Jack was saying be quiet and Jack himself was totally calm, because they both knew that no one was coming, they both knew exactly how this would end.

Joseph tried to breathe and his chest heaved and he turned around and looked at Jack and screamed again, looking up at Jack's face now, trying his hardest to scare Jack the way Jack had scared him, no no No NO NOOOOOO! But Jack just stood there and said dude, what are you doing, this is not a big deal, stop being a little baby what the fuck. All you have to do is touch it, all you have to do is touch it, all you have to do is touch it, and all he had to do was touch it, so Joseph took his right hand and extended his index finger and he pressed it against the mushroom tip of the penis and then he screamed let me go let me go let me go.

And Jack did. He took a step to the side. See. I'm a man of my word. That wasn't so bad was it. And Joseph tried to tell himself that was true, this was normal, this was fine, Jack was gross and wanted Joseph to do things he didn't like to do, but that's friendship right, we can't all want to do the same things at the same time. And so he kept coming back to the shop, again and again, just making sure not to go to the back room, because the back room was where the bad things happened, and for weeks he didn't, he just looked at his cards and talked to his friends and negotiated with customers and they all had so much fun. And sometimes Jack told him to go to the back and he said no, and then he told him again and Joseph said no again, until one time he decided it had been long enough and Jack was his friend and that was just a thing that used to happen but probably wouldn't happen anymore, and so when Jack told him to go back there again Joseph said okay whatever fine I'll go.

Someday soon this entire memory would vanish. Joseph would lose every single detail. He would forget the first time, when he escaped, and the second, when he touched the head of the penis and ran away. He would forget what happened now, when he turned around with that sick feeling in his stomach to see Jack standing there, stroking himself this time, hungry and smiling. He would forget what Jack said when Joseph tried to run again, when Joseph tried to scream again, when he banged the door as loud as he could and hoped that his mother or another grown-up might hear. He would forget that Jack told him he had a deal he wanted to make. That he asked if Joseph knew about that Fleer Special Edition Spring Training set, and Joseph said yeah, of course I know it, because they had a unique set for every team in the majors, with like four cards for every player, showing them at batting practice and in the field and at bat and in the dugout. It was cool because if you got the right team with the right players you knew you were going to get *four* cards of your favorite guys when usually if you opened a random pack you only got one. And Jack said you know we have the Oakland A's set and Joseph said yeah of course he knew it, he'd been staring at it for days, and Jack knew that Joseph knew that Jack knew that the A's were Joseph's favorite team, with three of the coolest players in all of baseball, Mark McGwire and Rickey Henderson and José Canseco, plus Joseph's very favorite Walt Weiss. Jack asked if he wanted the set and Joseph said yes and Jack said you can have it and Joseph said I don't believe you.

Joseph would forget the shape of the room, the size and slope of Jack's dick, the way it felt against his hand. He would forget about his fear and his screaming, about the way he ran again to bang against the back door. He would lose all of it, for decades, until the night of his thirtieth birthday party, Joe-a-palooza, when Pastor Mitch thumped his nads and Joseph laughed because it was so fucking funny dude, holy shit he got me good, and then wandered outside hammered and started talking to Alex and the memory came back as if politely stepping out of the dark caverns in his mind and nestling into his consciousness, and suddenly Joseph was speaking a simple and true sentence: "I was sexually abused as a kid too."

The memory came back in its entirety, from the broadest contours to the finest details, including this moment, trapped against the back door, when Jack told Joseph what he had to do to get the special edition set, and Joseph knew that he really meant this was what Joseph had to do if he ever wanted to leave this room. And when the memory came back Joseph would wonder how long Jack had known that someday this would happen, if Jack could tell from the first time he met Joseph that eventually he would be here, Jack standing over him calm and smiling, Joseph against the back door desperate and weak, and he wondered if Jack had always known what he would say next.

"Stroke it."

He wondered if Jack had always known how Joseph would feel now, so small and trapped and afraid, if that had been the point now and always, to leave this little boy so powerless to do anything other than exactly what he'd been told.

Nate

Long before a police officer patted down his chest, Nate had come to hate the breast binder he'd begun to wear. Not only for what it suggested to the roaming hands of that cop—that Nate was not who he said he was, that he was a *ma'am*—but for something simpler: It *hurt*. The straps dug into his sides. The pressure on his chest left him unable to draw a full breath. He tried switching back to sports bras but hated how they looked, those two small bumps still visible underneath his shirts. He tried taping down his chest, but the adhesives gave him rashes. He started googling top surgery. He wondered what it would be like to erase what he'd spent years trying to suppress. He thought back to his friend Austin running shirtless through his grandma's yard when they were kids. What would it have been like to join him? What would it feel like now?

Did he *need* the surgery? He wasn't sure. Every day since he'd first spoken aloud the truth of his existence, he'd felt more and more like a man. No excision of any piece of his body had been required. He'd still found plenty of interested romantic partners, had still been able to make friends who saw him the way he'd always seen himself. None of them had to be convinced of Nate's manhood. None of them cared what fatty tissue separated his sternum from his shirt.

And yet he longed to move through the world fully undetected, to feel supreme confidence that no one he met was secretly wondering, *What are you?* Online, he'd seen debates among trans people about whether *passing* even mattered. Why should *they* have to hide who they were? Shouldn't everyone else have to confront the fact that trans people *existed*? It had become fashionable to say that by trying to pass, they were "reinforcing the gender binary," or bowing to "cis supremacy," or upholding "heteropatriarchal norms." But Nate noticed something about all the people who made those arguments. Not a single one of them lived in *Youngstown fucking Ohio*. They were in places like Brooklyn, Portland, Oakland, even Atlanta. When they weren't posting screeds, they were posting pictures of themselves with all of their trans friends. Nate had only hung out with Ray three times. Besides him, he'd never even met another trans man. He knew there was more of a trans community in Cleveland, or even in Akron, but he'd never figured out how to get involved.

For now, his concerns were more immediate. He wanted to use a public bathroom without having to fear that he might get his skull cracked. Before he dropped out of high school, an administrator had declared that he would get raped if he ever went to the boys' bathroom. He'd seethed over this, but he knew trans people risked violence when they attempted to piss in public. He knew that his body, when studied closely, could still inspire confusion. And he knew that many men, when confronted with a challenge to their ideas about masculinity, became enraged.

—

There were, Nate had to admit, other reasons why he wanted top surgery. He wanted to take a shirtless selfie. Was this a horribly shallow thing to admit? If it was, should he care? This seemed like the most sublime imaginable act, to stare at himself in the mirror and not hate his reflection. To capture a brief moment of his body's existence, alone in his room, and maybe even to share that image with a girl he was talking to, or, fuck it, maybe even to post it online, to see what kind of comments the sight of his bare chest inspired.

He couldn't do that now. For one thing, Instagram made a clear distinction between a chest that could be displayed and a chest that must be hidden. But even if he *could*, he knew he didn't want to. He didn't even like to take off his binder during sex. If a woman ever tried to touch his chest, even gently, he removed her hand. "Not there," he said. "Anywhere else." How would it feel, he wondered, to let a head or a hand rest in the place that now made him recoil? Could he imagine inhabiting a body he felt worthy of being shared?

Was this *necessary*? Was it *vain*? Fuck it, who cared? Top surgery would make him feel better about himself. Weren't women pursuing the same goal every time they put on makeup or dyed their hair? And other men did the same thing, right? Nate's dad had pumped himself full of steroids until he looked like a pro wrestler. Nate knew scrawny dudes who tattooed themselves into the form of a perceived tough guy, letting the ink do the work of the muscles they couldn't build. Creatine, protein powder, hair transplants—the lives of many men were full of these self-modifications, all in pursuit of the very same standard that left Nate wanting surgery on his chest.

Right around the time of his twenty-sixth birthday, he made an appointment. When he met with the doctor, he heard all about the procedure and its attendant risks. He would have scars: two curved marks on his lower pecs, evidence of what had been removed. With time, they would fade, and new skin would grow over old. So his mother drove him to Cleveland, to the same clinic where he'd gotten his first prescription for T, and they took him to an operating room and put him under general anesthesia. When he woke up, he saw bandages across his chest and felt a throbbing all over his body. The doctor explained that he'd had a buildup of fluid on one side, and that they just needed a little extra time for that to drain.

They told him to wait a few days until he removed the bandages and sent him home. He lay in bed with a fever, which the doctor had assured him was normal, and watched anime until he finally woke up one morning and knew that it was time. His mom came into the room and watched him. He took off the bandages first, which were wrapped all the way around his upper torso, and then the gauze. *Oh, my god*, he thought, as he saw only two strips of tape across the sites of his incisions. And then he ripped those off and felt cold air on his skin. Where once there was fat, covered by fabric, now there was none. Pecs, nipples, everything, all of it bare.

He started shaking, with both pain and euphoria. He needed Tylenol and he needed a trip to the beach. This was *him*. He couldn't believe this was actually him. Scruffy beard and sharp jaw, mass in his shoulders, veins in his forearms, and now, *this*. A bare flat chest. He wanted to bench press and take selfies. He wanted to show off what he'd lost and work to gain something new. He wanted to lobby Congress to pass laws making shirts illegal. Was this how Austin had felt all those years ago on that summer afternoon at his grandma's? Was this how *he* felt, for those brief moments, just before his grandma had told him to stop because he was a girl?

He wept, for the man he saw in the mirror and for the versions who'd come before him, once a girl and always a boy.

Gideon

The drive from Albuquerque to El Paso feels like a tour through prehistory or postapocalypse. The land is dry and desolate, unsuited for human life. Towns are roadside blips, service stations scattered and barely functional. A few weeks after he and Caroline decided that they were done trying, and officially became separated, Gideon sat in the back of Matt's car, staring out the window at nowhere, hungover and filled with vague regret.

Not that he regretted splitting with Caroline. He didn't think so, at least. His anger toward her eased, but underneath it he found ambivalence. He'd had to admit an ugly truth: Once Connor was gone and Gideon could declare himself the winner, he'd no longer felt desperate to get Caroline back. And he'd asked himself a gnawing question: Why *couldn't* he imagine a life without her? If he had to be alone for a while, what might he discover about *himself*? So he had called her one afternoon and told her he needed them to stop trying. Maybe they didn't need to get divorced right away, but Gideon needed to be single for a while. "Sounds good," she said. Gideon realized then that he'd wanted her to fight for him, for them, but he realized, too, that neither of them knew what they would be fighting to save.

Now that Gideon was single, he knew two things. One, he could not imagine entering a serious relationship with another person anytime soon. Two, he still desperately wanted to have sex. It appeared he needed to sleep with a stranger. He'd never done this before.

Was Gideon any good at sex? He had no idea. Sure, Caroline had always seemed pleased, but she was also the one who'd taught him everything he knew. Gideon had memorized every slope of her body, knew how every part of her responded to varying levels of pressure, knew the rhythms she liked and didn't, how quickly she wanted the pace to build. And still, despite all of that, she fucked his boss.

Before he even worried about that, how was Gideon even supposed to *find* someone who wanted to fuck him? In high school, he'd just woken up one day and decided he had feelings for a girl he'd known since kindergarten, and then they had dated for three years. At West Point, he'd let his eyes linger on the tall blonde with the fuzzy slippers, and days later they were making out on the baseball bleachers. None of these scenarios seemed likely to repeat themselves. Besides his female colleagues, who were off limits, everyone else he encountered was a fleeting presence: women at grocery stores and gas stations, patrons of the same shitty downtown bars. What was he supposed to do? *Talk* to them? About *what*?

Online dating was still seen as pathetic. The apps didn't yet exist. So instead, Gideon started to pay attention to the world around him. When he stood next to someone in line, did she make eye contact? Smile? Did smiling mean something? Once, his cashier at the grocery store made a joke about his protein powder, something about how that must be how he got so big, and he'd just laughed and said he wasn't really sure, that he was just born this way, he guessed. Then in the car on the way home he began to wonder if she'd been flirting. But rather than go back, he spent hours trying to track her down on Facebook. He never found her.

—

In Albuquerque on a three-night trip to teach a course at the air force base nearby, he learned that having sex with strangers was actually quite easy. Here, a simple road map.

(1) Go to a restaurant. (2) When the waitress speaks to you, speak to her in return. (3) When your buddy Brad tells the waitress, who happens to be tan and brunette and gorgeous, that you're recently divorced, going so far as to use the words *on the prowl*, blush lightly, laugh playfully, and tell him to cut that shit out, let her do her job. (4) Return her smile with your own. (5) When she grazes your shoulder with her hand while delivering your second liter-sized Corona, lock eyes with her and don't look away. (6) When your group gets the check and she tells you to wait, that her shift is ending, do as told. (7) When Brad tells you, on his way out the door, that you cannot possibly fuck this up, because he's already done all of the hard work on your behalf, just shake your head

and say nothing. (8) After she suggests grabbing a bottle of Bailey's and heading to your hotel room rather than going out to another bar, and then when she sits on your bed and looks up at you and asks why you seem so nervous, just tell her. You haven't been with anyone since you and your wife split up. (9) When she tells you that you'll be okay, that your nerves are kind of cute, don't worry, and then when she grabs you and kisses you and puts your hand on her ass and runs hers up your thigh, just do what your body tells you. She'll make it clear. She is not here for conversation.

At least that's how it went the first night. The next night, he met another woman at the hotel bar, and they drank and flirted and soon loaded up with the guys and rode out to the casino, where she sat on his lap and they drank and flirted some more. But by the time they returned to the hotel, she'd had so much to drink that neither of them could feel good about proceeding with the things she'd whispered in his ear that she wanted Gideon to do. So he dropped her off at her room and returned to his own. And then the third night, yet another woman—this one a bit older, in her mid- to late thirties, with clearly articulated ideas about how and where she wanted Gideon to touch her—moved quickly with him from the bar to his room, then coached him through exactly what she needed and promptly left, seemingly pleased that he'd done as told.

And now they were headed back to El Paso, and he was looking out the window into the void of southern New Mexico, trying to figure out just why he felt so damn sad. Gideon wanted to feel the elation that his buddies had felt on his behalf. He wanted to live in their cheers when they saw him emerge each morning for the breakfast buffet. And, to be clear, he'd *enjoyed* himself—the feeling of being desired, the pressure of a strange body against his own. But he also felt himself being pulled downstream toward someplace he'd never intended to go, carried by the currents of his desire. He could see, out in the desert, a glimpse of his immediate future. He would be the guy who fucks. That was what life held for him. He pressed his forehead against the window, willing the throbbing in his skull to stop.

Ryan

There was so much, Ryan learned as a single twenty-something in Buffalo, that one man could do with another man's body. You could take an arm in your hand and apply the faintest weight of your fingers, sliding over the slope of the forearm's muscles and tendons, feeling each strand of hair. You could taste the sweat on a neck or back, smell the skin before or after or even while it's being washed in a shower, hear the way a heartbeat thumps when your hand moves off a forearm, down a torso, up a thigh, all of the movements, both yours and the other body's, carried by animal force. You could feel the way the body softens, undone by pleasure. How it lays on a bed, fully open, inviting you in.

More things Ryan learned one man could do with another's body: Square up outside a bar, shoulder facing shoulder, studying the venom on its face and contorting your own to match. Move closer to the body, voice raising, your volume meant to provoke, because you tell yourself that you do not start fights but you end them, and that this, for reasons you can't explain, is a code you absolutely must keep. You could stand and wait for the impact of the body's fist against your face, could stagger backward assessing the pain, before you exploded forward, carried by that same animal force, and hear the dull crunch of your knuckles on cartilage and bone. You could feel the way the body softens as it falls, undone by violence. How it lays on pavement, fully open, begging you to stop.

—

It would be nice, perhaps, if coming out as gay had dulled Ryan's pull toward barroom violence. If he had come into his own identity and found that he no longer held onto long-dormant anger, if he had found himself embraced and loved by those around him, and then released all that he'd held inside. But that didn't happen. If anything, he felt a thrill in owning both his sexuality and his violent impulses simultaneously. In squaring up against the kind of men who unironically called themselves "alphas," who joked with limp wrists and put-on lisps about men like Ryan.

After that first fight outside the Latin dance bar his junior year of college, it took a few years before the next one. He graduated and moved out and spent many months on dates with men from Gay.com, graduating from that first encounter with Michael into others that felt thrilling in some moments and tender in others. He had boyfriends, if only for brief spells. He joined a gay men's volleyball league and for the first time felt like he could finally unleash his competitive hunger without hiding pieces of himself.

Some parts of gay Buffalo, though, remained alien to him. He found himself shrinking into the background when he went out to gay bars. Those men wanted skinny and he was thick; they wanted tall and he was short; they wanted white or Black and he was Mohawk. But still, if he lingered near the bar long enough, someone handsome and interesting would eventually approach him. If he left his photo up on Gay.com, he got daily messages from men who wanted to meet him. He made gay friends and found his place in the community.

One of those friends was Jared. Jared was Mohawk, too, but he'd grown up in Buffalo, a "city Indian," as Ryan called him. He had barely ever been to a reservation, but he seemed at home in any room he entered. They met on Gay.com but never considered dating. Instead, they became roommates and friends. Jared pulled Ryan out to bars and parties, often on nights that Ryan wanted to hide alone at home. One night, Jared took Ryan to a house party hosted by a friendly acquaintance. It promised a good crowd and free booze, and Ryan ignored most of the crowd but took full advantage of the booze—until the moment, just as they were getting ready to leave, when he found himself hammered and talking shit.

As he walked behind Jared on their way to the exit, he heard yelling, the words indiscriminate but aimed vaguely in his direction. He asked Jared, is that fucking guy yelling at me, and Jared laughed and said oh my god I think he is. Ryan turned around and saw that yes, indeed, a very large and drunk man was yelling in his direction, was in fact pointing at Ryan, shouting you fucking pussy, you bump into people and aren't man enough to say anything, and now Ryan felt that this was it, the moment he'd been imagining ever since that night at La Luna, and now he stepped back toward the guy and they were both shouting, and Ryan would barely remember the next morning what they were yelling about, could barely understand the words as soon as they left his mouth. But still. The large man shouted and Ryan shouted back. You big dumb motherfucker. Shut your ass up you little bitch.

Jared grabbed his arm and Ryan said no, I gotta find out what this guy's fucking problem is, and he walked toward him with his arms spread wide and his chest puffed. The man was about six-two and white, with a thick body and thicker beard. He looked like he could be the older brother of the kids from just off the rez, who used to jump Ryan at school. Ryan looked up at his burly enemy and thought I'm gonna get my ass kicked, and somehow that thought propelled him closer, until he felt the guy push him, two arms to the chest, and Ryan fell backward, held up only by the crowd of people around them.

Technically, Ryan threw the first punch this time. Later he'd tell himself he'd been pushed, he'd been insulted, he didn't start it, he had no choice. A few seconds passed, fists rocketing back and forth between them, and then Ryan grabbed the big guy's shirt, pulled it nearly over his head, and was punching him again and again, until the guy shook loose and began pummeling Ryan in return. All around them voices shouted what the fuck is wrong with you two, stop it, stop it please, and now arms of strangers pulled Ryan backward until the two were fully separate, and Ryan looked up and saw that the big guy was splattered with blood.

A voice shouted.

"Somebody get a towel!"

"Yeah!" Ryan yelled. "Get that motherfucker a towel!"

But then Jared grabbed Ryan's arm and said no, Ryan, *you're* the one who needs a towel, and Ryan touched his face and found his hand covered in blood, and he realized that actually he was bleeding from everywhere, so he took the towel and wiped himself off, and then he and Jared finally left and drove home, and Ryan felt no pain then or for the rest of the evening. Instead, he found himself floating. Jared told him I'm gonna take you with me everywhere, you're my bodyguard now, I'm gonna talk so much shit until I make someone call me a slur, just so I can watch you kick some guy's ass.

Months later, that happened. Kind of. He and Jared and a few others were out at a bar called Q. Inside, there was a man sitting alone at the end of the bar, hunched over and talking to no one. He would glance around the room every few moments before returning his eyes to his drink. Jared and Ryan noticed him but had no reason to think much of it. Later, after they moved outside to the patio to smoke, the same man walked by and asked for a cigarette. "Sorry," Jared said. "These are our last three."

The man looked stung. And drunk.

"Fuck you," he said. "You fucking faggots."

This was the first time Ryan had heard that word, uttered with that intention, since his childhood. But here, coming from the mouth of a stumbling drunk who'd just spent hours sitting alone in a gay bar, it didn't sound menacing. It sounded pathetic and hilarious.

"You know you're in the gay part of town, right?" said Ryan. "If *we're* faggots, then what does that make you?"

The man swung, wild and searching, and his fist glanced Ryan's chin, just barely. Ryan took a step back, then returned with a right and then a left, sending the guy to the ground, and they all laughed while he fell, and then the man got up and moved to throw another punch before deciding against it. "Fuck y'all," he said, stumbling into the dark.

Here was the thing. Now that Ryan was out of the closet, he *wanted* someone to call him a slur. He imagined it sometimes when he went out, eyeing the men who reminded him of his bullies back home. But in Buffalo, other than that one man at Q, no one ever did. He was chasing imaginary revenge on bullies who didn't exist.

—

In total, Ryan only had a few proper bar fights. Four, maybe five, depending on which altercations truly counted. They all seemed to fit the same pattern. Alcohol, rising tension, a few words and then blows, repeat. They were mostly with bigger guys, the ones Ryan called "cornfed," guys Ryan knew believed they could kick his ass. Most were white, and almost all were straight, or at least seemed so to Ryan. Once, he hit another gay man after last call at a gay bar, some skinny white boy loudly mocking Ryan and his friends for the way they looked. Ryan delivered an open-hand smack to the face, and then, as the man fell to the ground, surrounded by gasping friends, Ryan yelled, "Keep talking, bitch!" *What the fuck is wrong with you*, Ryan's friends said as they helped the guy up, *that's not fucking cool, man, why would you ever hit some helpless little twink?* Ryan felt ashamed after that one.

And then there was the one that revealed to Ryan the ugly depths of his impulses. He was out with coworkers for an official work mixer at a private club one of his colleagues belonged to, drinking at its members-only bar. A drunk man tried to force his way in, though he didn't have a membership or an invitation. A couple of the employees, both older men, politely explained that he needed to leave, but the man refused. Then he put his hands on them and started trying to push his way in, and that's when Ryan stepped forward. The man grabbed him by the shirt, pulling them both outside onto the sidewalk. He swung at Ryan and clipped him twice in the chin. That was all the permission Ryan needed.

They wrestled to the ground, Ryan on top but the man still clinging to his shirt, and Ryan grabbed his head, lifted it, and pounded it on the pavement, and the man did not let go so Ryan did it again, and now Ryan felt blood on his fingers, pouring from the man's skull, and he stood and saw the man sprawled there motionless. *Oh, my god*, Ryan thought. *I'm going to jail. They're going to lock me away for what I just did.*

His coworkers told him to leave and so he did, shaking as he walked through the city, and he heard sirens and thought surely police were coming to arrest him for assault, but the cars sped past him and eventually he made it home. He spent the weekend waiting for the police to show up at his doorstep, too ashamed to call or text his colleagues and ask what had happened, and whether the man had gone to the hospital or died there in the street. Ryan realized, even after his coworkers told him the guy had gotten up and walked away without assistance, that he could no longer say he didn't start fights. He could no longer tell himself he abided by some unfailing code. His was no longer some inspirational story of a tough gay man defying stereotypes, standing up against bullies. Ryan was a fucking *menace*. "You need to stay away from us for a while," one of Ryan's colleagues told him that next week back at work.

–

Years earlier, after his very first fight outside La Luna, Ryan had lay in bed replaying the night over and over again in his mind. He'd thought about it many times since, and his memory had stretched back further, all the way to his childhood, when he'd get jumped by older kids. But now when he thought of those moments, he realized something. His mind shifted to a new perspective. He thought now about the boys who had pummeled him on the pavement and felt his bones crack against their fists.

Oh, he thought to himself. *Now I know why they did it. They wanted to feel the way I feel right now.*

Gideon

Back at the bars in El Paso, Gideon found that women appeared before him as if from nowhere, all of them staring up and smiling, how tall are you, six-six no way, my dad is six-two but I don't think I know anyone as tall as you, let me guess you're in the army, enlisted or officer, I bet you're an officer, I can wear heels around you! My ex always got weird when I wore heels.

One of the first times this happened, Gideon felt stupefied by the experience of having a strange woman leaning into his chest while she laughed at his dumb jokes. She'd look at his eyes and then his lips and then his eyes again, and Gideon felt thrilled but frozen, unsure of where things were supposed to go next. So he just kept buying and guzzling drinks and feeling the weight of her hand on his triceps, until finally she suggested they get out of here, and so he stood up, took a single step, and collapsed on the floor. He didn't remember most of this. His buddies reconstructed the story for him the next day. But all of it served as an education. Gideon could get hammered or he could get laid. Many nights, he wasn't sure which one he wanted more.

He learned to function best within a structure. Baristas, waitresses, cashiers. Anywhere he had a pretense to be addressing the woman before him. Talking to the hot bartender served a purpose: Gideon needed a drink. But maybe that drink would lead to him saying he liked her T-shirt, and maybe soon she'd start asking where he was from and what he did, and maybe when he came back for his next round he'd ask what she was doing when her shift ended, and maybe she would say that the two of them should hang out. Gideon heard people make fun of guys who thought bartenders and waitresses were flirting with them, but he never really understood it. Gideon's experience was different. Every woman was flirting with him, everywhere, all the time.

He fucked his way through the fall and then the winter, through a solo trip home for Christmas, though the announcement of Caroline's deployment and the filing of papers for their divorce, and all the way through the next spring. By summer, though, he began to grow numb to the routine.

When he'd slept with Caroline, Gideon had gotten naked and stayed naked. He was naked to fuck and to sleep, naked because he was next to someone whose body he'd long memorized, a body that felt safe when he held it and made his body feel safe too. When he slept with strangers, though, Gideon found himself reaching for gym shorts the moment he finished, desperate to cover up. With both his wife and his hookups, their nudity always felt purposeful, the energy between their bodies dissolving the room around them until everything else had vanished, nothing remaining but their own sweat and skin. But, afterward, the room came back into focus, the weight of the bed took a solidity beneath him, the fan continued to spin, and the pictures returned to the walls. When he was with Caroline, the world that rebuilt itself felt familiar, serene. When he was with one of the women he found in the bars on Cincinnati Street, the family photos on their shelves felt unbearably intimate, the sight of their uncovered thighs obscene. And his entire body felt like an exposed nerve, like he was Adam and Eve both, in the garden, desperate for foliage to cover shame. Do you want to go to the bathroom first or should I? Here's your bra. I think I left my shorts over there. So what are you thinking, I should probably get back home, right?

—

Gideon did not date. He met women in bars and took them to his place or went to theirs. Sometimes, he got phone numbers. Others, not even names. Occasionally, he texted and asked if they wanted to hang out, which typically meant finding some way to fill fifteen minutes or an hour before they had sex. He never told them, explicitly, that he was only interested in their bodies, but he believed his actions carried that message. He did none of the things he'd done for Caroline. Nothing that suggested he wanted a girlfriend.

Okay, sure, occasionally, he would make plans to meet with someone for a drink. And yes, of course, once they were drinking they would engage in conversation. He would ask about their parents and jobs and hometowns. He would tell them the quickest version of the story of his marriage—"She fucked my boss"—and shrug his shoulders to say this was no big deal, just the way life goes. And yes, he supposed he could understand why someone might see this hour or two of conversation over drinks at a prearranged location, with this exchange of banter and stories from each other's pasts, as some kind of a date. But that was their problem, right?

Gideon didn't give anything of himself in those conversations. He offered no window to his inner world. He didn't tell them that he ached over where his life had led and feared where it might be going, that he'd imagined that by twenty-five he'd be a Major Leaguer with a happy marriage and maybe even a baby, but instead had spent the previous night drinking half a fifth of gin and venting to his dog. He didn't tell them that fucking strangers had recently been his only hobby and ambition. Or that he'd begun dealing with its growing monotony by only trying to fuck the *hottest* strangers, certain that this would imbue these encounters with new meaning, not because sex with hotter women was *better*, necessarily, but because the fact that he could gain access to their bodies might say something meaningful about his worth. He said nothing about the fact that he'd recently started taking diet pills, not because he was overweight, but because his abs weren't quite fully visible, and because his torso offered more the *suggestion* of lean muscle than the sight of these muscles themselves, and he believed that this change, going from 14 percent body fat to 10 percent, while maintaining that muscle, would be the thing that unlocked his access to that tiny percentage of women who sometimes (and let's be clear—*only sometimes*) remained just beyond his reach.

He didn't tell them about the pressures he'd felt to succeed, that he worried he'd already failed his parents by not repaying all they'd invested in his baseball career. He didn't say he wondered sometimes what it might have been like if his big brother hadn't died in the crib, how Jackson might have outshone Gideon and made his parents proud in ways Gideon never could. He said nothing about the ache he felt over what his life could have been.

But he listened to their stories. He laughed at their jokes. He told them he liked their eyes or their dress or their hair. Maybe this felt to them like a date. But to Gideon it felt only like a way to keep another body in temporary proximity to his own.

—

They finalized the divorce. He sold the house. Caroline shipped off for the Middle East. They did not say goodbye. Through it all, he drank. Rarely during the week, but more and more each weekend. On Friday afternoon he would stop by the liquor store on his way home from work, and he'd grab a handle of Tanqueray or Sailor Jerry or something, and often, by Sunday morning, the entire 1.75 liter bottle was gone. Usually, no one else had touched it. Occasionally, Gideon wondered if this was not okay.

Which made it all the more noteworthy when, one night that next January 2011, Gideon experienced the rarest of occasions: a Friday night in which he was not drunk. This felt strange. He was, after all, back on Cincinnati Street, roaming from bar to bar. He was with a crew of ex–West Point athletes, some baseball guys and a few football guys, none of whom he particularly liked. They were marauders, hell-bent on conquering each bar they entered, demanding attention and guzzling liquor and leaving with new women on their arms. Yes, Gideon understood that he, too, was an ex-jock soldier, and he, too, was prone to blacked-out Friday nights, and he, too, was often in search of strangers with whom to have sex, but still. He was twenty-six years old now. He liked to think that he did all of this with a bit more dignity.

But whatever. It was either this or sitting at home with Charlie, where he'd probably drink more than he drank when he went out. He was trying to cut back. Somehow, going to bars seemed like the best way to accomplish this goal. All that money spent, those long walks back to the bar for another round, the knowledge that people could *see* him, all of it managed to slow his drinking down. For now he sipped his beer, and he hung on the periphery of the crowd. One of these guys was named Ethan. He was massive, a former defensive end or something, nearly as tall as Gideon and maybe fifty pounds heavier, most all of it muscle. Ethan was one of the dumbest West Point grads Gideon had ever met, a beautiful Neanderthal. He introduced Gideon to Sarah, the woman he'd been hooking up with, who had just shown up at the bar. Sarah was loud and her body language was louder, and tonight, which happened to be her birthday, she'd given herself license to turn her own volume well past ten.

"Gideon's not really drinking," Ethan said, and he rolled his eyes at this, conspiratorially, as if surely Sarah would think that this was the most absurd choice someone could make on a Friday night in El Paso.

"Oh!" Sarah said, and then she grabbed another woman who'd been lingering on the edge of the group. "She's not drinking either! You two, talk to each other. We're gonna go over here."

And with that, Sarah and Ethan took two or three steps in the direction of the bar, then stopped and began making out. Gideon took a quick glance in their direction, then shook his head. He took a sip of the Shiner Bock he'd been nursing for the past hour. "Well," he said, and now he looked at the woman, who was tall and brunette and outrageously fit, with eyes golden on the inside and green on the edges. "This is a little awkward."

"Yep," she said.

"Yep," he said.

He stuck out his hand. "I'm Gideon."

She stuck out hers. "I'm Addie."

"It's nice to meet you."

She looked up at him and kept her eyes locked on his, staring with an intensity that froze him, leaving him both unable to speak and unable to look away.

"I'm not going to fuck you," she said.

Gideon felt his cheeks flush. "Ummm," he said. "I didn't. I mean. Yeah. No. Of course."

She kept looking at him, waiting for him to say more, until she seemed to realize he was done.

"Just so we're clear," she said. "That's not happening."

"Okay," Gideon said. "Yeah. I agree."

Gideon didn't exactly have a *strategy* for sleeping with random women. He never professed to have what other guys referred to as *game*. He just went to bars and talked to the women who talked to him. And that was it. He never approached women. When talking to them, he never hinted at going back to his place. He would laugh if they made sexual jokes, but he never made any of his own. His whole thing was predicated on the fact that women believed the hot and tall and smart and curious man standing before them had so many better options for casual sex or even a relationship that it was incumbent upon *them* to continue being interesting enough for the kind, large man to continue asking for the names of their childhood pets. And then, eventually, they ended up in someone's bed.

But here was an anomaly: a woman in a bar immediately declaring her disinterest. Gideon was insulted by the premise of their interaction. And yet he felt thrown off-balance and pulled in closer all at the same time.

"Well," he said. "I'm glad we got that out of the way."

She nodded. "Yep."

"So," he said, "what should we talk about?"

She shrugged.

"What are you drinking?"

She was nursing a Shiner Bock, same as him. He asked why she was out tonight if she didn't feel like drinking, and she explained that she needed to celebrate Sarah's birthday. They were friends from work, both military contractors who ran a physical fitness program on post.

Gideon asked how she ended up in El Paso.

"It's a long story," she said.

Gideon looked over at Sarah and Ethan, now in the corner of the room, still making out. "It seems like we have time," he said.

"Okay, fine."

Addie had grown up in New Jersey but lived in South Carolina, California, and Japan. The army had offered to move her here for this job, so she took it. And now here she was. She loved the work but couldn't stand most soldiers. Same bullshit, every day. Boys who needed mommies. Men who still acted like boys. All of that aggression, papered over insecurity. She just wanted to lift heavy and run fast and teach others to do the same, but she hated that the job required spending her days with the kinds of idiot men who shared her interests.

She asked him about himself, and he told her. He was an officer. Air Defense Artillery.

"West Point?" she asked.

"Yeah. How'd you know?"

"You fit the type."

"Do I?"

"Yeah. I've known a lot of West Pointers. I never liked any of them."

And now Gideon laughed, a little exasperated. "So I already know you're not going to fuck me. And now you're not even going to like me?"

She shrugged. "I'm just saying. I never liked 'em."

"Well," he said, "we do get a bad rap. Pompous, egotistical, snobby."

"Yes, yes, and yes."

Addie didn't seem to care whether the conversation continued, as if she would find someone equally interesting the moment Gideon walked away. He felt a small rush of nerves, scrambling to find ways to keep watching and listening to her talk. He asked her about living in Japan. She'd been working at Kadena Air Base on the island of Okinawa, a place with its own distinct culture and identity, very different from the Japan westerners imagined. Typically, when Gideon asked anyone affiliated with the army about their time overseas, they just bitched about the food on post or the bars just off it. Addie talked about Okinawa as a place she had fully sunken into, taking long walks through its cities and markets, trying foods she'd never heard of, making local friends off post.

She did not flirt. He didn't either. They just talked. For an hour, then another, standing in the same spot in the middle of a crowded and sticky bar. Until finally, the lights came on and the bar closed and it was time to take their two friends, by now both obliterated, back home.

Together, they all piled into Sarah's 1990 Toyota Corolla, with Addie behind the wheel. She drove them back to the apartment complex where both Gideon and Ethan lived. When she pulled over in front of his place, Gideon paused as he opened the door. He looked at Addie.

"Can we get dinner sometime?" he asked.

Addie shrugged and suppressed a smile.

"Sure," she said. "I like free food."

What happened next would remain in dispute. They would argue about it on their first date, a few weeks later at a restaurant called Crave, minutes before Gideon's card was declined and Addie began to laugh as she paid the bill. They would argue about it before their wedding, on a cliff overlooking the Aegean Sea in Croatia, where they eloped thousands of miles away from family, vowing to create their own. They would argue about it in front of their children, who cackled as each parent made their respective case, sitting on the floor of their living room with the dogs they would adopt after Charlie died. They would argue about it so much that they'd memorize each other's arguments.

One fact, they would agree on. Gideon leaned in. He reached for a hug. But that's where their stories would differ. Gideon would argue that Addie's intentions had been clear, her lips on a direct path for his. Addie would argue that she'd just been trying to say goodbye, but then she looked up to find this man she'd just met "attacking my face." But they would agree that soon it was over, and Gideon was out the door and Addie driving the others home, and they each moved through the night in opposite directions but had to work to suppress a rising giddiness over what they'd just experienced and what might come next.

"I don't know what just happened," Gideon would admit he said to Charlie, the moment he settled on the couch in his apartment and poured himself a drink. "But I think she might be special."

Joseph

The image of the dick first arrived in September, eight years after he got back from Iraq and seven years after he married Emily, just a few weeks after his first semester of law school began. Joseph knew, the first time he saw it, exactly what he was seeing, exactly where he'd seen it before. The image was there when he closed his eyes and there when he opened them. To even call it an *image* felt incomplete. This was more than sight. This was panic, this was sweating, this was the buzz of familiar fluorescent lights and the enclosing walls of that same windowless room. This was his chest tightening and his body turning scared and small.

He rolled over, next to Emily in bed, and the image disappeared. But then, the very next time they had sex, it came back. And then again. And then again. Her touch was a time machine. He felt her hands running across his skin and he was eight years old and trapped, let me out let me out, what the fuck is wrong with me, am I a freak? After a few weeks, he learned to give himself a little compassion. Something terrible had happened to him. *Of course* he was going to experience flashbacks. This was fine.

In fact, Joseph told himself, if you really thought about it, the fact that he was seeing the dick all the time was a *good* thing. Clearly, he'd been repressing the memory for some reason. But now he remembered. And not only did he remember it, but now he was *reliving* it, and that had to mean he was *processing* it, right? He'd heard Emily and others talk about "processing" their own trauma, and it always sounded very hard and important. Mostly, people seemed to do this in therapy. Which he would do too, of course, totally no problem, except for the fact that here he was already *processing* it so well on his own.

Besides, as fall wore on, he found ways to avoid the image. Mostly, this meant avoiding sex with Emily. Sure, it was hard to say no. He never wanted to see her face drop when he told her he just wasn't in the mood. So he got creative. He would stay in the library until 9:05 p.m., knowing Emily couldn't function unless she went to bed by 9. Or he would devour a bowl of chili, let the beans do their work on his intestines, and then warn her to stay away. Often, he would just turn to the easiest and truest excuse. He was, simply, way too stressed.

But this could only work for so long. He knew she had an internal abacus, measuring the number of times she'd initiated without reciprocation, each one of them further evidence in her mind that she was an ugly bore who couldn't please her man. She remembered every time she'd kissed his retreating neck or run her hand up his unresponsive thigh. He wanted desperately for Emily to feel desired. He wanted her to know she lived in a home with a man who wanted her, but who was held back only by the chaotic texture of their new lives. He wanted to give her intimacy without requiring it of himself. These moments were difficult, not only because he hated to disappoint her, but also, more urgently, because he was horny, terribly so, all of the time. When he was away from Emily he wanted desperately to fuck her. When he was with her, he wanted to do anything he could to keep *her* from wanting to fuck *him*. Arousal was subsumed by the fear of what her touch would make him see.

Eventually, Joseph realized, knowing how to avoid sex wasn't enough, if he wanted to maintain equilibrium in their home. His most brilliant move wasn't about avoidance. It was *initiation*. If you picked the right time and the right methods, initiating sex could be just as effective as rejecting it. So he would wait until she'd had an overwhelmingly stressful day, or right until the moment before he knew she'd want to go to sleep, or five minutes before she had to leave for work, and then he would kiss her, slow and deep, knowing that she would say no, not now, but let's pick this back up later, and Joseph would say okay, feigning disappointment, but celebrating inside, because now Emily could not tell herself that *he* always rejected *her*. Then once they'd gone a week without sex, it was easier to go another, and soon the hands stopped rubbing thighs, the kissing turned perfunctory and polite, the marriage functional but chaste.

Still, on occasion, he knew he had to power through. Every now and then, Joseph would come home from class on a Friday for date night and immediately get a little drunk, substituting his typical Dos

Equis with higher-alcohol Dogfish Head IPAs. He'd put away four in quick succession to reach that delicate place where his mind was too dulled to conjure long-ago images, but his body was still alert enough to respond to the naked body of the woman he loved.

Other times, he would make himself respond to her advances while still sober, and when they moved to the bedroom he would close his eyes. Sometimes he could push the dick from his mind if he simply conjured another image to replace it. While he pressed his body against Emily's, he would close his eyes as tightly as he could, allowing in no light, and think about something else.

Think about titties, he told himself, and yes, in his mind, he really did say this exact sentence. *Think about titties*. And then, at least sometimes, there inside his eyelids, a beautiful pair of titties would finally appear. They arrived attached to no face, no torso, not so much as a rib cage or a clavicle. Just hovering there, two lights in the darkness, round and perfect.

Joseph understood the fact that while this was happening, two beautiful breasts, which happened to belong to the person he loved most in this world, were pressed against his skin. The problem, of course, was that focusing on the actual breasts would mean allowing the traumatic memory into his mind, and the memory would invite panic and sweating, the sense that the walls around them would swallow him whole. The imaginary titties somehow left no room for any other image, and so this, for now, was what he would do to reach completion during sex.

The strategy worked to perfection. At least once. Maybe even twice.

—

Joseph had never really been into porn. For most of his adult life, he could take it or leave it. He'd first seen it at too young an age, five years old, when he'd walked in on his babysitter showing his sister a video she'd brought with her to their house. Joseph was transfixed, crouching behind a chair, aware that he was seeing something he shouldn't, but unsure of exactly what it was. Later he would have no real memory of the acts or body parts he saw, only of what he felt as he watched—a dryness in his throat and mouth, a sense that he was slowly and gently choking on his own breath.

When he reached the appropriate age, he never picked up the habit. Part of this was a fact of timing. He'd hit puberty a few years before the proliferation of high-speed internet, back at a time when you had to steal your father's magazines if you wanted to see a pair of breasts. In high school and the years afterward, he'd entered young men's ministries at church, where they preached the dangers of masturbation. He'd jerked off plenty, but always filled with shame, and never as part of his regular routine. But now, in a moment when all sexual contact with Emily brought him images of his own abuse, he started watching it. Here was something that felt, at least vaguely, like sex, but that he could do without the anxiety or terror attached to actual sex. He'd been grasping for control, and here, finally, he'd found it. With porn, Joseph decided when to initiate, and Joseph decided how to continue.

Sex with Emily belonged to them both but also to the fear in his mind. Porn belonged to Joseph alone. Maybe this was what he needed. By starting with porn, he could readjust to sex. It was like exposure therapy, he told himself. Maybe the more he touched his own body, the more his body could handle being touched.

But wait, another idea, even better: What if he *used* porn in his sex with *Emily*? Not openly, of course. He knew there were couples who sometimes watched porn together, but those people would never be *them*. Instead, Joseph came up with another perfect solution. He would commit to memory the particular scenes he liked, and then he would close his eyes during sex and transport himself from their bedroom, where a real body was touching him and bringing back the traumatic memory, and into the porn scenes, where no one was real and everything remained under his control.

He settled into a routine. A few nights a week, they would sit on the couch together rewatching a movie or a TV show they'd already seen a million times. *Pineapple Express, Talladega Nights, Friends.* They both craved the comfort of old favorites, because their minds were not required to engage with anything new. Eventually, she'd fall asleep on the couch, then wake up briefly and move to the bed. Joseph would stay on the couch, watching the movie for another hour or so, before pulling up something else familiar and safe, a favorite scene, then jerking off and going to bed. He'd hold tight to the memory, knowing it would be useful the next time they had sex.

This was a sin. He believed that, even though he no longer really believed in God. The lust was a sin, and the secrecy was an even worse sin. The routine soothed and tormented him in alternate measure. But he couldn't tell Emily about it—any of it. The intrusive images, the stress brought on by physical touch, or his new ritual. If she knew any piece of what was roiling inside him, then she would think things were not fine. And everything, it was important to stress, was *totally* fine. But on some level, if he was really leveling with himself, Joseph believed that *she* was the one causing him to relive the trauma. If she would just not touch him for a while, then surely he'd get all of this sorted out. So if you really broke it down, he actually had no *choice* but to watch porn and then try to imagine the sex he'd seen on-screen the moment Emily touched him. This, obviously, was the loving thing to do, the *right* thing to do: to eject himself from his body so that his body could service her needs. Surely she'd understand.

Ryan

Coming out had felt at first like salvation, like he was reborn into a new world that accepted him, whole. But as Ryan grew into his late twenties and got more deeply connected to Gay Buffalo, he felt himself falling into a parallel universe governed by a familiar set of laws. The clothes and the affect and the cultural references had all shifted, but in many ways, the men who ruled this new world looked a lot like those who'd ruled his high school. The tall ones, the athletic ones, the mean ones. They bullied differently, but they still bullied.

The way Ryan saw it, all gay men wanted to be the men everyone else wanted to fuck, and if they couldn't achieve that, they wanted to fuck the men everyone else wanted to be. Jealousy blurred with desire. He knew plenty of men wanted to sleep with him. Even if they didn't fawn over him the way they did over taller and slimmer guys, he had no problem finding attention, either in bars or online. But every relationship seemed to fizzle after a few weeks. Ryan began to wonder if he might be attractive enough to grab attention but not attractive enough to sustain that attention. Maybe he didn't deserve to reach the stage when a man would introduce him to friends and family and proudly announce that Ryan was *his*.

How would Ryan find a man who wanted to keep him? He would lose weight. A lot of it. He started running, six or seven miles every day: a few in the morning and a few more in the afternoon. He worked and ran and went out most nights, barely taking any time for sleep and never taking time to properly eat. He dropped 20 pounds, going from 180 to 160. When he went home to the reservation, his mother and his aunts looked at him aghast and started shoving burgers and hot dogs and chips in his face, demanding that he eat every bite. He posted a photo on Facebook and immediately felt ashamed, studying the picture and seeing someone fat and pathetic. When the likes and adoring comments poured in, he didn't believe them. After a breakup, he took a week off work and went out every night, deciding in advance that he'd sleep with any man who showed him attention, desperate to see himself as those men saw him, as a body worthy of exploration and touch.

—

One day at work, his friend Mary popped by his desk. "I have a new obsession," she said.
"What?"
"Taekwondo."
Ryan was curious. He trusted Mary. She was Mohawk, too, and she was short and strong and fueled by a similar aggression. She was someone who reveled in, rather than shying from, Ryan's stories of his own scraps.

Taekwondo was a Korean martial art, built on "the art of fist and foot fighting." It was more than a combat sport; it represented a way of living and thinking, with a goal to achieve total mind and body happiness. All of that sounded fine enough to Ryan, if unexciting. What caught his attention was this: "It's really fucking intense," Mary said. Plus, the first class was free.

"You may have fought in the streets," Ryan's *sabom*, or instructor, told his beginners' taekwondo class on the first day. "But now you're here. And in here, you're going to learn to fight *my way*."

So Ryan committed to learning taekwondo. He began to love the technique, felt a rush anytime he landed a clean strike with his fist or foot. He came to appreciate the ritual, bowing to his partners before and after training, tying the belt and folding the uniform in a way that showed respect for history and tradition. His instructor had been right. Nothing he'd learned in bar fights translated into the *dojang*. And he'd passed up his father's boxing lessons the one time he'd been given the chance as a little boy—not that those lessons would have helped him now. Taekwondo was ordered, graceful. Sparring felt less like a fight than a dance.

Plus, it helped him lose weight. Between this, the running, the cigarettes, and forgoing meals, he began to wilt into a shape he found more appropriate, one he hoped others might find beautiful. His sparring suffered, though. One day he went to punch and found that he'd lost all his power; he lifted his leg to kick and saw that on impact, his opponent had barely moved.

"What's happened to you?" his instructor asked him. "You're wasting away."

—

Ryan got a new message one afternoon on MySpace. He loved MySpace. He posted pictures and sometimes shared blog posts. He wrote private and public messages to friends, a few of whom he ranked in what the site called his "Top Eight." And occasionally, he got surprising messages. Like this one.

Hey! I think you know my ex. I used to see you when I was with him, and I always thought you were cute. I just wanted to say what's up.

Ryan clicked through to visit the sender's profile. He recognized this guy, if only vaguely. His name was Anthony. Ryan wrote back.

Yeah. I remember you.

They had met years ago, back before Ryan came out, when Anthony was dating a guy who lived on Ryan's hall at Buffalo State. But they'd barely spoken then, just watched movies with large groups of friends in the dorm's common room. Anthony was Black, with a slender face, a wide smile, and eyelashes so long and gorgeous they seemed to stretch through the computer screen. As Ryan studied his photos, he felt something galloping in his chest. He left his computer to return to a workout in his living room, but then he heard a *ding* from the speakers, and he darted back to see if Anthony had replied. An introduction turned to small talk turned to casual and long-running conversation: about where they were from (the rez, California), how they liked Buffalo (it's cool, i love it!!), what kind of music and movies they liked (hip-hop, action), and whether they were single (yes, *yessssss*).

Anthony had grown up following his father to army bases across the country. His parents divorced, his mother settling on the West Coast and his father back East. Anthony had spent years splitting his time between both until going to Buffalo for college. Ryan tried to avoid being glued to his computer, but every time he heard a ding he came running back to see what Anthony had sent. Afternoon bled into evening, messages volleying back and forth, until Ryan mentioned that he was hungry.

What do you want to eat? Anthony asked.

McDonald's.
I'll come pick you up.

—

Anthony was the first man Ryan felt no need to impress, the first one who saw him, including the pieces Ryan found ugly, and who only looked closer, never away. He saw Ryan's Mohawk culture as fascinating but not exotic, unlike some of the white guys Ryan had dated, one of whom called him *my little Pocahontas*, and another who joked that he should dance to stop the rain. Anthony saw the rolls in Ryan's stomach, the mass in his ass and thighs, and he ran his hands over them tenderly, held the lumps of Ryan's body against the spindly muscles of his own. When Ryan mentioned needing to abstain from dessert, Anthony scolded him. "I like you thick," he told him. "In a zombie apocalypse, I'm killing you, and then I'll live off your legs for months." And then he laughed and tried to feed Ryan an extra bite.

As the weeks passed, they never spoke, explicitly, about becoming exclusive, but only found that they were spending so much time together that they had none left for anyone else. And then one of Ryan's friends introduced Anthony to another of Ryan's friends, and she used the word *boyfriend*, and Ryan felt a jolt of anxiety until he looked over and saw Anthony beaming. Later that night Ryan asked what he'd thought about that comment, and Anthony started giggling, until he said, plainly, "I guess that means I'm your man."

Anthony was expressive and outgoing where Ryan was quiet and watchful, Anthony passionate where Ryan was calculating, Anthony wild and adventurous where Ryan was brooding and stoic. He stretched the limits of who Ryan imagined he could be. Sometimes during movies Anthony would cry, and Ryan would sit there stone-faced; Anthony would look up through tears and declare that Ryan was not human, that he didn't have feelings, and Ryan would tell him that of course he had feelings: "I'm just not a cry-ass like you." Anthony had traveled the whole country and dreamed of skydiving one day; Ryan had barely left upstate New York and announced, passionately, "Indians aren't meant to fly." They took a trip down to Florida and visited a place called GatorWorld, filled with reptiles that Ryan deeply feared, and they went into a tent where they were allowed to hold snakes and alligators. When they took a photo together, Ryan was unable to open his eyes, and Anthony was grinning like a child who'd just reached undiscovered levels of joy. Ryan thought that this must be what love was, to find yourself thousands of miles from home and terrified, but delighted by the joy on the face of the man who sat next to you, deadly reptiles in both your hands.

Oh no, Ryan thought, one morning a few months into their relationship. *Am I going to have to introduce you to my family?*

—

Back when he'd first started college, Ryan had begged his mother to come back to Buffalo, pick him up, and bring him home. The thought of life without his family, away from the safety of the reservation, had seemed then like something he could never manage. As the years had passed, though, he'd begun to feel adrift from much of his family. His mother called him regularly, asking about his work and his friends, and Ryan reported back dutifully, talking about his boyfriends as if they were merely friends, talking about his volleyball team without mentioning he played in an all-gay league. When he talked to his sister, eight years younger than him, on the phone, she spent most of her time asking for brotherly advice, and he helped her navigate the social pressures of high school, listening to her stories about friends and parties and boys. His father remained distant but showed Ryan love in the ways he knew how, mostly at Christmas, the one day each year when he grinned from ear to ear as he watched his children open the kinds of presents his own parents had never been able to afford.

After Ryan's first fight outside La Luna, he told his dad the story, with a shy smile just like the one he'd seen on his uncles' faces when they told their own bar-fight tales. Finally, he imagined, he was showing his dad he was no longer the little boy who wilted, that he was now someone who knew how to defend himself, who could inflict more than he received. As he told the story, though, he saw that his father was not laughing or smiling, but looking increasingly concerned. "Why would you do that?" he asked. "You're going to get yourself arrested. I can't believe you would be so stupid."

"Seriously?" Ryan asked.

"Yes! I didn't raise you that way."

Well, Ryan thought. *You definitely tried.*

Once, Ryan brought Anthony home with him for a long weekend. All his life, Ryan had seen the way outsiders looked at the reservation. He knew there were people from Potsdam or Canton who warned each other not to drive too far north on Highway 11, fearing what might happen if their cars broke down on Mohawk land. Others would stop by for tax-free cigarettes and tax-free gas but barely considered the existence of the people in town. Anthony was different. He loved exploring the rez. Ryan took him along the invisible US–Canada border, which had no real meaning on Mohawk land, showing him where the border crossed through an intersection, ran down the street, and went directly through his family's home. He showed Anthony the local schools and lacrosse fields, the casino that had become the region's biggest employer. They spent a Friday night with Ryan's high school friends, drinking at The Brass Horse, which was the reservation's dive bar and its dance bar, its first-date bar and its solo bender bar, the classiest and trashiest and, save for the casino, which mostly catered to out-of-towners, the *only* bar in town.

Everywhere they went, Ryan introduced Anthony only as "my friend." One night, they sat up late watching TV on the couch, and Anthony stood to go to bed and asked Ryan if he was coming. Ryan hissed, "No, of course not," while darting his eyes around the room to make sure no one had wandered in and overheard them.

Then his cousin, Kyle, came out as gay. He was a couple years younger than Ryan, but they'd spent their childhood playing kickball and riding four-wheelers together, and digging in creek beds in search of worms and bugs. Ryan heard that his aunt had taken the news hard, but her husband had been supportive, and he wondered what it might be like if someday he came out to the family too. He tested the waters with his sister, Steevi. She was grown now, eighteen years old, out of high school and beginning her adult life on the reservation. She'd been a star hockey and lacrosse player her entire life. She was the son, Ryan joked, that their father never had. She and Ryan had remained close, and he imagined she was safer than any other member of the family. So one day he called her and said he had something he needed to tell her, and then he stammered his way vaguely in that general direction, until finally she told him just *say it.*

"Okay," Ryan said. "I'm gay."

He heard her smile on the other end.

"*Finally*," Steevi said. "I've been waiting *years* for you to say this."

—

As time passed, Anthony's place in Ryan's life became impossible for his family to ignore. Steevi told Ryan that their mother had been asking questions. Why was he so close with Anthony? What exactly *were* they to each other?

So one weekend Ryan drove home and asked his mother to meet him for lunch. She had him come to one of the restaurants at the Mohawk Casino, where she worked. They sat down at a table tucked in a stale room with faint music, where they ate sandwiches and salads surrounded by slot-playing Canadian retirees. They caught up for a while, talking about anything but the thing Ryan had gone there to say, until finally, with their meal almost finished, Ryan took a deep breath.

"So," he said. "I know you've been asking questions about me and Anthony."

She picked at her salad. "Uh-huh," she said.

"Well," Ryan said. "What do you think he is to me?"

She looked up. "Why don't *you* tell *me*?"

He heard in her tone a kind of challenge, a chastening. Ryan felt his insides twist.

"Anthony is my boyfriend," he said. "We've been together a couple of years now."

Her face showed the faintest confusion, as if she'd just recovered a long-forgotten memory.

"And..." Ryan started. "And I'm gay."

Here was terror, here was relief, here was the heartbeat leveling off but the sweat on the palms increasing, and here was his mother, standing up and reaching for her wallet, saying nothing as she dropped enough cash on the table to pay for the bill. Ryan stood with her and grabbed her, pulling her in for a hug. Her body stiffened, then relented, relaxing ever so briefly into her son's arms. He said to her a version of the sentences he'd hoped she would say to him.

"This doesn't change who I am. I'm still me. I love you."

She pulled herself out of his arms.

"I love you too," she said. And as she walked away, she added one more thing.

"I'm not telling your father. *You* have to tell him."

—

Months passed. His mom kept calling, checking on him several times a week. Ryan tried to conveniently edit Anthony out of his stories from Buffalo, but eventually his mom started to ask, her voice a little tentative, "Is Anthony doing okay?" Ryan just said, "Yep, he's great," and tried to steer the conversation elsewhere. But the very question served as an acknowledgment that she knew someone out there shared a love for her son. At the very least, she was curious to know whether that person was *okay*.

And then, one day, Ryan got a text.

> Need to talk to you ASAP.

Steevi. His sister. He called her right away.

"You're planning to come home this weekend, right?"

"Yeah."

He'd been planning the trip for weeks. They were throwing a big party for his mother's birthday.

"Well," she said. "If you come, I think you should probably find another place to stay."

Typically, his father loved hosting Ryan on his return visits. He made sure Ryan's bedroom was prepared for him, that he had clean sheets and enough towels, that their meals were all planned. He got frustrated when Ryan went out at night with his friends, only because he wanted his son to be at home with the family, even if that just meant eating dinner together in front of the TV.

"What?" Ryan asked his sister. "Why?"

"Mom told Dad."

Mom told Dad. He knew.

"He, um, didn't take it well."

Of course he didn't take it well. And yet, if Ryan was honest with himself, though he'd never once said it out loud, he had, on occasion, allowed himself to hope. Maybe, he'd imagined, someday he would sit down with his father, and he would look him in the eye and announce that he was gay, and maybe his father would respond as his sister and so many of his friends had, with a gentle smile and something like "I know. I've always known." Maybe he would tell him that he loved him and accepted who he was. Ryan had seen the movies and television shows where a son comes out and the father disowns the son, and he'd always told himself that his own father would never do that, that no matter what he felt about gay people, he couldn't bear the possibility of losing a connection to his eldest child. But now here he was, indirectly making it known that Ryan wasn't welcome in his home.

Ryan couldn't tell his father he was gay, and his father couldn't tell Ryan he wasn't welcome. The women of their family served as conduits between them, relaying messages and soothing raw emotions, shouldering the work required to keep their family at peace. Ryan daydreamed about sitting down with his father. "Listen, you heartless bastard," he imagined saying, before launching into all the ways his dad had failed him: Taking him to the heavy bag after Ryan got beaten when he stepped off the bus, instead of sitting with him and holding him, tending to his wounds. Showing up drunk on Saturday nights and yelling at Ryan's mother, leaving him to cower and listen in his room. Pushing him into sports, where Ryan never felt comfortable or accepted, rather than allowing Ryan to develop his own passions. He was not enough, Ryan thought. He'd never been enough. And now here he was, a grown man with friends and a career and a partner, who happened to be another grown man, who loved him deeply, and his father seemed to be saying that Ryan's successes and joys were still more failures, that the life he'd built for himself was something perverse.

Ryan felt, suddenly, a deep and enduring urge to drive to the reservation, find his father, and tell him to square the fuck up. Let's fucking *dance*, old man. This was the way. This was what it took. His father would only respect him if he showed up on his doorstep to kick his ass.

Nate

One morning, a few months after his top surgery, Nate saw a post from his friend Jay on Facebook that caught his attention:

Any trans guys out there who like thick girls?

Nate liked the status and commented immediately:

🖐 Right here

Jay said he had a friend. Her name was Mya. She lived in New Haven, Connecticut. She was interested in dating a trans man. Jay showed her Nate's picture, and she thought he was cute. What followed were the most thrilling and chaotic two years of Nate's life. Joys he'd never known he could feel, and pain worse than any he'd suffered before.

He started FaceTiming Mya for hours every night, sometimes while lying in his bed at home, others while working the graveyard shift at Walmart, where he stocked shelves. They told stories from their childhoods and shared memes about life as an Aquarius; they recounted mundane details of their todays and fantasized about the future they could build starting tomorrow. Sometimes, they sat in silence, or she watched him work. Other times, he watched her sleep. In the early mornings, he saw her toddler son, Trae, playing with toys in the background.

"Who's that?" he heard Trae ask her one morning over breakfast.

"That's my boyfriend," she said. "His name is Nate."

Nate went to visit her after three months, then moved to Connecticut after six. "I'm not gonna be his dad," he told Mya about Trae, and she said that was fine. Nate had never imagined himself as a parent. For so long, the only vision available to him had been one of motherhood, a vision he never allowed himself to fully see. Besides, he'd had a hysterectomy a few years after he started testosterone. He couldn't get pregnant if he tried.

The idea of fatherhood terrified him in altogether different ways. For one thing, he barely had a model. He hadn't ever seen a father he could imagine himself emulating. He thought, sometimes, of the way his own father had been when he was little—tender but strong, playful but firm—but that man was gone now. He'd gotten a new home, a new wife, and new children, and all of them had already been abandoned just like Nate and his mom had been abandoned before them. When Nate went to visit, his father usually wasn't home. After starting steroids, Nate's father had dealt with pain that had led to prescription opiates, which had led to addiction, which had led to heroin, and now staying one step ahead of getting dopesick had crowded out his dad's desire to be a father.

And yet here, in the apartment he shared with Mya, a tiny and voracious brain, a body in perpetual motion, this small but whole human, followed him from room to room. Trae asked Nate impossible questions and gave him wobbly high fives. He begged for him to sit and read in his lap. They colored in coloring books and dribbled basketballs, studied Pokémon and T-Rexes, belted every single word to "Itsy Bitsy Spider" and "Baby Shark." The first time he called Nate "Daddy," Nate corrected him. The second time, he corrected him again. But at some point, he asked Mya if she thought that word was okay, and she said yeah, sure, and then, for a while after that, "Daddy" felt more natural than any other name, male or female, he'd ever been called.

That's when things were good between him and Mya. It lasted almost a year. They fought, often—petty jealousies over someone the other was texting or whose pictures they'd liked on social media—but they always made up. Then the fights grew more frequent and more venomous, and they decided they couldn't do it anymore, that their shared fear of losing the relationship left each of them unable to keep it.

But even if they couldn't be together romantically, they both thought they had a good thing going, sharing rent and responsibilities. They decided, for a while, that Nate would stay in the home and continue helping to care for Trae. He and Mya would sleep in separate rooms. They would date other people. They would be roommates and functional co-"parents," even if Nate was only a dad by name and function, not biology or law.

The jealousies lingered, though, and they still argued several times a week. And then one night, Mya hosted a party and got drunk and angry, and anger turned to aggression, and she started hitting Nate, over and over again, in the face and neck and ribs. Because Nate knew that a man does not ever hit a woman, even if that woman is six inches taller and forty pounds heavier, he cowered in the corner, begging her to stop.

Police arrived within an hour, and Mya left in handcuffs. She spent several nights in jail until she could put together bail money, and this was followed by court-mandated counseling and anger management. Trae went to stay with his grandmother. Nate flew home to Ohio. Sometimes, they talked on FaceTime.

"Daddy," Trae would ask him, "when are you coming back home?"

It took more than a year for Nate to realize the answer was never.

Gideon

Days after the night they met at that bar on Cincinnati Street, Gideon and Addie went out to dinner. They talked for hours, both at the table and outside in the parking lot, standing together long after closing time at her car. She thrilled him. He liked finding the places where they disagreed, because he liked watching her mind at work. Addie cut through Gideon's performance, calling him out when he was full of shit. She spoke with an unnerving directness, which left him struggling to project a confidence to match her own.

He never felt the need to splay himself open before her with the details of his divorce. They'd each emerged from their own marital wreckage. She had a seven-year-old son, Theo, from her marriage to a soldier who had struggled with PTSD and alcoholism, and her ex was now a sporadic presence in her child's life. Gideon met Theo for the first time a few months after they'd started dating. At first, it was just a brief hello, but a few weeks after that he spent some time helping Theo with his math homework. Then one night when Gideon was at Addie's apartment, Theo asked for a bedtime story, and so Gideon took him to his room and proceeded to tell him the entire plot of the Denzel Washington film *Man on Fire*, in which Denzel goes on a murderous rampage after a little girl he loves is kidnapped by members of a drug cartel. "And then they all lived happily ever after!" Addie shouted as she barged into the room. She sent Gideon back to the living room, saying he'd done a wonderful job but she could take it from here.

For as long as he could remember, Gideon had wanted to be a father. He remembered watching his own dad crouch down into a catcher's stance, out in their big front yard, catching pitch after pitch as Gideon threw the ball as hard as he could, and occasionally he thought to himself, *Someday I'll catch pitches for my son too*. He imagined driving future daughters to dance recitals, or sitting at the kitchen table at night while getting peppered with questions about math homework. He wanted to teach them how to dress wounds and divide fractions and throw a punch. He wanted to hold them while they wept.

As he fell in love with Addie—a process including late-night revelations of the insecurities he'd never shown anyone else, debates over politics (just like with Caroline, she was more liberal, he was more conservative), and early-morning CrossFit workouts—he found himself feeling a love for Theo too. He loved the child as an extension of Addie, sure, but he also came to love pieces of him that belonged to Theo alone. He was observant and curious, deeply sensitive to the pains of all creatures he encountered. He would climb to the top of the swing set, not to jump down, but just to sit and admire the view.

That summer, after Gideon and Addie had been together about six months, Gideon was assigned to attend an army training program in Fort Sill, Oklahoma. Addie took Theo to Florida, where they could be closer to family support. Every Wednesday afternoon while they were apart, Gideon called Theo. He asked him about his day at school and he said that it was fine. He asked him about soccer practice and he said that was fine too. Despite the one-word answers, Theo made it clear that he didn't want to get off the phone with Gideon—"I like talking," he would tell him—he just didn't know what else to say. So then they would read together, *Little Monsters* or *The Berenstain Bears*, or they would play a game of "I Spy" in which they each had to picture the other's room. Sometimes they would just sit on the phone in silence while Theo colored and Gideon studied, listening to each other breathe.

"Hey, Small One," Gideon said one afternoon that fall.

"Hey," Theo said.

"I've been thinking about something. Do you think you can keep a secret?"

"Yeah. What is it?"

"Well," Gideon said, "if I tell you, you have to keep it a secret, and if you *do* keep it a secret, then I'll give you a special present when the time comes. What do you think?"

"I can do it!" Theo said. "I know I can."

And so Gideon told him what he'd been thinking, since moments after he met Addie; what he'd been thinking on their first date and all through that spring and summer; what he thought every time he talked to Theo on the phone. "I really love your mommy, and I want to be with her forever. So I'm going to ask her to marry me."

"Really?"

"Really. What do you think about that?"

"I think you should do it."

Gideon told him that he would, as soon as he knew the time was right, which didn't arrive until several months later, over Christmas. When all three of them had just finished watching a movie, Gideon turned to Theo and asked if he was ready for his present, and Theo said yes. Addie watched them, confused, and Theo started to jump up and down with excitement. Gideon started to shiver, and then to shake, as he handed Theo a chain necklace and then pulled out another jewelry box and got down on one knee.

"Can I call you 'Dad' now?" Theo asked after Addie tearfully told Gideon yes, and then Gideon started crying too.

"If you want to, Small One," he said. "If you want to, I would love it if you did."

—

A year after they got married, Gideon deployed to Qatar, and a year after he returned, they moved to Louisville, Kentucky, where Addie promptly got pregnant and gave birth to a baby boy. Parker was born loud and ornery, plagued by colic and screaming all day and night. He was perfect. And soon Gideon officially became Theo's dad too, sobbing in the courtroom while the judge declared him father to another son.

Even though Theo was not his flesh, Gideon saw so much of himself in his child. He had the mind of an engineer, relentlessly curious to learn how things worked. He was stubborn and sarcastic and wholly immune to fear of authority, demanding that grown-ups prove themselves worthy of his attention. He also saw, in his child, so much of what he loved about Addie. A deep capacity for self-reflection, a willingness to love with full abandon and no fear.

Gideon loved the chaos of their home, but the pressures of fatherhood wore on him. Right around the time Parker was born, after nine years of service, Gideon left active duty. The deployment to Qatar had been fine, if at times frustrating in the ways all jobs are often frustrating. He had clashed with authority. He didn't get the leeway to run his unit the way he wanted. He felt daunted by the task of trying to please one commanding officer after another in order to keep climbing in rank. More than that, though, he no longer wanted to be subject to the army's whims, or to face the possibility of uprooting his family at a moment's notice or deploying again. It was 2016. The war in Iraq was long over, and the American presence in Afghanistan had decreased steadily over time. Gideon had faced no real danger when he deployed, but he hated the thought of spending another year away, parenting his children over FaceTime.

So here he was, at home in Kentucky, transitioning to the civilian world and raising two kids. His biggest stress: money. Gideon had taken for granted how much financial stability the army gave him—not only through the paycheck, but through health insurance, hazard pay on deployments, and even a housing allowance. Now, he had to find new ways to cover everything: rent, day care, food. It was impossible math, floating through Gideon's mind every moment of every day. Addie had started a small skin-care business, but she wasn't yet making a profit. She mentioned picking up shifts as a waitress. Gideon hated that thought. The possibility of her going back to a job she'd last held as a teenager, all because he couldn't make enough money to support their family, felt humiliating. "We're fine, babe," he told her. "I've got this."

Parker seemed to have a preternatural ability to continue existing in this world despite never, under any conceivable circumstances, during the daytime or at night, going the fuck to sleep. His screams were the soundtrack to their lives. They wore down Theo, who was now nine, and left him resentful toward his brother and pissy toward his parents. They wore on Addie, stripping her of any of the patience she once had with Gideon.

But in truth, Gideon was less concerned by Parker's screaming than he was by the fact that he needed to drink formula and eat food that Gideon was required to buy. That he needed to sleep in a crib in a nursery in a home Gideon must rent. That he needed to ride in a car Gideon still paid hundreds of dollars for every month. Gideon wasn't sure if money could buy happiness, but he knew a few hundred extra dollars each month could stop the constant buzzing in his ears and pounding in his chest.

Booze helped. Sometimes, at least. He'd give it a chance to help when he was on his lunch break from his first civilian job, selling insurance, as he sat in his car at a gas station about a mile from the office. There, he'd guzzle a couple of forty-ounce bottles of Steel Reserve malt liquor. But even Gideon had to admit, sitting in the driver's seat, the engine off to save gas, windows open, staring at the dumpster of a Kentucky Circle K, that this was potentially alarming behavior.

He'd always been able to tell himself he had a perfectly normal relationship to alcohol. In high school he'd stolen his mom's wine coolers from the fridge because that's what you were supposed to do in high school. In college he'd drunk no more or less than every other member of the baseball team, which, because of the demands of their sport and the rules of West Point, he felt confident was much less than the average student at any other school. When he and Caroline were married, they'd always started Saturdays with Bloody Marys and kept a steady drip of Coors Lights going all day. That primed them to go out on weekend nights, where, inevitably, in El Paso's bars, he ran into every other soldier he knew. If Gideon was a drunk, then all of them were drunks. America's freedoms were kept safe by young men and women who could quickly put away four to fourteen beers. After the divorce, he'd started blacking out alone with Charlie every weekend, but he managed to make it through the week without a drop.

Drinking on the job felt like a different kind of choice. Still, Gideon could explain it. For starters, he was stressed. He'd been discharged from the army less than three months previously, and he'd watched the number in their savings account dwindle as he struggled to find a job. And then he'd finally gotten hired selling stop-gap workers' compensation coverage to companies around the state.

His bosses told him it was a numbers game. He would call companies and ask to talk to human resource directors, and on some days those calls would lead to meetings that would lead to sales. He'd be paid no salary, just 100 percent commission, but the upside was high. He heard of salespeople who made multiples of six figures. His bosses drove Mercedes and referenced "going out on the lake," which, to Gideon, implied possible boat ownership.

And yet, the first few days on the job were brutal. Gideon's entire identity rested on earning praise from friends and family and strangers. Sales was all about weathering an endless barrage of the word *no*. That required confidence. Wasn't everyone a little more confident after a few drinks? Gideon just needed to relax.

He followed the same routine for about a week. Steel Reserve in the car at lunch, back to the office to make a few tipsy sales calls, chest tightening with each new rejection, then guzzling water and chewing a handful of mints on his way home. That's how it went until that Friday, when he decided on his break that maybe he needed a little more than usual. So he bought a second forty, then maybe a third, and he let his lunch sit there uneaten, the booze swimming in his empty stomach until it was time to drive back to work.

Soon after he got back to his desk, his boss walked into the room, a short, pudgy man with a strangely deep voice.

"What's wrong with you?" he asked Gideon.

"Huh? Nothing. I'm good."

"You're drunk."

This was ridiculous, Gideon said. He'd just had a couple drinks at lunch. No big deal. But no, his boss said, and soon he brought in another boss to confirm it, this one even shorter and meatier, and the shorter and meatier one nodded his round head and said yep, you're definitely drunk. He needed to go home, but they couldn't let him drive. And so one guy drove Gideon, and the other drove his car behind them, and on the way Gideon thought about how he'd finally and fully fucked everything. One marriage had dissolved because his wife was a cheater, and now another would dissolve because he was nothing like the man his wife had hoped him to be. When he got there, Addie was standing outside waiting, because one of the two bosses had called ahead and told her to expect them, and she smiled and thanked them for getting him home safe. When they drove away, Gideon found that he couldn't quite look at her, could only look at his feet as they took wobbly steps toward the front door, but then he felt her, as she slowly wrapped her arms around him and pulled him into a hug.

She didn't tell him about her rage, not then. She didn't tell him about her fear. She didn't tell him that she was wondering if *she* was the one who'd fucked up her family—her worry about how, after the dissolution of her marriage to Theo's biological father, who had become a depressed alcoholic, she'd found a kind and gently powerful man with whom to build a family, and now *he* was a depressed alcoholic too. She said nothing about how her mind played images of her childhood on a loop, the daughter of *still another* alcoholic, or about how she feared she had a "type" that she could never escape. How maybe her life was a series of failed attempts to save sad drunk men. Instead, she told him one thing she knew was true: "I love you." And she told him what she believed, what she *had* to believe. "We will get through this. Everything will be okay."

—

They fired him by Monday. Afterward, he spent hours each day applying to anything that seemed like it might be a fit. He looked for freelance jobs and part-time jobs. He took online quizzes that paid him a few bucks at a time. They sold Parker's crib, and Parker slept on a mattress on the floor in their room. They sold Addie's ring, and instead she wore his Pappo's aviator ring to show the world that she was Gideon's. His little sister sent him some money. His parents sent him money too.

One day, he got a call from a recruiter.

"I don't know what you're doing this weekend, but there's a hiring fair in Virginia Beach. One company is hiring for a job based in Louisville. I think you'd be a great fit."

They didn't have enough money for a hotel, so Gideon drove to Virginia and slept in his car. He showed up for the interview without a shower, having brushed his teeth in the parking lot. The company was an "industrial solutions provider." Basically, they sold stuff that other companies needed in order to build more stuff. They were looking for someone with the technical knowledge of an engineer and the people skills of a marketing director. Gideon told them he'd operated large-scale weapons systems and managed more than a hundred soldiers under his command. They offered him the job right away.

He liked it. He made $80,000 a year as a base salary, with bonuses that could push that higher. But that was still less than he'd made in the army, and it didn't come with all the other perks of a soldier's compensation package—the housing allowance, the hazard pay, the health insurance that covered any need his family might have. Addie went back to school to try to finish the college degree she'd never made it through as a single mom. Degrees cost money too, though. They were more stable now, but Gideon knew they needed more.

Every night, Gideon put Parker to bed around 8 p.m., gave Addie a kiss goodbye, and then hopped in the car, turned on the Uber app, and waited until he got called for a ride. He drove college kids out to the bars at the beginning of the night and back home at the end of it, with a few airport trips and commutes for workers sprinkled in between. Once, someone tried to get in with a cigarette. A few times, lovers fought in the back seat. But mostly, the nights passed with small talk or silence. He drove from 8 p.m. until about 3 a.m., and then he went home and slept until Parker woke up at 6. Then, he'd guzzle some coffee and make it to the office by 8. He was home by 5 to spend time with his kids and eat dinner, before putting the baby down for bed and firing up the app for another night of giving rides.

—

For the Fourth of July that year, they drove north to Madison, Indiana, a little town full of antique shops and cafés, to watch the annual regatta, a daylong event of speedboat races on the Ohio River. Everywhere they looked, they saw American flag T-shirts, American flag bandannas, American flag bikinis, and occasionally, actual American flags. Vendors, food trucks, blue jean shorts. T-shirts with the word FREEDOM emblazoned across Under Armour logos.

Scattered throughout the crowd, there were also young men selling toys. They worked to capture the attention of the kids first, then waited for the kids to pressure the parents, offering anything the kids wanted, all of it glowing. Gideon walked with Theo over to one of the vendors, and Theo pointed at a lightsaber and said that one, and Gideon asked how much it cost, and the guy said thirty dollars, and Gideon felt something lurch inside him and nodded and said okay. Then he kept looking, and soon he saw another toy, a light-up spinning contraption. He asked how much that one cost, and the guy said ten dollars, and Gideon thought okay, they could spend ten dollars, and so he told Theo let's get this one instead.

Theo looked up at Gideon, eyes big and blue and a little sad. "Okay," he said.

"Okay," Gideon said.

And that was it. Theo didn't press the issue. Didn't say *please*. Didn't pitch a fit that he couldn't have the lightsaber he wanted. And Gideon wondered if this was because he was well behaved and considerate, or because he had learned to expect less than other children, had come to accept that his father could not give him the same toys as luckier boys. And so Gideon felt himself breaking, just a little, as he handed the cheaper toy to his son, and as he watched his son run away and start playing with other kids, and then he felt himself breaking a little more when Theo came back with the toy no longer glowing, now cracked open, broken too.

Theo handed it to Addie, and then he turned around and ran back to the other kids, the ones with lightsabers, and it looked to Gideon like they wouldn't let him play, like he was just standing on the periphery and watching them, invisible without a glowing sword in his hand. Gideon watched the other children running around and screaming and laughing, and he knew that he was the reason his son wasn't screaming and laughing too, that if he hadn't been terrified by the thought of spending thirty dollars, his child would be happy now, would be making new friends and having a night he would think back on fondly for the rest of his life.

Gideon stayed quiet the rest of the night. They watched the boats race down the river and the fireworks detonate in the sky and then they rode back home in silence. When Addie asked what was wrong, Gideon said nothing, it's fine, I'm fine, it was a fun night, and then he lay awake in bed, desperate for a drink.

Ryan

Even after he started training in taekwondo, Ryan still occasionally found himself squared up with another man outside a bar. He couldn't help it. Wednesday nights at the dojang, bowing to opponents before sparring, held none of the electric danger he found on streets just minutes after last call. Taekwondo felt too ordered. There was a beauty to it, grace and precision.

Often, Ryan did not want grace. He wanted to fucking *hit* someone. He wanted to leave a man broken and bleeding, unaware of the day or time. He wanted to know that he was now the instrument of violence, that he held within him the power to inflict what he'd once received.

Still, he kept training at the dojang. He held more strength in his legs than almost anyone else he encountered. Just one clean low kick could bring opponents to the ground. He took first place in a regional competition in his weight class. He earned a blue belt. He told no one at the dojang that he was gay. But everyone in gay Buffalo knew that he could fight. He became transfixed by the idea of becoming, as he put it, "a gay lethal weapon." Jared told him that he'd never make it on ESPN, because he believed no gay man would ever appear on that channel. "But someday," Jared said, "you could be in a Lifetime movie. The faggot who can fuck you up." Ryan liked this idea.

—

As years passed, Ryan and Anthony settled into the rhythm of a shared life, rotating holidays with Anthony's family in Florida or with Ryan's, with or without his father present, up on the rez. Ryan sank into the quiet pleasures of domesticity: cooking with Anthony on weekend evenings—Hamburger Helper or spaghetti and meatballs—then drifting to sleep next to each other on the couch to the sounds of a movie they'd already seen a dozen times.

Here and there, they would argue. About the dishes and the laundry, about the way Ryan responded too kindly to a stranger flirting with him at the bar, small grievances that vanished into the air around them within minutes. Usually, at least. But occasionally their conflicts lingered, turned uglier with time. Anthony refused to come out to a group of his closest friends in Buffalo, insisting on introducing Ryan as his friend and roommate, even years into their relationship. One night they went out with a group of Anthony's straight friends to a gay bar called Roxy's, and even there, Anthony continued to play straight. And so Ryan retaliated by declaring himself single for the evening, saying that if a man flirted with him he would flirt right back. In the quiet moments that night, they hissed at each other in the bar's corners or behind the closed doors of Ryan's car. In Anthony's voice, Ryan heard a panicked fear of being rejected by these straight friends, and in his own voice Ryan heard a desperate anger and the belief that he was unworthy of being claimed.

And then, all at once, their lives began to fall apart. Ryan was laid off from his job with the local office of Native American Community Services when the organization lost some of its funding. Anthony was struggling at work too, afraid he might soon be fired. They had to tell their landlord they wouldn't be able to afford their next month's rent, and she let them out of their lease. Ryan moved in with a friend on a nearby reservation and lived with members of the Seneca nation. Anthony stayed in Buffalo, crashing on another friend's couch.

Ryan woke up each day with a low-simmering panic. He'd never been unemployed before. Now he had to ask his mom to pay his car bill. He ate Dollar General ramen and Kraft instant macaroni and cheese. He could spend forty dollars a week on food and not a single dime more. Every night, he lay alone in the dark on a friend's couch, homeless and jobless, staring at the ceiling, unsure how he'd get through the next day. Every time he bought groceries, he knew the number in his bank account was dwindling near zero. But he couldn't make himself check it, didn't want to know just how close to the edge he'd reached.

Then one night his cousin Kyle came to town. Ryan liked Kyle, even if his joys threw Ryan's misery into relief. Kyle was three years younger than Ryan, and he'd come out of the closet years before Ryan ever imagined doing the same. Ryan knew his parents had struggled with that revelation, but they'd seemed to move past it. At family gatherings, while Ryan flew past his own father without risking a second of eye contact, Kyle and his parents seemed fully at peace.

Kyle wanted to go out. Ryan obliged, and Anthony joined them. They started at a lesbian bar, a relaxed place with music Kyle liked, somewhere a little more appropriate for a family gathering than the bodies and leather on display at Marcella's. They drank. A lot. Captain and Cokes, one after another, until the room swam and blurred. The more Ryan drank the more he seemed to forget the life he would return to when the night ended, the couch waiting on a reservation that wasn't even his own.

Last call approached, and Ryan stumbled to the bar. When he closed out, his debit card was declined. Ryan tried to take out cash, but the ATM declined him too, and then he went back to the bartender, explained that he wasn't sure what was happening. Could he just come back and pay tomorrow?

Kyle stepped in and offered to pay the tab, and Ryan waved him off. He wouldn't dare accept help from his little cousin. It's fine, he said, I promise it's fine, don't worry, we do this all the time, and Ryan meant that they knew the bartender and she sometimes hooked them up with free drinks, but Anthony overheard and took Ryan to mean that all the time they went out to bars and then bounced without paying their tab, and so Anthony said what the fuck Ryan, we don't do this all the time, and once Anthony interjected Kyle interjected too, and soon all three of them were yelling over nothing, until security was gently nudging them, come on guys, settle this later, it's time for you to leave.

They stepped into the cold and Ryan felt that familiar anger, crackling and malevolent. He saw his cousin near the door and he rushed in his direction. Maybe he could hit Kyle and still tell himself he didn't start this fight, either, because Kyle had been the one to come down here, demanding that they go out. But now he heard the security guard nudging Anthony in Ryan's direction, saying to calm that fucking guy down, and so Anthony walked toward Ryan and Ryan screamed at the love of his life whatever words passed through his mind, what the fuck are you gonna do bitch, do you want me to fuck you up because I will.

Anthony took a couple of steps toward Ryan, then stopped, shook his head, and began to walk away. But this was unacceptable, so Ryan grabbed Anthony by the shirt, don't you fucking leave me, and Anthony turned around and shoved him, and Ryan fell to the ground. Falling was release, hitting pavement was freedom, because now Ryan could spring back up, knowing he *definitely* didn't start it, was in fact blameless, his fists could find a face, slim and dark with gorgeous lashes, and could pound delicate bones.

Ryan tried to stand up. He felt his traps and lats tense, preparing to coil with the first punch. The alcohol slowed his movement, but finally he reached his feet and prepared to charge. As he moved toward Anthony, Anthony remained still, watching. He did not prepare for impact, did not coil himself to hit Ryan before Ryan could reach him. He just looked at him, with confusion and perhaps a flash of fear. And only now did Ryan stop. Here was a face, awaiting impact, belonging to the man Ryan most loved. Anthony remained still, and they stared at each other for just a second, until Anthony turned around and got in his car and sped away.

Joseph

A few pieces of evidence for the fact that Joseph was, as he entered his first winter in Seattle, still doing just *fine*.

(1) He survived the fall semester. Two As, a B-plus, and a B-minus. He was making it. Maybe not at the top of his class, but at least in the top half. He was on his way to becoming a lawyer. This was an indisputable fact.

(2) He had at least three friends. How many thirty-one-year-old men had at least *three* friends? There was Rex, whom he'd met the first day of orientation. Rex was an ex–Division I linebacker who seemed fast-tracked for some high-billing corporate job. Then there was Danny. Joseph didn't really know Danny all that well, but they both really loved Dogfish Head IPAs, and that by itself seemed like enough basis for a proper friendship. Finally, there was Alex, back in Atlanta, who worked at the psych hospital. Joseph called him every few weeks so they could talk shit about fantasy football. Alex didn't know anything about what was happening inside Joseph, but there was something comforting about talking to the person he'd first told about what he had once suffered, that night at Joe-a-palooza, even if the only thing they discussed now was the totally unfair trade the commissioner had just approved in their league.

(3) Joseph and Emily had had a single, extraordinary date. It was Christmas Eve. They'd gone to breakfast, someplace nice they could barely afford, with mimosas and everything, right off Denny Park. They'd sat across the table and told each other about the moments from the past few months that they'd missed in each other's lives, and Joseph felt that he was looking at Emily, really *looking* at her, for the first time since they'd arrived in their new city. She was living an entire *life* here, with her own friends and joys and anxieties, a life that seemed only rarely to intersect with his own. "We can do big things," he told her, and she nodded and said she already knew that was true.

Here, a lone piece of evidence for the fact that Joseph was, as his spring semester began just a couple weeks after Christmas, very much *not fine*.

He saw Jack's dick everywhere. Not only when he and Emily were having sex. It had started that way, during sex, but now, a few months later, he started to relive the abuse anytime his body touched another person's body. He would shake a professor's hand, and there it was. The same thing happened when he offered Rex some dap when meeting for beers. Each time he saw it, the panic rushed in: a tightness in his chest, runaway fidgeting in his fingers and toes. He felt his face trying to respond to ebbs and flows in conversation the way he imagined a face should. He nodded at the stories, laughed at the jokes, and tried to keep his eyes focused on the speaker rather than turning glassy and faraway.

Every time the memory overtook him, it brought with it a singular desire: to cleanse himself. He washed his hands compulsively, maybe twenty-five times a day, rushing to the bathroom before and after classes, or the moment he arrived at the library or back home. There was heavy scrubbing between each finger, deep in the folds of every knuckle. With the approach of any friend or stranger, he felt rising fear. With each washing, he felt release.

It was stunning, just how thoroughly the handwashing soothed him, but he knew he couldn't run away to wash his hands every five minutes. So Joseph came up with an alternative solution. He would simply never touch another human person. This would be easy. Whether a handshake or a kiss, a back pat or a blow job, he would, as often as possible, find a way to escape.

He had his strategies. First, he'd never enter a room first. Whether it was a class or a study group or a happy hour, he'd always linger nearby, just outside the door, watching and waiting for others to go in before him, then slip in at the apex of the greeting ritual, the exact moment when every other person had found a hand to shake or a neck to hug. Simple. Then, while the bodies were still in contact with the other bodies, he would just slide around the edges of their movement, still saying hi enthusiastically but moving with a quickness and false sense of purpose, always just out of reach from anyone who might be tempted to reach out for his hand.

Second, when he showed up to a bar, and a table of friends waved in his direction, he would wave back, but then he would point in the general direction of the restroom, where he would go not to pee—because why would he ever pee in public?—but simply to wash his hands. Water and soap between the fingers, intense scrubbing on the palms, a quick release, deep exhales. And then he'd return to the table, where no one would reach for him, because everyone knew that you did not shake hands with someone just back from the restroom. No one wants the unpleasant sensation of shaking a still-damp hand.

Third, if he ever *had* to enter a room before others, he would simply pull out his laptop and pretend to do some work. Better yet, he would *actually* work! Then when they arrived he could say sorry, just give me a sec guys, which of course they would do, because all of them were law students, predisposed to admire anyone who was visibly working, and prone toward feeling a deep shame that they were not presently working themselves.

Unfortunately, though, there sometimes is no escaping the touch of another person. He went to networking events. He applied for jobs. He entered rooms and locked eyes and shook hands with all who stood before him, because this was America, and these were potential employers, and this, simply, was what culture had deemed he must do. So before entering the room, he'd prepare himself for the horror, and then he'd shake the hands and pat the shoulders, sometimes at the same godforsaken time. Then, when the image of his abuser's penis arrived in his field of vision, when he felt the tightness and the sweating and the desperate need to escape, he would strain with everything inside him to remain still in his seat until the meeting finally ended and he could find the nearest faucet to cleanse himself in an office-park automatic sink.

—

Early that spring semester of the first year of law school, Joseph started to relive the abuse in his sleep. In the night terrors, he was both victim and observer, both the small child in the corner of the room and someone else watching from the edge. The physical act never occurred in his dreams. He never watched or felt himself touch what he was so afraid to touch. But he was overwhelmed with the feeling of being trapped, stuck in that corner with a larger body before him and no way out.

When he woke up, he was drenched in sweat, grasping to find his voice, to shout no and run simultaneously from his bedroom and the stockroom with the fluorescent lights and brown walls. He felt, for a moment, a sense of relief, the knowledge that he was not a trapped child but a grown man in bed with the woman he loved. But then he felt wracked with a new terror, that if he fell back to sleep the nightmare would resume, and so instead he lay there, remaining as still as possible so as not to wake Emily, until he saw light creeping in through the window and he could rise and shower and prepare for his day. But then the next night he would lie in bed and will his eyes to remain open, terrified of what would appear the moment he lost consciousness. He started staying out on the couch long after Emily had gone to bed, the idle noise of the TV keeping him upright, then playing in his mind as he listened to it while he slept.

And sometimes he would watch porn. This served two functions: It helped him relax and it gave him new images he could escape into the next time Emily's touch brought back the images of his abuse. Really, he told himself, he was doing it for her, making sure their marriage didn't slip into celibacy. And yet, every time, he felt like he could drown in his own shame. Sometimes he wanted Emily to catch him. Once, she fell asleep on the couch and he decided not to wait for her to go to bed, but to watch it then and there. She slept right through it. Another night, after she went to bed, Joseph pulled up a video on his phone and cast it to the TV. He felt disgusted with himself from the opening seconds, revolted by his own desire.

He turned up the volume. Joseph could turn this off right now and go wake up Emily and tell her he wanted her, and he knew she'd be turned on by his urgent need. All he had to do was stop, walk ten feet into his bedroom, and lie down next to his wife. Instead, he turned the volume up again. On the screen, he saw a woman in a silver sequin bra, leaning over an exercise bike, a man positioned behind her, each one playing their assigned roles, you're fucking sick, he told himself, you hate yourself and you hate your wife, and if she's smart she'll catch and leave you, and he undid his pants, what the fuck is wrong with you, you piece of shit.

Joseph didn't really believe in God anymore, but when he got scared, he still prayed. Only in silent words sent up to nowhere could he unleash the force of his desperate need. Now, tonight, he prayed that Emily would catch him, that she would see what a piece of shit she'd married and leave him like he deserved. He turned it up louder again. Emily is a heavy sleeper, she'll never wake up, but what if she does, maybe she will, maybe she should. He turned it up louder still. He watched, aroused and revolted by his own touch.

And then, he heard a small voice.

"Joseph?"

He wanted, right then, to die.

"Babe?"

Not a painful death, he wasn't *that* sick, just something quick and efficient that would grant him the release of no longer having to live.

"Joseph, what are you doing?"

He scrambled for the remote. He turned off the TV, but now the moans and screams continued on his phone.

"Joseph, are you watching porn?"

And just like that, shame evaporated, replaced by fear. *No!* Of course he wasn't watching porn! Why would she think that? He had no idea what was happening, how this had ended up on the screen. He was just scrolling through something on Facebook and all of a sudden this popped up, he couldn't believe it either, it's so gross, right? Well, okay, yeah, now that he thought about it, he guessed that he did see a pop-up ad for something, and because he was a dumb man who didn't know what he was doing, he clicked, I mean yeah, these pop-up ads are evil the way they make you look at something you never wanted to see. But he of course didn't mean to, was at that very moment figuring out how to make it stop. This was the kind of thing they'd always warned about back in his youth group. Porn was everywhere, a danger lurking behind every one of the internet's corners. You never knew what kind of thing you'd be looking for and all of a sudden this filth was on your screen. It was shocking how quickly it could appear from nowhere.

"You were watching porn," she said. Her voice was quiet, calm, her eyes still adjusting to the light.

"No," he said, and he could hear how pathetic the lie sounded. "No, no, I really wasn't."

She turned around, went back to the bed, lay down on her side, and began to wail. He followed behind her, a pathetic horny failure.

"What's wrong?" he asked, not because he didn't know, but because he wanted to hear himself speaking over the sound of her wails.

"It's okay," he told her. "I promise it's all okay."

Joseph patted her head. "Yeah," he said. "Yeah, it's okay."

"Were you watching porn?"

"Well, I mean…"

And then more wails, heavier this time. The dogs crawled over, jumped up to her lap, tried to soothe her as she cried.

Finally, she managed another sentence. "You crushed my heart."

She asked him if she was ugly and he said no. She asked him if he really loved her and he said yes. She asked why he had to watch porn then, and he said nothing. Then she went back to wailing, and eventually she asked him if she was ugly once more. He told her that he'd been praying she would walk in, that he wanted this to happen. This was a good thing, didn't she see? Nothing he said changed the reality before him. Words kept coming out of his mouth, any thought that entered his mind immediately spoken aloud, all frantic attempts to craft a story of what she'd seen that didn't make her body heave with shock and pain.

"You crushed my heart."

"No. It's okay."

"I'm too ugly for you."

"No. No, no, no, you're beautiful."

"You're a pervert then."

"No, that's not it either."

"Why," she said, pausing for a moment to let her chest heave, "won't you ever have sex with me?"

Finally, desperately, he decided to try telling the truth.

Nate

Back in Ohio at his mom's house, Nate watched the news sometimes. He didn't really mean to. He'd never been into politics, hadn't voted a single time. But sometimes he'd scroll Facebook and the news just found him. He'd grown up barely aware that trans people existed; now their bodies were debated daily on his feeds. There were new laws banning minors from receiving the hormone therapies he'd gotten when he was seventeen. A trans boy had been beaten to death at a high school. A congresswoman had declared that trans people shouldn't be allowed in the bathrooms that matched their gender identity. The president had been elected after running ads targeting trans athletes, and had immediately enacted policies deleting evidence of trans Americans from government documents and websites, and even from national monuments and parks. In the voices of those politicians and pundits, he never heard an ounce of curiosity. Only disgust. That's what gnawed at him. The sense that no one was arguing about sports, or about bathrooms, or about consent to medical care. That they were arguing, instead, about whether he even belonged in this world.

Sometimes, the news left him sad and afraid. Mostly, it left him numb. He had spent so much of his life fighting for the right to inhabit this gender. To feel the scratchiness of his beard, the hard slope of his chest. To hear the rumble in his voice and the familiarity of his chosen name.

Besides, the truth was that the biggest problems in his life had nothing to do with politics. At this point, the biggest problems in his life were barely even related to being *trans*. And that part kinda fucked with him. It's not what he was used to. For nearly two decades, his life had been dominated by one central concern: that he felt alien in the body he'd been given and that this was confounding to the people he desperately wanted to see him for who he was. The problem of his gender extended from his face to his underwear. It governed the shape of his body and his friendships; the way he spoke and bled and fucked; the way his Black skin functioned, making him feel invisible in one gender and threatening in another; the way he was or was not offered comfort by his mother and respect by his father; the way his own eyes either darted away or remained fixed straight ahead when meeting a mirror that reflected back his flesh.

But now? He'd dealt with that shit. At least most of it, in ways he'd never imagined possible when he was younger. But now he'd spent his entire life obsessing over how to inhabit his gender, only to find that he had no clue how to inhabit anything else about who he was. Nate had loved school, but the torment he felt over finding acceptance left him unable to function within its walls. He'd found easy success with women, but he was coming to realize that he'd been blinded by the exhilaration over his ability to attract them and left without a sense of how to build healthy relationships. He'd spent so much energy on his gender-affirming health care that he'd neglected the care he needed for *everything* else. That included the seizures he'd suffered since adolescence, which were now diagnosed as symptoms of epilepsy, and the spells of crippling anxiety and depression that he now knew were born of bipolar disorder.

So here he was, twenty-nine years old, ten years on testosterone, three years after top surgery, wearing what he wanted, talking how he wanted, and going by the name he wanted. And yet, so often, Nate struggled to feel like the man he wanted to be. He was small. Shit, he was tiny, shorter than most women and the vast majority of men. He felt weak, like no matter how much his muscle tone developed, he couldn't compete with the hulking trans fitness influencers he saw online, or the meatheads grunting their way through squats on the rack next to his at the gym. Men protect themselves, Nate believed. With intimidation, with fists, with the threat they carried in their voices. Men protect their families. Nate still relied on his family to protect him. Men imposed themselves on the world around them. Often Nate felt he was floating to nowhere, carried by the wind.

Nate had filed a restraining order against Mya, so they never spoke, but he stayed in touch with her mother. Mya's mom told him how sorry she was for what her daughter had done, how much Trae missed Nate, and how she wished there was still some way for Nate to be his dad.

He thought about visiting for Christmas but couldn't save enough money. He told himself he was going to move back, but he couldn't figure out a way to co-parent with a woman who'd inflicted on him the most severe violence he'd ever endured. He missed Connecticut. It wasn't just Trae, or even just the brief period when he and Mya were happy, but the entire community. It was the first place he'd ever lived where he had regularly encountered other trans people. He had even met some of the more flamboyant and gender-fluid queer people he'd always tended to judge online, the ones from liberal cities who posted about destroying the gender binary. In person, they were kind, thoughtful, grounded. He wondered what it would have been like to grow up trans as they had, where "passing" didn't seem like such a matter of life and death, surrounded by people who didn't see their gender as a problem to be solved.

For months, he told himself he'd go back. He stayed in a spare bedroom upstairs at his mom's house, with her husband and his daughter and their dogs. He collected food stamps, which he gave his mother to pay for groceries, and he collected disability checks, half of which he paid her in rent. The seizures had gotten worse since Mya had attacked him. He saw something online about trauma living forever in the body. Maybe his convulsions were his body's way of revolting against all he'd endured.

Nate wanted to work and thought maybe he would stock grocery shelves, like he had before. Or maybe he would study to become an exterminator. He also thought about becoming a machinist down at one of the steel mills. His grandma had worked on an assembly line, doing backbreaking labor that drove her to drink, but she'd always talked about how jealous she was of the machinists. "Button pushers," she called them. Maybe Nate could learn how to do that. He heard it paid well.

Mostly, though, he sat in his room. He was well more than a decade removed from the middle school days he'd spent on Gaia and spelunking the depths of YouTube, but now, lying in bed and staring at his phone, he found himself pulled even deeper into his screen. He scrolled the endless stories about hate crimes and bathroom bans. He swiped through Tinder and got plenty of matches, but none of them went anywhere. The problem wasn't that he was trans; plenty of women seemed to be into that. It wasn't that he was short; he'd found it easy enough to find women who didn't care. It wasn't even that he was unemployed and on food stamps. Thoughtful messages and kind eyes seemed to make up for being broke. Instead, the problem seemed to be that after exchanging a few messages, Nate would just *forget* to text back. His matches didn't seem to like that. But he'd lost the energy for human interaction, and he found the stress of coming up with clever replies far less soothing than just scrolling through his phone.

Did he have a rock bottom? Who knew. It's hard to feel the bottom when you don't feel anything at all. Underneath the numbness, one terrible certainty ate at him: He'd failed Trae. It didn't matter that his ex had beaten him, didn't matter that he'd never held any official claim to parenthood. That's how he saw it. A child had called him "Daddy," and now Nate was no longer in that boy's life. The more time passed, the more Nate realized that relationship was over. He could not speak to Trae without speaking to Trae's mother. And Trae's mother was barred by law from contacting Nate.

He thought about suicide, occasionally, but it just required so much *effort*. He would have to make a plan, figure out a method, and then risk botching the attempt, and living the rest of his life permanently maimed. Besides, at least some of the time, he actually liked being alive. Even now.

—

After he was back at his mom's for nearly a year, his psychiatrist tweaked his meds. Nate's seizures became less frequent, his energy more robust. Weeks passed, and he spent a little less time upstairs scrolling, more time downstairs cooking, cleaning, and caring for his stepdad's grandchildren. He watched daytime TV with his mom. He smoked weed with his friend Wanda, an old white lady who used to live next door to his family's old house, and he hung out sometimes with Carol, the old lady who ran the corner store down the street. Wanda said some racist stuff from time to time, and Carol said transphobic stuff so often that he genuinely believed she'd forgotten he was trans, but he decided to take this as a sign that he was fully passing. He'd just tell them both to get the fuck out of here with that ignorant bullshit, and Carol would give him a discount, and Wanda would smile and pass the blunt. Sometimes, at night, he hung out with his mom's husband, Travis. Travis was a big dude, six-something and two hundred-something, with callouses on his hands from his work at the dairy factory and muscles still imprinted on his body from his linebacker days. Nate and Travis fought a lot, about dishes and laundry, but at night they sometimes sat and talked for hours. Travis liked to write poetry, but all the guys at the factory gave him shit for it. Nate told him it was beautiful. Travis seemed to appreciate that. It felt good, Nate thought, to affirm the parts of another man that he sometimes preferred to hide.

Whenever he had enough energy, Nate went for walks alone. He liked the Ohio air in all its forms: sticky and wet in the summer, bitter and frigid from November through March. He walked down to Big Lots or Walmart, to McDonald's or Panera, sometimes did laps around the ocean-sized parking lot that surrounded a Target, a Planet Fitness, and the mall. When friends were buying, he stopped in the food court to grab something from his favorite spot, Asian Chao Oriental Eatery. The old lady who owned it smiled whenever she saw him coming and started scooping up his favorite dish, bourbon chicken with rice, no sauce.

In all of these rituals, he found flickers of comfort. Maybe he could stitch together more of these moments. Maybe they could add up to a full life.

Ryan

The road was narrow and winding, two lanes between endless miles of forest, stretching toward the reservation, leading Ryan from Buffalo past Syracuse and Watertown and still farther north, taking him back to his old home.

He'd never imagined this day was coming. He was thirty now and had spent over a decade in Buffalo. It had been more than a year since the night he'd nearly hit Anthony outside the bar. He'd gotten a new job within weeks, working in HIV and sexually transmitted disease testing at a health clinic. He and Anthony had found a new apartment and moved back in together, resettling into their shared life. Anthony never even knew how close Ryan had been to hitting him. Their story of the evening was one of drunken messiness, not of suppressed violence.

They had remained in love with each other, but less in love with the city where they'd met. Anthony had spent long hours on the phone with his mother, who called from her home in Florida, lazing at the pool or beach while her son trudged through snow. She missed him. Aside from Ryan and a few friends, Anthony had no reason to stay in Buffalo. He decided to give life in Florida a try, for at least a few months. They would remain together long-distance.

Ryan had begun wondering, too, what it might be like to move home. When he got bored, he looked at job listings on the rez. At first all he saw were the menial tasks done by so many of his high school friends who'd never left: gas station attendants, janitorial services, cigarette factory gigs. But then he saw a job as a program manager at the Akwesasne Boys and Girls Club. He'd spend his mornings on administrative tasks, his afternoons playing with kids. He got the job.

"I'm thinking about moving back," he told his friend Callie.

But he had concerns. How could he live among the same people who'd made his life miserable when he was a child?

"There are plenty of assholes," Callie told him, "But there are assholes everywhere. At least here, there are plenty of people who love you too."

—

Ryan found a trailer in a small town just off the reservation, and he settled into his new job and life. He saw his family several times a week and spent Friday nights at the Brass Horse with old friends. He and Anthony broke up, got back together, and broke up again. Ryan thought about dating on the rez, but small-town dating was tough, and small-town gay dating even tougher. Besides, he decided, the other Mohawk guys weren't his type. Some were too effeminate, others too sheltered and naive. He longed for Anthony. He thought, occasionally, of moving to be with him in Florida, but over time the distance between them took on its own kind of immovable weight.

And then Steevi, his sister, got pregnant. For years, Ryan had wanted desperately to be an uncle. So many of his favorite childhood memories revolved around his own uncles and aunts, their family a tangle of caretakers floating in and out of each other's homes. Mohawk families seemed to grow closer as they grew in number, and Ryan felt he could be one of his own family's pillars, even without children of his own. Steevi gave birth to a beautiful girl named Brynn, and Ryan swore to her that he would never leave her, that he would love and hold her and shepherd her through this world.

His life came to revolve around Brynn and Steevi and the rest of his family. He and his father settled into a tense stalemate, acknowledging each other's presence and making polite small talk, but never daring to invite each other into their inner lives. He and Anthony occasionally gave it another shot, visiting each other at their respective new homes, but eventually they always seemed to break up. Ryan ached at times for the life he'd found in Buffalo, with volleyball and taekwondo and the presence of a man who loved him. But he felt that this was his home now, that wherever his niece lived, there he must live too.

One day, scrolling through Facebook, he saw a page that grabbed his attention. Killer Beez MMA, a gym run by Mohawk fighters, sat just a few miles off the rez. He began to follow the gym's page with curiosity, liking its posts, wondering what it might be like to step onto the mat himself. Then one day his phone buzzed with a Facebook message from the gym's owner, a man named Sheldon. They were looking for new students. Did Ryan want to try a class?

He showed up to a warehouse on the edges of the mall in Massena wearing a baggy T-shirt and baggier shorts. Before he even entered the gym, when he was walking through the parking lot, he felt his heartbeat quicken and his throat go dry. He'd never endured or inflicted violence this severe in a setting this controlled. MMA promised the brutality of bar fights paired with the order of taekwondo. He'd decided that perhaps he would like to begin a regular regimen of feeling and delivering enormous pain. But could he? Ryan had never even *heard* of a gay cage fighter. Did Sheldon know about him? Ryan wasn't sure.

He walked through the door and saw a squat rack off to one side, free weights piled on another, a few box-jump boxes and stair-run stairs, large mats lying empty in between. There he saw Sheldon, an oak tree in gym shorts, taller than any other Mohawk man Ryan knew and a mass of tattooed muscle. Sheldon approached him and shook his hand, Ryan's eyes downcast and Sheldon's direct and piercing. When Sheldon said hello, his tone was warm and his pitch much higher and gentler than Ryan's own, and when he heard him, Ryan relaxed just a little. He thought that maybe he could survive this day of learning violence from a man who looked like he'd mastered its form.

First, Sheldon told Ryan everything he was not allowed to touch: the diesel-truck tire, which was meant for flipping; the barbells and free weights; the heavy bag meant for punching and the heavier bag meant for kicking. "You're not ready," Sheldon said, and he smiled. "You won't be ready for a long time."

Sheldon explained how this was going to go. Though MMA, or mixed martial arts, allowed for any martial-art discipline, they would focus on Muay Thai, the most versatile one, and then build his skills from there. It was fine that Ryan had never trained in an MMA or Muay Thai gym; his taekwondo training gave him more experience than plenty of others who'd walked through those doors. But they needed to start with an assessment, to see what kind of shape Ryan was in, what kind of force he could pack when striking pads or a bag. None of this would be easy.

"I'm gonna break you," Sheldon said.

Ryan nodded, feigning nonchalance. They were alone. Ryan had booked a private session, too nervous to jump directly into group training. But now he took in the vastness of the gym, the mass of Sheldon's body, and the sharpness of his words, which seemed to promise and threaten in the same breath. He mustered only a single nervous, high-pitched laugh.

"Okay," he said. "In what way? Physically? Mentally?"

Sheldon smiled.

"Just go with it. We'll have fun."

—

Sweat pooled under Ryan's arms and in between his shoulder blades, started to drip from his forehead and make small puddles on the mat as he moved.

"What the fuck, bro!" Sheldon shouted. "This is just the warm-up!"

Ryan had no energy to respond but just kept following Sheldon's instructions: shuffling laps around the mat, then going into high knees and straight-leg kicks and low shuffles, quads aflame and lungs weak, until Sheldon asked, "Did I break you already? I thought it would take a little longer." Ryan heaved with each breath but managed to shake his head and offer a short and feeble no.

Finally, they stopped. Sheldon set the timer for a one-minute break.

"Warm-up over," Sheldon said. "You ready to start?"

Ryan was not ready to start.

"Yes," Ryan said.

"Good. Let's start."

And now, finally, Ryan got to hit something. Sheldon put on punching mitts and set the timer for three minutes, then called out what he wanted Ryan to hit. It was simple at first, right and left crosses and jabs. He talked through the eight-limb striking system of Muay Thai, both arms and legs, elbows and knees. When that round ended, they took a quick break and began another, and soon they moved on to combos. Jab, right cross, left hook. Again, jab, right cross, left hook, as fast and as hard as Ryan could go. Again. And again. "No breaks until the bell!" Sheldon shouted.

Every now and then, Ryan felt his technique and power align to deliver a perfect punch, the force of its violence told in the sound of the smack of fist against pad, loud and clear and true. Nothing in Ryan's life had ever felt like this. Not in his muscles: He felt tired in fibers he never knew existed, small sinews on the edges of his shoulders, new layers deep in his lats. Not in his mind: He'd never *chosen* this kind of pain, never blurred the lines between misery and ecstatic delirium, never felt himself so desperate to stop something, and then, the moment it stopped, to begin again. Not in his lungs: He fell into what Sheldon called "panic breathing," hyperventilating as the room spun and his vomit reflex started to lurch inside him. Not even in his ears: He *heard* each heartbeat, a bass thumping inside his skull. When he slowed down, allowing even half a second between strikes, Sheldon would shout, "I didn't hear no fucking bell!"

They ended with kicks. High, fast, brutal, exhausting. Ryan delivered ten with the right leg, ten more with the left. At the final bell, Ryan collapsed, his body doubled over, his hands on his knees, and Sheldon told him good job, that was it, they were done, and now Ryan found his chest heaving, every gulp of breath pulling in too little air, until Sheldon taught him a breathing technique: deep breath, hold for three beats, exhale as hard as you can, again and again, until your lungs catch up. And now Ryan felt himself returning to his body. He'd survived one session but didn't know if he could survive another.

Sheldon tossed Ryan a towel. As they walked off the mat together, he patted Ryan on the back. They said little as they caught their breath, little as they packed their bags and wiped off their sweat. They walked past all the equipment Ryan was not yet allowed to touch, out the door and into cold air and bright sunlight, toward their cars, and now Sheldon patted Ryan on the back yet again.

"Not bad for a gay guy," he said.

—

In the end, that was the thing that did it. That one comment guaranteed Ryan would come back. There'd been something light in Sheldon's tone. When Ryan looked up, he was grinning. "Fuck you," Ryan said, and Sheldon cackled.

"See you next week?"

He returned, session after session. He paid extra to keep taking private lessons so he wouldn't have to step onto the mat with men he didn't know. With each session, the intensity increased. "You're in gym shape," Sheldon would say. "That's not fighting shape." He promised to break Ryan of "that taekwondo bullshit," the way he kicked with his feet and not his shins, the way he punched, loose and snappy, instead of high and tight and fast. "We build pillars," Sheldon said, "not pyramids." Ryan nodded, pretending he understood what this meant. A few weeks into his training, Ryan walked in one day and saw a smile stretching across Sheldon's face.

"You ready?"

"For what?"

"We're sparring today."

Ryan looked around the room. No one else was there.

"Who's *we*?"

Sheldon began taping up his own wrists and ankles, then tossed Ryan a roll of tape of his own.

"Come on. It'll be fun."

They would go slow, Sheldon promised. They circled each other, pawing carefully in the other's direction, until Sheldon struck, and then Ryan struck too. They exchanged light jabs alternating with hooks and occasional kicks. After weeks of hitting nothing but bags and pads, here was a live wire of coiled muscle, moving with Ryan around the mat. In the first round, Ryan made contact on a couple of light blows, and Sheldon made contact on many more.

"Okay," Sheldon said after a couple of rounds. "Let's speed it up a little."

Now the blows came quicker and harder, Ryan working to return them in kind. And then, a couple of minutes into the round, Sheldon hit him with a jab to the left eye, and Ryan saw a flash of light as his head snapped back, bright and sudden. He stumbled, vision blurred, and Sheldon dropped his fists to his sides as Ryan tried to blink his way back into his body, to recapture his balance before he tumbled down to the mat.

"You good?" Sheldon asked.

Ryan stood up straight, blinked his eyes a few more times, and the flash disappeared, replaced by the shapes and colors of the mat and the walls and the body that stood before him.

"Yeah," Ryan said. "I'm good."

He could take a punch. He could last a round. He was not going to curl up and prepare for the impact of future blows. This, Ryan would later think, was the moment the sport captured something inside him it would not let go.

"I'm good, I'm good, I'm good."

They went on like this for months, three or four sessions a week, then sparring on Saturdays, just the two of them. After the sessions they would make small talk, Ryan chronicling his journey away from the rez and back again, Sheldon sharing his own funny stories from a former life of petty crime. Ryan tried never to reference his sexuality, but every now and then Sheldon joked about it.

"You still gay?" he asked from time to time, and Ryan said yes.

"Cool. Just checking."

Once Ryan slipped and fell during an exercise, and Sheldon helped him back up. "I'm cutting you some slack because you're gay."

And then, another time, Sheldon went quiet, contemplative.

"You know," he said finally, "I saw two fags bang one time."

Ryan was too stunned to be offended.

"What?"

Sheldon nodded, eyes distant.

"Yeah," he said, voice gentle. "I saw that shit."

"Huh," Ryan said.

"Yeah," Sheldon said, and he shrugged his shoulders. "Decided it wasn't for me."

"But you stood there and watched?"

"It was in prison! There's no porn! What the fuck was I *supposed* to do?"

—

After a few months, Sheldon started asking Ryan when he was going to come to a group class. "You can hang with those guys," he told him.

"I don't know," Ryan said. "I just need more time."

"You have to trust yourself," said Sheldon. "Besides, what good is being a fighter if you're just gonna fight me all the time?"

Week after week, the same conversation, until finally Ryan said it.

"I don't want to be around those guys. I can't go back in the fucking closet."

He knew a few of the guys who came to the gym. Some were white, some were Mohawk. But all of them were, truly, and Ryan meant this with a perverse kind of admiration, *complete fucking Neanderthals*. They were men who lived for the chance to beat the shit out of other men. One was a bouncer, another one a biker. One guy, perhaps the scariest of all, worked as an engineer. Ryan could only imagine what that guy did the moment he got off the clock. Many were misfits who fit in nowhere besides the gym. Ryan couldn't imagine those guys training with an out gay man.

"*Bro*," Sheldon said. "Who fucking cares?"

Sheldon seemed unable to understand the world Ryan had conjured in his mind. "If someone gives you shit, fuck 'em," he said. "They can go find another gym."

A few weeks later, Ryan showed up to a group class. They started with the same warm-up as in the individual sessions, then paired off with someone of similar height and weight and ran through striking drills. He made it through. At the final bell, Ryan did not linger. He did not make small talk with the other guys. He did not need new friends.

He returned, week after week. He insisted to himself that he wasn't going back in the closet, but here he found himself being extra careful to project from the chest when he spoke, to avoid any upturn in his tone. He wore his biggest and baggiest shorts. He kept quiet.

As weeks passed, he got follower requests from his training partners on social media. There was the biker, Dan, and the bouncer, Eric, and the in-house pro, Brett, who traveled the region fighting competitively. Colin, a kid in his early twenties, worked at a local grocery store and was on his way to becoming a black belt in every martial art. On their Facebook and Instagram pages, they all seemed to live normal, stable lives, some with girlfriends or wives, a couple with kids. Ryan felt a rush of nerves every time he got a request from one of them, tried to view his page through his gym-mates' eyes. On Facebook, he was fully out. Here they would see pics of him and Anthony, could scroll back and see him on his volleyball team in Buffalo. He accepted each request. Better for them to find out this way than for him to make some grand announcement.

But every time Ryan walked in, he wondered if today would be the day. Maybe Sheldon would take him aside quietly and say that some of the guys had concerns, that they didn't like the way Ryan looked at them, didn't want to be forced to touch a man who slept with men. Or maybe he would square up to spar against someone who would go 100 percent against Ryan's 50 percent, pummeling him into the ground while shouting familiar slurs. There were so many ways for them to tell Ryan he no longer belonged. They just had to pick one.

But for months, the fact of Ryan's sexuality hung in the room unspoken. Until one day, when they were all warming up, shuffles and high knees around the mat, and they moved into a wide sumo squat, designed to open up the hips, dropping as low as possible on every rep. Ryan struggled.

"Come on, Ryan!" Sheldon shouted. "Lower!"

Ryan had always had stiff hips. No matter how much he stretched and strengthened the muscles around them, he never seemed able to get as low as the others.

"Lower!"

The others in the room got all the way down, ass nearly scraping the floor, like baseball catchers. Ryan hovered higher, just barely below parallel. Sheldon paced back and forth, shaking his head.

"What the fuck, Ryan!"

His legs burned. His hips felt locked into place. He sensed Sheldon looking straight at him.

And then Sheldon said it.

"Squat down like you're squatting on a dick on a Saturday night!"

Now Ryan felt that flashing light, the same one he had seen when taking a jab to the eye, shooting through every cell in his body. They were laughing. Everyone was laughing. He was in a gym surrounded by straight men and all of them were laughing because Ryan was gay. He stayed in his squat, struggling to get even lower, and he fixed his eyes on the wall ahead, and he started to wonder if this was the moment all his sparring had been building toward, if now he was going to have to try to fuck someone up.

And then, within a fraction of a second, he glanced up and saw Sheldon looking at him and smiling, and something in that smile seemed to invite Ryan to join him, to acknowledge the absurd delightfulness of the fact that here he was in a gym with men all learning to brutalize other men, but that sometime later, he would enter another room, with another man, for a different purpose. Sure, Sheldon had wildly overstated the acrobatics involved in Ryan's sex life, but come on, his smile suggested, it's all a little funny, right?

Ryan looked around at the other fighters, and he saw them looking back at him and stifling laughter, and he decided to take that laughter not as a taunt but an invitation, and so he started laughing too.

"Fuck you guys," Ryan said.

At this, they laughed harder, and so did Ryan, until he nearly fell out of his squat and onto the ground.

"Fuck every last one of you."

Gideon

Gideon once read something that said a wildly disproportionate number of veteran suicides happen within the first ninety days of leaving active duty. He couldn't remember all the reasons. But he knew, now, that by leaving the army he had already experienced one kind of death, an end to everything that had constituted his identity through most of adulthood, and that made a second death seem, if not quite attractive, at least a reasonable endpoint for wherever he was headed.

He tried calling one of his childhood best friends, Kenny. He didn't answer. He tried another, Jason, but he didn't pick up either. They lived in other states, with their own families and jobs. The three of them used to call each other often. Lately, it just seemed like it was only on birthdays, or on the anniversary of their *other* friend's death. Now, when they didn't answer, he didn't know who else to call.

Throughout their marriage, he had watched Addie, a self-described introvert, find and nurture new friendships everywhere she went. She had coffee dates with other moms, went to gallery openings with people she'd met at the *last* gallery opening she'd been to, who would now inevitably invite her to the next. Small talk after workout classes led to playdates for their kids. The world, to her, seemed full of potential friendships. She stitched together a community for herself simply by going out into the world and saying, "Hi, I'm Addie," again and again. Before Addie, he'd watched Caroline do much the same thing.

Gideon had no idea how to do that. He'd never needed to. Pile twenty-five fourteen-year-old baseball players onto a bus, send them to a Fairfield Inn for a tournament in a small town in East Texas, and they will return with a sense of shared intimacy that would take most grown adults *years* to foster among themselves. There is no bond like that between children who have battled faraway opponents on the field and watched each other chew tobacco until they vomited in the bathroom of their budget motel.

Gideon had started that sort of ritual as a boy, and everything about his life had been another version of it, all the way until now, in his early thirties. The baseball teams at West Point were slightly more grown-up versions of the Little League and travel teams, and even though baseball left a void, the army itself had provided the same kind of structure. Pass the physical training test, shoot down the simulated missile, complain about chain-of-command bullshit, and along the way, listen to stories about weddings and births, divorces and deaths. Structure forced proximity; proximity begat intimacy. He loved the men next to him because he knew the men next to him, because they shared the simple goal of keeping everyone in their country alive.

After he left the army, Gideon stopped getting invited to barbecues and poker nights, the social rituals that were part of his life as a soldier. He texted army friends to propose trades in their fantasy football league, and that was it. Now, loosened from the structures that had upheld his friendships, he found those friendships slipping away. Gideon was on his own to figure out a new purpose. That seemed simple enough: He had to feed his wife and children. This was what he was for. Here was a family, made up of various members, and at its center, Gideon. The boy who saved his parents. The man who would provide.

Still, even with his new job, Gideon was failing. Addie disagreed—she insisted they had everything they needed. But the number in their bank account showed that they were one emergency away from having nothing. Every two weeks, he watched the number trickle down into the triple digits before resuscitating the moment each direct deposit hit. Gideon knew, too, that many of his West Point classmates were making a killing, whether it was on Wall Street or as defense contractors in the Middle East. None of his teammates had ever made it to the Big Leagues, but a couple of them had worked their way up through the minors for a few years and would at least be able to tell their children they'd played pro ball—all while Gideon was here, explaining complicated industrial tools to Midwestern businessmen so his family could live paycheck to paycheck.

In his down moments, he drank: In hotels, away on work trips. In his car, before going into the house at the end of the day. And occasionally, yes, on his lunch break. And when he drank he felt himself descending into the sadness that he spent most of his days pushing away. Sometimes, he drank to indulge that feeling. Mostly, he drank because he had to. Alcohol was the thing his body most craved.

Gideon had been on medication for anxiety and depression for the last several years he'd been in the army. Since his discharge, he hadn't been able to get the same medication covered by his new insurance, at least not without paying more out of pocket, and so he'd decided he didn't need it. He would wait until he could afford it—he'd be fine until then. Alcohol filled the gaps. And then it began to spill over, filling everything. One night he got home from driving Uber and he drank in the parking lot of their apartment for an hour or so, and then he woke up three hours later and drove to work and kept drinking there, and by the time he got home he was rose-faced and wobbly, and when he walked in to find Addie rushing around making dinner and caring for the kids he decided he was not needed, and so he told her he was going to go ride his bike.

"Gideon," she said. "No."

For one thing, Gideon didn't own a bike.

But he told her it was fine. "Don't worry, I'm good."

"Gideon. Please."

"Love you babe. I'll see you later."

And he walked out the door and found a bike in a neighbor's yard, and he rode it downtown to the pedestrian bridge, and when he got there he fell down a couple of times but got back up and kept riding until he was in the middle of the bridge, and then he stopped and began to cry. He had no articulable reason. He couldn't have explained it if someone had asked. He was just crying, and then he was crying *because* he was crying, and then he was crying because he was starting to think about jumping off the bridge.

He had some Steel Reserve. Maybe that would help him stop. He pulled it out of his pocket, took a few sips. This would calm him down, maybe even put him to sleep. He'd probably be fine if he just lay here on the bridge and took a nice little nap. One problem: He couldn't sleep because he was too busy drinking, and the more he drank the more he thought about jumping. There was no reason for this. His family was beautiful. They loved him, no matter how fucked up he might be. And yet the lure of leaping off the bridge stayed with him. He would stop crying if he stopped breathing. Everything would be just fine.

He looked out over the bridge, from Kentucky into Indiana. It was late evening, and the sun had turned the sky a million shades of red and orange, colors he'd never seen before, slicing through the clouds. How gorgeous it was, this tiny pocket of the planet, and he thought that this would be good, this would be okay, to leap from this bridge and down into the beautiful earth.

In his pocket, his phone buzzed.

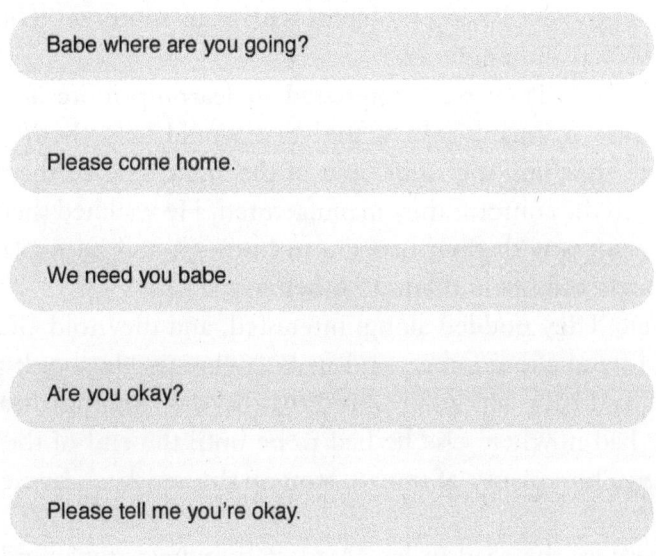

Addie had told him once that with her ex-husband, it had been so easy to decide to leave. He suffered, and then he spiraled, and then he drank, and when he drank she felt unsafe, and she knew this was not a man she could live with, not someone she could allow to raise her child. But Gideon did none of that. He drank and he sobbed and he begged not to be seen. He drank and he tried to vanish and thought only of hurting himself.

She found Gideon there, sitting and sobbing on the bridge, after she'd tracked him using an app on their phones. When he saw her, he tried to run away but didn't get far, tripping, and when she finally reached him, she hugged him, again, and she told him that she loved him, that they needed to go home where he would be safe.

The next morning, he had a project scope at a factory in Illinois. He was up by 6 a.m., on the road by 7. This left him plenty of time to stop along the way and pick up a couple Steel Reserves for the drive. By the time he walked into the facility, around 10 a.m., he was hammered. This was fine. He popped a few mints and took a swig of water. He walked inside a cavernous space, with stacks of equipment from floor to ceiling, and heard the sounds of machines whirring and pounding in every direction.

"I hear you guys are having problems with your sunroofs," Gideon said to the sales rep and engineer.

They explained. They were interested in learning more about a product Gideon's company sold, a tool that would help them make sure they were attaching the right bolts at the right time to the right specifications on the sunroofs they manufactured. He watched them go through the process with their existing technology, and he explained how his product could help them do it better.

It went well. They nodded along, interested, and they told Gideon they needed to run the numbers and make a choice. He shook their hands and walked back out and realized that he was running ahead of schedule. He had nowhere else he had to be until the end of the day. This would give him plenty of time to stop on the way back home and grab a drink.

He got back on the road in his Mazda 6, windows down and hot air whipping past him, as it does in July in the southern Midwest. He turned on a mix CD that Addie had made him, and he felt the air on his face and saw the trees blurring together, everything hot and wild and green. The roads were dry, the black leather of his seats and his steering wheel warm against his body, the bottle of Steel Reserve cool in his hand. When he finished one Steel Reserve he drank another, and then another, and then he started to wonder how fast the car could go, so he edged it past 80 and then 90 and then 100 and then a little more, touching 110 and edging faster still, cars and trucks vanishing in his rearview. He laughed as he drove. He called the people he loved most in this world—his childhood friends and his West Point friends and his parents and his siblings—and he told them he didn't care if he lived or if he died.

He called everyone except for Addie. Never Addie. He couldn't bear to hear her voice, knew she would say something unbearable, I love you, we need you, please come home. *No.* He would just drive, and he would crack another bottle, and maybe he would see her again or maybe he wouldn't, maybe he would vanish here, screaming down the highway, finally and fully obliterated by the open road.

Joseph

Joseph liked to get a little drunk before therapy. He found a bar across the street from his therapist's office, something generic with a nautical theme. He sat alone, at the end of the bar, in silence, and he drank two high-gravity IPAs in quick succession. Drunk therapy required sophisticated calibration. Stay sober and he might turn around and drive back home before ever setting foot in the shrink's office. Get anything more than a light buzz, and she would notice, and then they would have to do therapy about *that*.

Her name was Lauren. She was the third therapist he'd tried. If he had his way, he never would have tried any of them, given the fact that he was obviously fine, but Emily seemed to think otherwise. After she'd walked in on him watching porn, he'd told her that he was reliving his sexual abuse every time they touched, and then she had left him with no choice. No matter how much he protested to the contrary, he was, quite clearly, *not* fine.

And Emily was miserable. She'd left her life in Charlotte to follow Joseph across the country. She'd begun a job that thrilled but overwhelmed her, and then had to come home at night to a marriage with no sex and barely a shred of emotional intimacy, to a husband who was always studying or trying desperately not to relive the most terrifying moment of his life. After he'd opened up about the effects of the trauma, she'd softened toward him, but that only made her more adamant. Joseph was not okay. He needed help, or their marriage might not last.

It wasn't until he said he would go to therapy that he'd begun to think that maybe Emily would stay with him. For days after the night she caught him, she'd barely spoken. She hadn't left him only because she had nowhere else to go. Everyone who loved her lived thousands of miles away. But he would say anything and she would say nothing;

he would reach for her body and she would recoil and walk away. She'd looked at him, briefly in the eyes, when he'd told her that he thought he was struggling with the effects of his abuse. She seemed to take this as the first honest thing he'd said in months. And then she told him, "You have to go to therapy." So fine, fuck it, whatever, here he was.

The first therapist he met was an older woman with close-cropped gray hair. She greeted him by reaching out her hand, and he took it, and then he saw flashes of the trauma, a small terror, before settling himself down. She asked him what brought him there and he told her. "I'm having a lot of stress and anxiety. I'm having trouble sleeping. I think it's mostly related to childhood sexual trauma." She said okay, and that she was sorry that had happened, and then she asked him for more details on the ways the anxiety had impacted his life. He told her those things, dutifully, in part because Emily was sitting right beside him listening, and he knew that meant he had to tell the truth. And then finally she asked him about the trauma itself. "Can you tell me what happened?"

And so he did. He kept it vague. There was an older boy. He trapped me. He made me touch him, multiple times.

"Well," the therapist said, and her voice held a chipper lilt. "You must feel really lucky. That could have been so much worse."

What the fuck, Joseph thought. *That could have been so much worse?* He may not have returned to any therapist at all, if not for the fact that he knew, due to Emily's training and Alex's training and his own common sense, that this was among the worst things a therapist could possibly say to someone who'd been sexually abused. Surely, he had stumbled into the office of the only therapist anywhere on the planet who would listen to a grown man describe the terror he felt reliving the worst moment of his childhood, and then tell that man just how lucky he was.

Also, no matter how shameful it had felt to hear those words, Joseph realized, walking out of the office, that he was okay. He could tell the story. He could sit with the fear. He could withstand whatever reaction it might draw, even a reaction like that. He would try again.

He went without Emily the next time, confident he could manage on his own. The next one was a middle-aged man, about six-three, with a big beard and wild curly hair. When he reached out his hand, Joseph shook it. Again came flashes of terror, the dick in his vision, his heart rate spiking, until he could sit down and breathe his way toward relative calm. The big bearded man said nothing offensive. He never made Joseph feel panicked or small or ashamed. And yet, when Joseph left, he still thought, *fuck* that guy. He had brought out a "feelings wheel" and asked Joseph to point to what he felt as he was speaking. He seemed, to Joseph, like a man who believed that no other man on the planet had ever understood emotions quite like him. His questions felt basic, overly gentle, like he was talking to a child. Joseph was sure it all worked well for some people. But not him. A *feelings* wheel?! Get the fuck out of here.

Before Joseph registered the presence of the ivory-colored couch or the plush green chairs, before he met her dark brown eyes or noticed the half-sleeve balloon tattoo running down her arm, before he even saw her smile, kind and welcoming, he was struck by something else that calmed him the moment he walked in through the third therapist's door.

Her hands. He couldn't see them.

He'd looked for her hands, of course, right away, preparing himself for the way they would soon be reaching for his own. But instead she held them behind her back, out of sight. She held that smile, and she said hi, welcome, it's so nice to meet you, and she invited him to take a seat. He felt his chest uncoil. He sat.

In his email to Lauren, Joseph had tried to be as direct as possible. "For a long time, I had repressed a memory of childhood sexual abuse. I recently recovered the memory. It's causing me anxiety and stress, including a lack of sleep."

She had written back quickly. "I think I have the skills to help you with this."

And now here they were. Lauren asked how long he'd been in Seattle and where he'd moved from. She asked him which sports he liked, about Emily and the dogs. When she asked about his upbringing, he said he wasn't close to his family, but she did not make him explain why. He told her he'd grown up in church and then gone to war, and eventually he'd gone to seminary to see if he could reconcile what he'd experienced between the two. She asked if he wanted faith to be part of his therapeutic process, and he said absolutely not. She didn't ask about his trauma. She did not require a description of the abuse. She just talked to him for forty-seven minutes as a pleasant and curious stranger, and then, just before their time expired, she said, "Let me explain a little bit of what I do."

"How was it?" Emily asked when he got home.

"Great," he said. "It was easy."

"What did you talk to her about?"

Joseph thought for a second. "Honestly? I don't even really know. But I'll definitely go back."

And so he returned, time and again, and every session reached just a bit further beneath the surface. They talked about his marriage, about his parents, about old resentments that covered even older wounds. Usually, she let him guide the conversation, never demanding that he talk about anything in particular. Therapy, Joseph decided, was great. Even more than that: Joseph, he decided, was great at therapy. Smart, introspective, ready to cut to the core of the issue. She was good, clearly, but so was he. Together, he imagined, they could get him fixed up in three or four weeks.

Lauren was smart and patient and funny, pretty in a way that made Joseph want very badly to impress her. He was not drawn to her sexually or romantically, only with an energy compelling him to show that he was the best client she would ever have. Yes, sure, he'd suffered debilitating childhood trauma, but look at all the ways he already knew how to fix himself! He could self-diagnose with PTSD, could talk through the kinds of treatment he'd researched online. He could point to this event from this stage of life and explain, in detail, exactly how that outcome had resulted from the aforementioned trauma. And did he mention he was crushing it in law school? Even while seeing images of a dick!

But that only went so far. Lauren didn't seem interested in being impressed. Sometimes, he gave vague answers, because the more specific answers might feel humiliating, and then she would press him to be more specific. When he couldn't be more specific, she would tell him to think about it, and then he would sit there in silence until he either gave a better answer or their time ran out.

Other times, he would try to fill the time with small talk. But if you talk long enough, about small enough things, eventually that conversation opens up a window to something you'd rather not see.

Like the time that he mentioned, casually, that it took him an hour to get to her office.

"What?" she asked. "Are you serious?" This made no sense. Her office was in Fremont. His law school was near downtown. He drove here from campus. "Do you *walk* here or something?"

Joseph tried to explain. When he left the law school, he drove south on I-5, which took him all the way around the full perimeter of the city, rather than going north. "But if you go north," she said, "it just takes fifteen minutes." Her tone softened, from chiding to curiosity. "Why are you doing that?"

Joseph shrugged. "Oh, I don't know," he said. "It's just the way I go."

She looked at him, clearly confused.

"Yeah," she said. "But why?"

Why? Who the fuck did she think she was, asking him *why*. Joseph drove that way because he drove that way. But then the silence lingered, and then he allowed himself to continue thinking, and to begin wondering, and then to concede in his mind that yeah, sure, it was kind of weird that he would voluntarily take a much longer route than necessary, and he sat with that thought for a moment, Lauren still looking at him while he looked at the ceiling or the furniture or the floor, and then he realized, suddenly, oh shit, I know what it is.

Joseph was afraid to turn left. Every week, when he left the garage at the law school library, he turned right to get on I-5, going south. He did this because that's how he'd done it the very first week he'd gone to Lauren's office. But that was back before she'd moved to a new office on the northern part of town. Because he had turned right out of the garage the first time he had come to see her, he turned right every other time after that. Turning right meant going to a ramp that led only onto I-5 south, and so week after week, that's what he did. When he turned right, he knew exactly where he'd go, how he'd merge lanes, when he'd prepare to hit the on-ramp, how he'd weave in and out of the slowdowns when interstates merged. If he turned left, then sure, he knew the route was quicker, but he didn't know that route, couldn't imagine what dangers it might hold. As he realized this, this clearly very reasonable and *obvious* reason for driving one hour to her office instead of fifteen minutes, he felt, suddenly, that he was going to erupt into tears.

He went quiet. No. He would not do that, could not relinquish that sense of control. And so he sat. He waited. He watched the clock. He said nothing and she said nothing in return. A simple question about directions had paralyzed the room.

The clock hit 5:50.

"Okay," he said. "See you next week."

"See you next week."

—

The next week he left an hour before the session, as always. But this time when he arrived at the exit of the garage he found himself turning on his left blinker and then making a left turn, and then suddenly he was riding north on I-5. It was simple and quick, with minimal traffic. He arrived forty-five minutes before their appointment. And that's when he decided to start a new tradition of drinking pre-therapy beers. It was a good tradition. Two beers in, he could talk without crying or cry without panic. He could peer into himself with only the faintest fear of what he might see. Within a few weeks, he walked into the room and told her, "I'm ready."

"Are you sure?"

"I'm sure."

And so he told her. He started by describing the baseball card shop. He'd barely started talking, and already he was about to cry. He told her about Jack and the other boys, teenage gods. About the ways Jack would pull out his penis around everyone, fucking hilarious dude, why is your dick out, what the hell bro come on. Joseph looked at Lauren once, her eyes wide and earnest, and then he felt himself welling with tears, so nope, he couldn't look at her, needed to stay focused, to keep his gaze on the floor or out the window while the story poured forth from his chest. He told her about the way Jack had first asked him to go to the back room, how he'd met him there, dick in hand, telling Joseph to touch it, touch it, touch it, just touch it you fucking baby what's wrong. When he looked out the window from her office he saw that the city was dark, late afternoon in the maw of a Seattle winter. The darkness pushed him forward, because he loved this time of year, how the sky turned gray but the city stayed green. So he told Lauren about how stupid he felt for returning to the shop, what is wrong with you dude, but he loved his cards and his friends and he wanted to get away from his mom. Outside the office he saw lights, flickering red and green and hinting of Christmas. He told her about the second time, when he'd tried to run away but couldn't, when Jack had told him chill out dude just touch it, and so he did. Joseph could feel the IPAs swimming around in his gut, and as he stared out the window and listened to his own words, he felt he wasn't the one speaking but was just watching a sad movie, a character narrating a scene of pain and terror while the camera showed streets bright and shining gold. Finally, he told her about the third time, the one Joseph felt most ashamed of, when he had screamed let me out and cowered in the corner, while Jack closed the distance between them, telling him to touch it, then telling him to stroke it, you want those cards right so just stroke it, it's no big deal. And how Joseph felt he could drown in that moment, flailing beneath the weight of a teenage boy's grotesque desire.

When he finished, she sat still for a moment. He could hear her breath. He looked from the window to the floor, worried what the quiet would do to him. He heard her sniffle, then saw her reach for her box of tissues to wipe away her own tears, and this felt like a gift, that someone else would hear his story and allow themselves the emotions he couldn't bear to indulge. When she spoke, her voice was soft, calm.

"Joseph," she said, "that is so awful." His eyes met hers for a brief moment, then flitted away. "I am so, so sorry that happened to you."

And then, silence. For five seconds, then ten, then a minute, then more. Joseph wanted to break the silence but didn't know what to say. He tried whatever words he could grasp for. "So, the whole not-sleeping thing," he said, "it's because of this, I think."

"Yeah," she said, but then she was quiet.

Joseph scrambled to keep talking. "And honestly," he added, "even before this whole thing came back, I've never been comfortable with sudden change. So."

She nodded. "Change is hard." Then nothing.

Every time he tried to say something else, she answered in a way that didn't ask for any response, and they fell back into that silence. They sat and listened to the hum of the heater, to the sound of cars outside. She did not tell him what was wrong with him. She did not explain exactly how she would go about making it better. She sat in his wreckage, and she looked around, not even studying it, just letting it take shape all around her. If he had more to show her, she seemed to trust that he would. But if not, then she would just continue to sit with what he'd already revealed.

Joseph thought of Macy and Hobbes, his and Emily's two dachshunds. Adorable, tiny, fascinated by the world around them. They'd gotten them when they were puppies, littermates who immediately injected unimagined energy and joy into their daily lives. Back when they were young, Joseph would put them in their crate, and at first they would panic, barking and clawing at the gate and looking at him with desperate eyes. But then they would go quiet. They would sit and watch him, their caretaker, still in the room with them, absorbing their panic, and watching him watch them seemed to slow their breath. Seven minutes, then ten. Finally, they would lay down, bodies curled, eyes still on Joseph. Fifteen minutes, then twenty. They let their eyes drift away, then close, and over time they learned that in their crates, they might be constricted, but they were in a place designed by a person who wanted to keep them safe.

He rested in the silence of her office. The clock hit 5:50. He stood, thanked her, and drove the fifteen minutes home.

—

A couple of years after the visions overtook him, Joseph stepped on the gas of his gold Chevy Cobalt, windows down and wind whipping past him, wondering what his life might hold next. For now, the thought sat in the air, light, not like it had sat so often before, as a weight pushing down on his chest. He and Emily were driving down to the coast. They'd lived here three years, and they'd still never seen the Pacific Ocean.

A few things had happened since that afternoon in Lauren's office. First, she had recommended Eye Movement Desensitization and Reprocessing therapy, known as EMDR. This breakthrough treatment for post-traumatic stress aimed to train the brain to reprocess trauma in a safe, controlled environment. The sessions were grueling, forcing Joseph deep into his most terrifying memories, but cathartic, and the longer he went, the more the intrusive images slipped away.

Next, Joseph decided to file a lawsuit. The criminal statute of limitations had long ago run out, particularly since Jack had been a minor, but there might be other ways to claim some sense of justice. Joseph decided he would like that. After lawyers served Jack the papers, thousands of miles away in Florida, he admitted what he'd done, and they settled for $15,000. Joseph decided the money didn't matter, that he would blow it on frivolous things. Whenever he wanted something, *anything*, he would buy it.

Was the therapy and Jack's admission of responsibility enough? Was Joseph *healed*? He didn't really know exactly what that word was supposed to mean, but if he had to answer, he would say, kind of, yeah? Did *healing* mean no longer seeing his abuser's dick every time he touched another body? Did it mean no longer going to extreme lengths to avoid sex with his wife? Because he seemed to have moved past those things.

After the night she caught him watching porn, Emily had demanded two things: Joseph would go to therapy, and they would take a trip. She would no longer let his anxiety tether them to the apartment. And so one Saturday morning they piled into the Cobalt and drove down to Cannon Beach on the Oregon coast. They let the dogs roam through the sand and splash in the water. The sky was cloudy, the air cool, the coastline gorgeous and brutal. This was exactly what Joseph loved about the Pacific Northwest, its austere beauty. It was a land designed to enrapture and pummel you at the same time.

He took a photo of Emily that day, in a quiet moment when the dogs were resting. In the image, her dark hair is wild, lost to the wind. The rocks rise up from the sand behind her and the water sits just beyond, the sky above a pale and stagnant gray. He would see a sadness in that photo every time he took it out in the years to come. He would see her there on the beach but also in their bedroom on that night months before, mourning what she believed she'd just lost. Underneath the sadness, though, he would see something else. A kind of *will*. A bullheaded faith that Joseph was not a man she should give up on. A desire to look at him, clearly and fully, and to find him worthy of continuing to share these kinds of moments, whether here on this beach or anywhere else in this world.

They would be leaving soon. Joseph had finished law school. So they'd drive back across the country to Alabama, out of some strange pull to live near the families they'd both once tried to escape. They would drive many of the same roads they'd taken to Seattle, and this time he would think nothing of the Cobalt's routine rattles and pings. Months after they arrived, he would pass the bar, and they would settle there. She would continue social work, and he would find a job as an associate in a small firm, and then there would be other jobs, bigger jobs, in other states. By his forties he would be making more money than he ever imagined possible, and yet, strangely, he would want more. He'd long ago given up collecting baseball cards. But the money represented now exactly what it had represented then: the chance to buy safety. And the truth is, it kind of worked. The more he saw his student loans decrease, and his savings and investments increase, the more he felt a version of calm. He would credit his months in therapy for the peace he started to feel as he climbed toward middle age, but he would also credit the growing number in his bank account. Was that something he should feel bad about? Who cared. It was true.

One day, he would be on a work trip, and Emily would call to tell him she was pregnant. By this point, they'd have had arguments about this possibility. She wanted children badly. He did not. But after getting the news, he would sit in a faraway hotel room, and he would know, immediately, that everything would be okay. That they would have a baby, and that she would be a girl, and that Joseph would protect her, because if there was anything life had prepared him for, he believed it was this, the chance to keep a small child safe.

Nate

Another day, lying in bed, and another Facebook post, demanding his attention.

> BLACK TRANSMEN OF OHIO
>
> WELLNESS AND RESILIENCE RETREAT
>
> Group activities, good food, and brotherhood
>
> September 20–22

It was the first few words that he had to read over and over again. *Black Transmen of Ohio*. He knew, obviously, that he wasn't the only one. He'd even started following this particular page years ago, but he'd never noticed many of their posts. Right now, though, the existence of such a group felt like a miracle. Other men like him, who rooted for the Buckeyes and had wrangled binders, who'd searched for creams to help post-op scars fade and who rolled their eyes at their own racist Wandas, who'd searched everywhere for barbers who wouldn't make some obnoxious comment while delivering a clean fade.

    A few weeks later, he was riding to Dayton, piled in the back seat with strangers, laughing and talking shit. There was Chris, the driver, veering in and out of traffic and occasionally crossing the rumble strips and swerving back into his lane, shouting, "I'm getting us there, dammit!" whenever he heard gasps or yelps from the back seat. As they rode, they divided themselves among fans of the Browns, Bengals, or Steelers; traded tips on beard and acne care; clowned one another over their universal shortness and the still-high pitched tones in everyone's voices. Nate was the shortest, of course. But this was the first time he could laugh along with jokes about his height without feeling defensive. He looked around the car, at guys barely taller than him, maybe five-three or five-four, some with voices higher-pitched than his own, a couple with beards that weren't quite lumberjack-thick and others with no beards at all, and he never questioned, once, whether any of them were sufficiently masculine. So why would he think anyone judged those parts of *him*?

They arrived at an Airbnb and unpacked, twelve guys spread across seven bedrooms, then hung out in the hot tub, and there Nate saw bodies that resembled his own across different eras of his life. Post-op guys with fresh scars and others with massively built pecs, guys who hadn't had top surgery or didn't even want it, some in sports bras or binders, others with their chests uncovered, because fuck it, if ever there was a place to feel at peace with your body, it was here.

They grilled burgers and hot dogs and gathered in the living room for something they called "reflection time." Chris, the driver, told them how it would go. They would take a handheld mirror and slowly pass it around the room. They would stare in the mirror and say three things.

1. I'm proud of myself for _____.

2. I forgive myself for _____.

3. I promise myself I will _____.

Nate sat in the corner, watching the mirror travel around the room, listening as the other men spoke. Some were proud of how they'd handled their transitions, others for ways they'd supported loved ones. They forgave their own botched relationships and perceived shortcomings, vowed to be better about fitness or meditation, listening or communicating, finding beauty in pieces of themselves they'd been conditioned to loathe. A few stared at themselves in silence and said nothing. A couple guys stood up before they could speak, just handed the mirror to the next person, and walked out of the room.

Finally, Nate took his turn. He gazed into the mirror. He'd hated his reflection so much when he was younger. Now, as he held the mirror up to his face, he knew he looked good, but he still felt his insides twisting. He couldn't bear to watch himself speak the words he was now supposed to say. He was proud of himself for... *what*, exactly? Some of these guys had college degrees, stable jobs, loving families. Nate saw nothing in his life that deserved that kind of pride.

He tried to think of one true sentence.

"I'm proud of myself for having the courage to transition," he said. The same answer could be given by every other man in the room, he knew, but still. He *was* proud.

He looked back in the mirror. He saw a quiver in his lip, then felt his eyes drift down to the floor.

"I forgive myself for…"

He added nothing. His chest was heavy now, and he watched its rise and fall. He started to cry, just a little, but he took a deep breath, dried his eyes, and composed himself.

"I forgive myself for fucking up my relationship with my son."

There. He said it. Now he felt he had to explain it. He told the story about Mya, about meeting her son, about how the word *Daddy* had felt like a title that bound him to Trae for the rest of his life. That he'd sworn no test of blood or law was needed to cement him as Trae's father. That those months had given him a sense of duty and purpose unlike any he'd ever known. And then he told the story of how things ended. The fight, the beating, the arrest, the move back to Ohio. By staying in this state and not returning to Connecticut to repair things with Mya, he felt he'd broken a sacred duty to the boy who'd loved him in ways he never imagined he might be loved. He owed Trae that kind of love in return, and now he didn't understand how he was supposed to live with himself. So you know what? Fuck that. Maybe he didn't actually forgive himself at all.

And then he left. He didn't mean to. He knew the other men deserved his attention just as he'd been given theirs. But allowing himself to be seen by others felt intolerable. He said he was sorry, so sorry, he'd be back soon, and then he rushed up to his room and dove into the bed. A few minutes later, he heard a knock.

"Yo." The door opened before Nate could answer. It was a man named Charles. Besides Chris, he'd been the chief organizer of the retreat. He was older, maybe forty, bald with a thick beard.

"Hey," said Nate.

"How you doing?"

"I'm all right."

"You sure?"

"I think so. I don't know."

Charles asked if he could sit and Nate said sure. He took his place on the edge of the bed.

"Listen, man," Charles said. "The way you were talking out there had me a little worried. Everything you were saying sounded so *final*. And, like, dude, you're twenty-eight years old. Your life is *not over*. Believe me. I've lived lifetimes in my lifetime. You've got a lot of life left. You're gonna mess up plenty of other relationships."

Nate laughed at that part, at least a little. And then Charles told him a truth that delivered heartbreak and release in equal measure. "I know it doesn't feel like it, but you don't have the same responsibility that Trae's biological father has, or his legal father would. And if you're ever in a spot where you're getting abused, you gotta get out, man. How could you possibly stay in that situation? You deserve to be able to move on and not make yourself miserable."

Nate nodded, said yeah, but he felt, at first, a searing rage. How could this man come in here and tell him whether or not he was Trae's father? How could some stranger possibly know what Nate owed that little boy? Charles didn't get it. No one got it. And because biology had left Nate incapable of impregnating a woman, he would never get to be a father in a way that people would understand. He thanked Charles, and Charles left. Nate went to sleep, angry and ashamed.

—

Light sliced through the windows just before 7:30 a.m. Nate had no blackout shades here. He got up, and walked downstairs and poured some coffee, then headed out to the porch to listen to the birds. He sat and he wondered: *Was Charles right?*

When he got back to Youngstown, Nate started wondering something else. What might it be like to be happy? What might it be like to have friends? He knew he couldn't re-create the experience of a weekend in the woods with twelve other Black trans men. But could he construct a life where he did more than smoke weed with racist Wanda and watch TV with his mom? He reached out to friends from high school. He asked if they wanted to hang out, and they said yes. Then he met their friends, and he asked those friends if they wanted to hang out, and they said yes too. Had it always been this easy? Nate struggled to remember.

And then when he made friends, he started thinking about getting another girlfriend. He messaged girls on Facebook and Instagram, and with the fog of depression now lifting, he managed not to ghost them this time. He went on a few dates. Then a few more. Relationships started, then fizzled, but that was okay. At least he was out there. Someday, he imagined, he could love deeply and enduringly and could feel that same love in return.

And then he started wondering: How might things be different if he had a job? He didn't want to give up on his dream of a career, and he still hoped to go through vocational training. But in the meantime, why not get back to stocking shelves? He reached out to a regional grocery chain, and they offered him a few shifts a week. It was a union job, starting at $15 an hour, with promises that his pay could rise, and he could receive health care and earn overtime once he started taking on enough shifts. He worked graveyard, 10 p.m. to 6 a.m., stocking and arranging, going aisle by aisle through the store.

He loved it. He could lose himself in his work, forget that anything else existed but these pallets of water bottles that needed to find their place on the shelves. His forearms ached his first night, and toward the end of the shift, he wobbled on weary legs. He loved that feeling of purposeful pain. He loved his coworkers, all of them burly dudes, some with the same taste in music and anime. None of them seemed to care in the slightest when Nate walked past them into the men's room during the middle of a shift.

—

Nate still scrolled through the news sometimes. He couldn't help it. All those trans pages he'd started following soon after he came out, the ones filled with tips on name changes and beard oils, now bombarded him with new messages about how the second Trump administration had begun to target people like him. A ban on trans soldiers. An executive order barring trans women and girls from playing women's sports. It wasn't just the actions themselves. It was their language. Trans teens had been "mutilated." Trans women athletes had a "corrosive impact" in locker rooms. Trans soldiers lacked the "humility and selflessness" required to serve.

Nate made himself a rule. Every time he saw a new headline, he would ask himself, *Does this news impact me, right now?* If the answer was no, he told himself he had to wait seventy-two hours before he could freak out. As a poor Black trans man, relying on Medicaid for his health care and Social Security for his disability income, he knew he was more at risk than almost any other American. That's why he had to make the rule. Eventually, he thought, the administration would come for him. But for now, he had to keep living his life.

Here's what helped: He became convinced that none of this reflected the America he inhabited, not even here, in small-town Ohio. Online, it was different. He got plenty of harassment; behind screens, confusion fueled hatred. He knew millions of people who would never meet him believed he should not exist in the body he'd learned to love. But when he moved through his small sliver of the real world, he found that in the flesh, confusion fueled curiosity. The Americans Nate knew wanted to find a way to keep loving the people they encountered, no matter their gender, or how they arrived there. He thought of Carol, the old lady from the corner store. She'd once told him she didn't "accept" that he was trans. But recently she'd stopped him one morning on his way out the door. She had a family member with a teenager whom Carol had always known as a girl, but now wanted to be seen as a boy.

"How do I refer to this person?" Carol asked Nate.

"If you really care about them, then you say *he*," Nate said.

"Okay." She nodded. "I think I can do that."

—

He'd been thinking about something lately. Growing up, he'd never really had a model for how to be a man. He'd chosen to inhabit the gender that had felt like home to him, but that choice was born of a kind of faith: that he could become a man worthy of emulation, without knowing any man he could emulate himself.

Over the years, though, he'd found himself grabbing pieces of the men who'd floated in and out of his life. He could think back to the father he'd had as a small child, long before the drugs had made his dad unrecognizable. This was the man who had held him in his lap and braided his hair while they watched TV, who had taught him about the vast reaches of the solar system and the inner workings of a car's transmission. They fell out of touch and his dad had gone to prison, but now he was out, and lately, they'd reconnected. The other day Nate posted a selfie on Facebook and his dad commented: *My first love. My son.*

He could think of Dante, his friend from high school, who'd defended Nate when other guys tried to insult him, demanding that the world show respect for his most vulnerable friend. And he could think of Travis, his mom's husband, the boulder of a man who'd once been uncomfortable with Nate's trans identity. Now, sometimes when they sat and watched news of new anti-trans laws going into effect, Travis moved to sit closer to Nate, and he put his hand on Nate's shoulder, and while Nate sat stoic, Travis cried.

And ever since the retreat, he could think of Charles, Chris, and the other trans men who'd been with him in the woods. He admired their openness and candor, the way some had built careers and families. But mostly, he admired the fact that they continued to *exist*. He admired the gray in some of their beards, the wrinkles in their foreheads, the clichéd wisdom they'd dispensed, all signs of the choices they made daily to continue to live in the bodies that felt like home.

On the last day of that retreat, after breakfast and a morning hike, Nate had gone kayaking down a river with them. He'd never done that before. Only a couple of them had. It scared him a little. But he hopped in his solitary vessel, and the other men paddled up around him, and then there was a group of Black trans men floating down a river in rural Ohio, staying connected to each other but each in their own boats. Nate paddled until the sweat began to pool underneath his arms and on his chest, and then he took his shirt off, and he lay back and closed his eyes. He floated like that for a while, face to the sky, and he felt the sun beating down on his bare skin, everything hot and alive.

Ryan

"You will have a secret."

That's what Sheldon told him, sitting on the mat moments after one of their first training sessions. Whenever he met someone new, or even when he saw a stranger across a crowded room, Ryan would know how, exactly, he could dismantle that person in combat. It was amazing, what bodies became once you knew how to bend them to your will. He eyed a cashier at the grocery store and saw a long reach he would have to get underneath, but a skinny trunk that could easily be dragged to the ground. He saw a meathead filling up at the gas pump next to him, and he knew exactly how long it would take those heavy muscles to tire—how, if Ryan made the guy work for even thirty seconds, he'd become breathless, putty in Ryan's hands. Anyone under six feet, he knew he could reach with a kick to the face. Anyone under 250 pounds, he knew he could get them to the ground and pound them into submission.

He daydreamed about it. He just needed one boy who had bullied him when they were children to see him down at the Brass Horse and try to start some shit. Many of them were now doughy, balding men racing through early middle age. The suffering he would inflict now would even out the suffering he'd endured then. Justice could be dispensed on a beer-soaked bar floor. He just needed one of them to give him the chance.

There was one problem. Since he'd moved home, no one seemed to care that he was gay. When he saw his old bullies at the grocery store, they gave him respectful head nods, holy shit, good to see you, dude, I heard you were back in town. He saw pictures on Facebook from a pride parade down the road in Massena, and there were the faces of women he'd once heard using antigay slurs, now smiling and waving rainbow flags. One of Ryan's oldest friends, Jill, had a son who came out in middle school, wore nail polish, and played with makeup, leaning into the parts of his identity that Ryan had always worked to suppress in himself. Jill worried about her son.

"Can you teach him how to fight?" she asked Ryan.

"Of course I can," he said.

But when she went to her son, he just laughed at her. "*Fight?* Why would I ever need to learn *that*?"

Anthony was down in Jacksonville, living near his mother. He and Ryan had tried to make it work long-distance and they'd failed, multiple times. The last breakup had felt permanent. They'd deleted each other's numbers from their phones and blocked each other on social media. Ryan considered dating in the North Country, and, alternately, to embrace the idea of being single for the rest of his life. Until one day, he got a text:

> What's up? How r u?

"Who is this?" Ryan responded.

> You know who it is.

"Do I?"

> I know damn well you don't know anybody else with a Florida area code.

They caught up, casually, about jobs and families, searching each other's messages for evidence of new boyfriends.

Anthony wrote again right before bed that night:

> I have to say something
> I miss you

Anthony flew north a few weeks later. Immediately, Ryan remembered what he'd missed. Those eyes and their lashes, the devilish laugh, the sense that here was the one person who loved all of him, every piece, even the ones he didn't yet know.

"Could I live here?" Anthony asked. "On the rez?"

"Yeah," Ryan said. "I think so."

Only a few dozen non-Mohawk people lived on the reservation, but it was possible. He would have to apply through the tribal government, get character references from Mohawk friends. He could work in government, or a local store, or the casino. There wasn't much, but there was Ryan. There was the chance for years and years of McDonald's anniversary dates.

"Let's do it," Anthony said, and so they did.

—

One night, Ryan went out to the casino with his sister and a few friends from work. They crowded around the U-shaped bar, throwing back shots and beers, migrating to and from the slot machines and the tables, then back again for another round. That's when Ryan saw him: Dillon Gallagher, sitting at the other end of the bar.

Ryan hadn't seen him since high school graduation more than fifteen years ago. But immediately, he knew. Dillon Gallagher had been Ryan's most consistent tormentor, from fifth grade all the way through high school. A farmer's kid, a sniveling country white boy, neither particularly smart nor particularly athletic, and to most people, Ryan later realized when he mentioned the guy to other friends, Dillon Gallagher was not particularly memorable at all.

But Ryan held a catalog in his mind of every interaction they'd ever had. Dillon Gallagher had started with standard-issue movie bully stuff: elbows to the sternum when passing in the hallway, smacks across the face and then a sprint in the opposite direction. No proper ass-kickings, really; looking back, Ryan now realized, Dillon Gallagher had never been physically imposing at all. Just mean.

Of everyone in this town, Dillon Gallagher was the kid Ryan had dreamed about taking revenge on the most. This was the face he'd seen at the center of the heavy bag. These were the ribs he'd imagined in Sheldon's chest when they'd practiced kicks. This was the body he'd held in his mind when he'd left all those other bodies lying on pavement, bleeding and dazed. Now, he was *here*. At the Mohawk casino, maybe fifteen feet away, totally oblivious to the violence he was about to endure.

Dillon Gallagher looked up, caught Ryan's eye for just a second, then looked away. He did not look back. Ryan stared, willing himself not to blink. He started drumming his fingers on the bar, doing calculations in his mind. This would be easier than he'd even imagined. Could a man be both scrawny and a little fat? Because that was Dillon Gallagher. Ryan would walk right over, say nothing, and pop him once, good, square in the face. Then he would grab his head and knee him in the stomach, letting him fall to the ground, and Ryan would join him there, pounding his face until it was unrecognizable, before standing up and saying, "Remember me, bitch?" while he walked away.

All of a sudden, though, someone was blocking Ryan's view. The bartender.

"What can I get you?"

Ryan had not yet considered this. The fact that he was here, standing at a bar, because the bar is where you stood when you ordered a round of drinks.

"Oh," he said. "Sorry. Just a second."

He turned, asked his friends what they wanted, then put in a round of whatever it was that they had said. And then the bartender turned to get the drinks, and that's when Ryan looked back at Dillon Gallagher, only to see that he was gone. He scanned the bar, and saw him nowhere, then he took the drinks, downed a shot, and walked down every row of the casino, and still didn't see him. Then he went out to search the parking lot, and still couldn't find him, until he almost began to wonder if Dillon Gallagher had ever been real at all.

—

Years slipped by. Ryan competed in MMA tournaments, then retired from competing, sparring only when he was healthy enough to get on the mat. And then he retired from sparring and turned to teaching, helping Sheldon train young fighters and leading a self-defense class for women on his own. "You're a gold mine," Sheldon told him. "You're handsome, but you're gay, so they know you're not gonna hit on them, and every single one of them wants their ass and thighs to look like yours."

On Facebook, soon before their twenty-year high school reunion, he saw the news that Dillon Gallagher had died. Cancer or something. And Ryan wondered what he'd ever really been chasing, why he had ever needed so badly to inflict pain on a boy who'd grown into a man who was now dead. He wondered if it ever could have been as satisfying as he'd imagined. He wondered that until he hit forty and he stopped drinking, and his back and neck started hurting, and he spent his days at home with Anthony and their dog and cats and realized that his anger was now slipping away from him, and he didn't know if it was even worth it to wonder at all.

—

Some nights, Ryan liked to go dancing down at the American Legion. These days, his sister was busy with her kids, and Anthony was usually working late in his job as an auditor at the casino, so Ryan would meet up with old high school buddies, listen to a couple of bands, and if the music felt right, move his body. His hips were still stiff, but he had rhythm. He'd remained light on his feet. Besides, he'd long ago given up trying to impress anybody on the dance floor.

One night when he was out, he walked by a table, looked down, and saw five faces grinning back at him.

"Oh shit!" Ryan said. "You guys aren't in bed yet?"

His Uncle Les pulled out a chair and told Ryan to sit down. He grabbed a spot between Les and his Aunt Elaine, his cousin Kyle's parents, and across the table from his Uncle Gordy and Aunt Donna. He'd seen them a couple weeks before that, at a cookout for somebody's birthday, but those crowded family gatherings were more about managing chaos than actually catching up with anyone. So Ryan sat down for a rare opportunity to have a conversation with his aunts and uncles.

"You know," Uncle Les said out of nowhere, after a few minutes, "when Kyle came out to us, I accepted him." Then he pointed at his wife, Aunt Elaine, Ryan's father's sister. "*She* had a really hard time with it. But eventually she came around too."

Ryan didn't know what to say. He'd never actually *come out* to anyone in his family except for his sister and his mom. They'd just had to get used to Anthony as a part of his life. Mostly, this had gone fine. Anthony was one of the best cooks in the family, someone whose laugh matched the volume of anyone else in any room. Some nights, he hung out on the porch with Ryan's cousins, smoking weed and listening to music, with or without Ryan even there. He'd learned a few Mohawk words, understood the history, and had encyclopedic knowledge of rez gossip. Sometimes, Ryan joked that most of his family would choose Anthony over *him*.

But still. Ryan didn't know where this was going. He still felt nervous when the fact of his sexuality was spoken aloud. So when Uncle Les brought it up, he just looked down at his drink. "Yeah," he said. "I remember."

Uncle Les continued. "We love you," he said. "You know that, right?"

"Yeah," Ryan said, nodding gently, still looking at his drink. "I know. I love you too."

His Uncle Gordy leaned across the table. "Hey!" he said. "Look at me."

Ryan looked up. He might as well have been looking at a future version of himself. Gordy looked just like Ryan's father, and Ryan had gone his entire life listening to everyone on the rez tell him he looked just like his old man. Ryan had always loved Uncle Gordy. He was loud, boisterous, a monologue in search of an audience. Of all Ryan's aunts and uncles, he was the most loving, the most hotheaded, the one who could knock you out or suffocate you with the force of his hugs.

Ryan looked at him. "You hear what he's saying?" Gordy said, a rumble in his voice. "You know that's true, right?"

Ryan nodded. "Yeah," he said. "I know."

"No," Gordy said. "You don't. So listen to me. We love you."

"Yeah," Ryan said.

"Fuck this," Gordy responded, shaking his head. "Stand up. Right now."

And so Ryan stood, and Gordy came around the table, and Gordy grabbed Ryan by the shoulders and pulled him close, into a hug. "You listen to me," he said. "We love you." Ryan said he knew, and he tried to let go, but Uncle Gordy asked where the fuck he thought he was going and said, "We love you for exactly who you are." He pulled him tighter now, and Ryan felt tears creeping in near the edges of his eyes, but he fought them off and he just stayed there, holding his uncle until finally his uncle decided he could let go.

"Thank you," Ryan said, and Uncle Gordy nodded.

"You know," Ryan continued, "that's the sort of thing I would love to hear from my father. But I don't think I'm ever gonna hear it."

Gordy nodded. "He'll come around," he said.

"If he's ever going to," Ryan said, "one of you is going to have to talk to him."

Gordy nodded again. "All right," he said. "Trust me. He'll come around."

—

For the most part, Ryan's father had solved the problem of his son having a male partner by pretending that Anthony didn't exist. He seemed to manage this easily enough. If you never look at someone, are they really even there? He scooted past him in the kitchen, eyes on the floor, and looked beyond him during conversations in the living room, talking only to other people. When they sat down for family dinners, he ate as fast as he could, then left the table to watch TV while the rest of the family laughed and told stories from their week. Ryan tried to tell himself that it wasn't *just* about the fact that he was gay, and he had at least a little bit of supporting evidence. His dad treated Ryan's sister's husband the same way.

It's hard to remember when it was, exactly, when Ryan looked over at his dad during dinner and saw something he hadn't seen in years: an empty plate. He'd finished eating, put his silverware down, and was just... *still sitting there*. He didn't say much of anything. Not then, and not for the next few family dinners. But he sat, and he listened, and Ryan could have sworn he even saw him look in Anthony's direction when he was talking, at least once or twice. Months passed like this, his dad lingering at their family dinners, and then one night Anthony told a story from work—how someone had asked him for the Mohawk name of something, and when he tried to read it, he'd mangled the pronunciation so badly that his colleagues called over *their* colleagues to listen to him butcher their native tongue. And Ryan looked over and saw that his dad was laughing, big and loud, with his whole body, and this seemed something of a miracle, their shared laughter filling the room.

As years passed, there were still more small miracles. Such as a family group text, and his father asking whose number is this, and then someone said it was Anthony, and his father said let me save it to my phone. A birthday dinner, where his father said that rather than going out to eat, he wanted Anthony to cook his famous shepherd's pie. A steady barrage of texts to Ryan asking how his HVAC and his transmission were doing, wondering if he needed anything from the Walmart down in Massena, gossiping about tribal bullshit, seemingly searching every single day for new ways to connect with his son. When he dropped by the house on Saturdays, he'd declare that Ryan and Anthony needed a new screen door, or repairs to the roof, or maybe a whole new kitchen, and then he spent days or weeks working on those projects, complaining the whole time but quite obviously delighted to be there, in that shared space. There were still more grand Christmases, his dad beaming like a little boy as he watched everyone, including Anthony, opening his extravagant gifts.

Ryan would watch his dad with his grandchildren, Ryan's niece and nephew, Brynn and Kingsley. He would watch the way his father scooped them up and squeezed them tight until they started laughing and tried to wriggle out of his arms. How he smothered them with kisses, turned silly and sappy in equal measure, told them I love you more times in five minutes than Ryan had heard in his entire life. *What would that have been like?* Ryan wondered. What version of his life might have been unlocked by that kind of love?

—

Ryan and Anthony had long ago decided they didn't want children. Now, in his mid-forties, Ryan is no longer a fighter, neither in competition nor in bars. The young man once full of fear and anger feels familiar to him, but far away. He still lifts weights on his lunch break, as many days a week as he can. He can still squat more than 300 pounds but knows the day is coming when he'll max out at 295.

Lately, he's been trying to access parts of himself he long hid. He has a close friend who designs clothes. He models for her sometimes:

high-fashion stuff, ornate capes and experimental coats, clothes he'd never wear in real life that become a kind of costume when he steps on the runway, transforming him into a character that long existed only in his mind. He's done location photoshoots, fashion shows across the region. Before the camera and on the runway, he looks good and he knows it. Once, just a couple years ago, he got invited to walk the runway for a show at the Indigenous Arts and Fashion Festival in Cannes, France. He'd never left North America before. Neither had his mom, his sister, or his dad. But they all drove to Montreal and boarded a plane to the French Riviera, and he walked out in front of a room of designers and actors from across the world. Martin Scorsese was sitting in the audience, right in the front row. Ryan heard he had a blast. He hoped that was true.

Mostly, though, his life is here, with Anthony and their dog, Kubo, and cat, Smoke, on this plot of land at the edge of the rez. He got invited recently to speak at an event at the community center on a panel for *two-spirit* members of the community. The term has become popular over the decades since Ryan was a child, a way to reclaim an ancient heritage of LGBTQ members of Indigenous communities. Ryan had never really connected to the term. He thought it implied that he was equal parts masculine and feminine. Lately, though, he doesn't mind it. The older he has gotten, and the more certain he has become of his ability to beat up any man who bullied him, the more comfortable he has felt embracing the feminine pieces of himself that he once hid.

Sitting on the panel, Ryan told stories from his childhood and talked through how he'd found peace training in martial arts. And he admitted that he was jealous of the others on the panel who'd grown up here in the decades since, of how easy it seemed for them to be their whole selves. He wondered what it might have been like not to carry such old wounds.

And yet, he is proud. Ryan thinks, sometimes, about the idea of legacy. Even if he has no children, he longs someday to leave something behind. He will leave this land, this small plot of the reservation that he owns. The government put his people there many years before he was born, but he has come to love this place, to feel a deep connection to its soil and trees. Sometimes, when he walks around the edge of the property with his niece and nephew, a full acre, he tells them someday, when I'm gone, all of this will be yours. Maybe they will live here.

Maybe they'll rent it out. But somehow this land will help them to create a life with a bit less struggle, will tether them for generations longer to this slice of earth.

And he will leave his story. He will leave it to them, his niece and nephew, and he will leave it to the next generation of gay Mohawk youth. He can look at their lives and tell himself that his suffering held purpose: that because he emerged at the end of all that darkness, they could grow up in light. He's never been to one of the local pride parades; they're just not his scene. But the fact of their existence seems like a testament to his own. He will leave behind a community willing to love boys who need the kind of love he once needed, a corner of the planet made just a little bit better by the fact that he made it his home.

—

But all that's still a long way off. He has plenty of decades still left on this earth. And besides, he might not be done writing his story. He has to confess something. There is still one daydream that gets him excited, pumping blood to every extremity of his body.

It involves his dad. Every now and then, here on the rez, people talk shit about Ryan's father. Usually, it has something to do with tribal politics, somebody jockeying for power by trying to smear his dad's character. That's the one thing that can still trigger Ryan's long-dormant rage. Even though he doesn't drink anymore, sometimes he pictures himself down at the Brass Horse or the Legion with his father, running into an old nemesis who starts to mouth off. Ryan would say something back, and he imagines his dad would say something back too. Maybe things would get heated, and then there would be a push, and Ryan and his father both could say we do not start these fights, but we can finish them, and then father and son would square up together, shoulder to shoulder, and fucking *swing*.

Gideon

Eyes closed, head heavy, a pool of liquid on his chest, Gideon heard a strange tapping noise, and his eyes opened to flashing lights. *Oh shit*, he thought. *I made it.* He saw cars whizzing past and buildings stretching high above, the sky in new pinks and blues. It was late evening in downtown Louisville, maybe a mile from his home. Gideon just needed to shift the car back into gear, and maybe he'd be back in time for dinner. He reached for the Steel Reserve sitting there in the cupholder, but before he could take a sip he heard that strange tapping noise again, and he turned to see a police officer, staring at him, knocking on the window.

"Sir," the officer asked, "have you had anything to drink?"

He blew a 0.34 on the Breathalyzer. This was four times the legal limit: enough for a coma, enough to kill. They drove him back to the precinct and locked him up while they typed up their incident report. An army friend brought him home around 3 a.m., still drunk, and he got out of the car and walked to the door. There, again, he saw Addie waiting. He couldn't bear for her to touch him. And yet she insisted, brought him inside, and put him to bed. He woke the next morning with her arms still wrapped around him. But when he turned over, she sat up, and he saw her face harden.

"Call your boss," she said.

Gideon struggled to keep his eyes open, powerless to stop his body from shaking.

"Call him right now."

"Why?" Gideon asked.

"You're going to tell him you can't come in today. I'm going to get our children fed and ready for the day. And you're going to sleep this shit off. Okay?"

"Okay."

"Good," she said. "And then we're gonna have a fucking talk."

Hours later, he blinked his eyes open and let the world come into focus.

"Look at me," Addie said, sitting next to him on the couch.

He looked, for just a second, but nope, that wasn't gonna work, because looking at her only served as a reminder that she was looking at *him*, and Gideon could not bear to be seen. So instead he studied the floor.

"Fucking *look* at me," she said.

Fine. He would try. He raised his eyes to meet hers, bottomless, and instantly he loved and feared whatever was behind them. "I love you," she said. "I *want* to be married to you. And I know you've been dealing with a lot."

Gideon nodded, weakly, then looked back down at the heart pine floor.

"You hear that," Addie said. "Right?"

He nodded again. "Yes."

"Good," she said. "Now, with that said, I don't care *what* you're dealing with. If you *ever* drink again, I am *gone*. I am taking the kids. *We* are gone. I *will* get custody. We will be out of your life. Do you understand me?"

In her words, Gideon heard, first, a shred of hope. If she was threatening to leave if he ever drank *again*, that meant she was not yet gone. There was still a chance that this life they'd built could remain his.

"Okay," he said.

She had more conditions. He would find a therapist and start going to Alcoholics Anonymous meetings. He would face whatever legal charges would be brought against him, and they would not spend a dime of their family's money on his defense.

"You're going to get help," she said, "or you're going to get out of my life."

Gideon nodded. "Okay," he said. He went quiet for a moment. Addie sat there, waiting for him to say something more.

Finally, he spoke. "What if I can't?"

"Can't *what*?"

"What if I can't do it? What if I can't stop drinking?"

Later, Addie would say that she became certain, then, of something she had long suspected. Or maybe it was when she'd gone to pick up the car, and the police officers couldn't help but grin when they reported his blood alcohol level—*0.34!*—as if reporting a sighting of Bigfoot. Or maybe it was when they said, solemnly, we know he just got out of the military, and that can be so hard, and she told them yeah, he got deployed to Qatar, it's not like he fought in *Nam*. Or maybe it was later, when Gideon's parents had arrived, and they'd told him this was no big deal, that he was gonna be just fine, everyone has a few too many sometimes, right?

Gideon had been *coddled*.

From the moment he got accepted to West Point and became a hero, or the moment a girl first strained her neck to look up and meet his smile, or maybe even the moment he first threw a baseball harder than any other boy he knew, the world had worked to make way for him, lavishing praise on his accomplishments and explaining away his mistakes. The scouts saw his frame and trusted they could mold him into a star; the women he slept with and conveniently forgot to text back probably told themselves he was just busy; the parents whose marriage he'd long ago saved trusted that any consequences he faced were cruel overreactions from a too-harsh world. Even Addie had allowed herself to look away from some of his recent benders, using the stress of raising kids as a distraction from the alcoholism that threatened to swallow her family.

But now he was sitting before her, still unable to look her in the eye, her leviathan of a husband who'd never before looked so small. *What if I can't do it?* They would both realize, sometime later, that this was the first time he had ever acknowledged the possibility that he might fail at anything.

Addie held his hand in hers, for just a second, then stood up and walked toward the door.

"Fucking figure it out."

And so he did. Gideon saw a psychiatrist who prescribed an antidepressant and naltrexone, a drug that helps reduce alcohol cravings. Then he found a meeting at a church in a corner of the city where he'd never been. He entered a room bathed in fluorescent light, sipped weak midafternoon coffee, and stared at his feet while he listened to middle-aged men in suits and teenage girls in sweats all tell stories of how drinking had ruined their lives and sobriety had saved them. The whole time he said nothing. But at the end, they asked if anyone there was celebrating one month sober, or six months sober, or one year or five years or ten, and then they said that the next question was the most important one of all: Is anyone here celebrating twenty-four hours without drugs or alcohol? Gideon almost didn't stand up, because to stand up would be to admit that he belonged here, among the drunks and druggies. But then he was standing, and he was walking to the middle of the room, and he was taking that twenty-four-hour chip, and he was fighting back tears while he listened to applause.

-

From the first time he had picked up a baseball until he'd pitched his last inning, success had always held the same marker. Throw a strike on the next pitch. That was it. Strikes added up to outs, which added up to scoreless innings, which added up to wins. He had built his entire life around throwing that next perfect pitch.

Adulthood had robbed him of that single, clarifying quest. He was still obsessed with chasing success, but now he had no idea how to measure it. He had the same question at age thirty-three that he'd had at twenty-three and twenty-seven: Now that baseball was gone, what the hell was he supposed to *do*? For a while, success meant climbing the ladder of army rank, chasing the promise of a general's star on his chest. For spells of time, success had meant winning back Caroline, or getting the attention of the hottest woman in any room, or doing enough cardio to carve his abs into their most desirable form. After he got married, he wondered if success meant watching the number in his bank account rise, with each extra digit representing new levels of security for Addie and the kids.

Now, though, success held a simple definition: Get through the day without a drink. If that meant finding a midday meeting, if it meant sitting in his car and turning his chip over and over in his hands outside the gas station where he used to buy Steel Reserves, then success meant *that*. Sometimes, a day felt too long. So he changed the definition of success to surviving the next *thirty minutes*. He stacked half-hours into hours like he'd once stacked strikes into outs, days into weeks like outs into innings, weeks into years like innings into wins.

He watched Parker grow from a toddler to a preteen, Theo from a boy into a man. Gideon's hairline receded. Addie's love for him grew. Charlie the pit bull died, and they all mourned her. Gideon felt staggered by the loss of this creature who'd sat next to him in the wreckage of one marriage and had seen him all the way through to the repair of another.

Sobriety hadn't given him any easy answers. It only quelled the chaos in his home. Occasional loneliness persisted, and so did the nagging fear that whatever Addie and the boys needed, Gideon couldn't provide. His childhood favorite team, the Atlanta Braves, won a World Series, and Gideon couldn't watch a single pitch. Whenever he turned on a baseball game, he was reminded that some men's dreams were being fulfilled on that very diamond while his had vanished nearly twenty years ago.

When he was married to Caroline, he'd become convinced that she loved him for the ways he towered over every other man in their orbit—taller, smarter, better looking. This, after all, was why *everyone* had loved him: He was a human trophy, always on display. And maybe he was right. Maybe she had cheated when she'd encountered the one man who outshone him. Or maybe it was something else. Gideon knew that he had lost himself in their relationship, let his identity become subsumed by hers until he was no longer growing. "Our lives," she told him once, "got boring."

Gideon wished he could say that he knew from the beginning that Addie's love for him held a different shape. Or even that he'd learned it on that day that his buddy dropped him off drunk at their home. But really, it took years, and there was no single clarifying moment. He just began to wonder if maybe she'd been telling the truth on that first night when she had expressed her disinterest in his credentials, if she'd chosen him not for the ways he outshone lesser men, but for his empathy and curiosity, for the ways he cared for their children and noticed the parts of her that she kept hidden from everyone else.

And so, as the years passed, he still celebrated familiar markers of success. He got promotions and raises at work, became a key piece of a growing company, and lifted his family to greater financial security; he returned to the army as a reservist and climbed the ranks to lieutenant colonel with still more promotions on the horizon. But he tried to find other markers too. He built a retaining wall in their backyard, relying only on how-to videos he found on YouTube and the advice of a couple of employees at his neighborhood Lowe's. He raced to the top of Diamond Head crater while on army orders in Oahu. He learned to cook an absolutely perfect *risotto alla carbonara*.

A phrase worked its way into their shared language, a quick mantra whose surface meaning paled in comparison to what it meant in their home: *Lucky little life*. A Tuesday night at home, kids in bed, books in hand, fireplace burning. *Lucky little life*. A family hike on a Saturday morning, then everyone in the kitchen cooking together in the afternoon. *Lucky little life*. Maybe success meant finding more of these moments. Maybe it meant appreciating them whenever they arrived.

—

He asked Addie about it once. He couldn't help himself. They were lying in bed one night a few years after he'd gotten sober. They'd just had sex, and Gideon had felt particularly proud of his performance, and so he brought up her ex-husband and asked her the same question he'd asked Caroline about Connor all those years ago.

"So," he said. "Who has the bigger dick?"

"What?"

"Come on. Who's bigger? Me or him?"

Addie sat up a little. "Oh," she said as if she barely had to give it a second's thought. "His dick was definitely bigger."

And then she laughed, and Gideon said what the fuck, and she told him he shouldn't have asked if he didn't want to know the answer, and now she started laughing harder, and Gideon relented and started laughing too, you really know how to make a man feel special, and then she grabbed him and pulled his body into hers, and they lay like that for a while, and she said who cares, I like yours better, and Gideon supposed that he could accept this, that maybe his presence in her bed and his children running around the halls of her home all added up to some kind of victory, and he said whatever, okay, fine, as long as everyone is crystal clear that I *won*.

Acknowledgments

I am writing these words after I've just finished my final edits on this book, feeling overwhelmed by the courage, vulnerability, and trust offered to me by the four men whose stories fill its pages. *American Men* has taken me five years to complete, which has meant five years of me asking for access to the innermost pieces of Ryan's, Gideon's, Joseph's, and Nate's lives.

I will cherish the time I've spent with each of these men: Sitting in Ryan's living room, with Smoke curled up on the couch beside me, listening as Ryan wrestled with his relationship with his father and himself; walking by a pond near Gideon's home, four years after we'd begun this process, and peppering him with questions about the size of his penis, each of which he answered with laughter and without a moment's hesitation; sitting on the patio of a brewery in Joseph's city, listening to him recount the most horrific trauma a child can endure, then grabbing another round so we could talk soccer and politics for a while before parting ways; walking around the mall or sitting in its food court with Nate, eating bourbon chicken and drinking Pepsi, while he showed endless patience for my questions about his transition.

To each of these men: I am eternally grateful for your time, your generosity of spirit, your openness, and your friendship. Telling your stories has been one of the great honors of my life.

I'm also deeply grateful to the families of these men for the ways they invited me into their lives and granted the time and space required to tell these stories the way I believed they should be told. In particular, thank you to Anthony, Addie, and Emily.

My agent, William LoTurco, pushed me to pursue this project from the moment I mentioned it. I'm so thankful for his belief in me and in these stories, and for his work to help me hone what began as a vague idea.

From the moment I first began talking to Colin Dickerman at Grand Central Publishing, he asked the kind of incisive and probing questions that I knew would make this book the best version of itself that it could be. His patience, guidance, encouragement, and thoughtful edits were vital. I'm also grateful to Katherine Streckfus for her copy edits, to Albert Tang for designing the gorgeous jacket, and for Sean Moreau, Ian Dorset, and the whole team at Grand Central. I'm grateful as well to the team at Ringer Books for their support of this project and my other work at The Ringer, particularly Bill Simmons, Sean Fennessey, and Geoff Chow.

Rafe Bartholomew did a first pass of edits when this book existed in its rawest form. There are very few people on earth I would trust with my writing at that stage of the process, but Rafe has been a steady presence in my life for more than a decade, making me a better writer at every step. Shaker Samman fact-checked this book on an exceedingly tight deadline, saving me from myself at several points along the way.

I owe so much to so many of my colleagues at The Ringer for making me a better writer, reporter, and thinker every day. Mallory Rubin, may all writers be so lucky as to have an editor-writer relationship like the one I've had with you. Special thanks to the others who have edited me over the past few years: Vikram Patel, Ben Glicksman, Justin Verrier, Matt Dollinger, Isaac Levy-Rubinett, Megan Schuster, and Conor Nevins.

Even though this book is built on the stories of four men, so many other books helped to inform the approach, the questions I asked, and the ideas I explored.

American Men draws enormous inspiration from *Three Women* by Lisa Taddeo. That book showed me what fully immersive narrative nonfiction can look like, and how telling the stories of ordinary people and their relationship to gender can illuminate universal truths. Other books that shaped my ideas as I worked on this book include *The Will to Change: Men, Masculinity, and Love* by bell hooks; *The Right to Sex: Feminism in the Twenty-First Century* by Amia Srinivasan; *To Raise a Boy: Classrooms, Locker Rooms, Bedrooms, and the Hidden Struggles of American Boyhood* by Emma Brown; *Know My Name* by Chanel Miller; *Entitled: How Male Privilege Hurts Women* by Kate Manne; *How We Fight for Our Lives* by Saeed Jones; *Gender Trouble* and *Who's Afraid of Gender?*

by Judith Butler; *Female Masculinity* by Jack Halberstam; and *Heavy* by Kiese Laymon.

The following books informed the way I told Ryan's story: *There There* by Tommy Orange; *Carry* by Toni Jensen; *The Rediscovery of America: Native Peoples and the Unmaking of U.S. History* by Ned Blackhawk; *Indigenous Continent* by Pekka Hämäläinen; and *How to Be Gay* by David M. Halperin. Thanks also to the folks at the Akwesasne Cultural Center.

The following books informed the way I told Gideon's story: *Absolutely American: Four Years at West Point* by David Lipsky; *Beyond the Point* by Claire Gibson; and *The Art of Fielding* by Chad Harbach.

The following books helped to inform the way I told Joseph's story: *Trauma and Recovery* by Judith Lewis Herman; *Repressed Memories: A Journey to Recovery from Sexual Abuse* by Renee Fredrickson; *Redeployment* by Phil Klay; *The Forever War* by Dexter Filkins; and *Jesus and John Wayne: How White Evangelicals Corrupted a Faith and Fractured a Nation* by Kristin Kobes Du Mez.

The following books informed the way I told Nate's story: *Pretty: A Memoir* by KB Brookins; *Before We Were Trans: A New History of Gender* by Kit Heyam; *She's Not There: A Life in Two Genders* by Jennifer Finney Boylan; *Chef's Choice* by TJ Alexander; *Becoming a Visible Man* by Jamison Green; *Fairest: A Memoir* by Meredith Talusan; *The Myth of the Wrong Body* by Miquel Missé; *Transgender History* by Susan Stryker; *Conundrum* by Jan Morris; *Second Son* and *Transforming Manhood* by Ryan Sallans; and *Ponyboy* by Eliot Duncan.

During the years I was working on this book, the community around the Dayton Literary Peace Prize gave me experiences that deepened my passion for this work and sustained my energy to pursue it. I'm thankful in particular to Sharon Rab, Nick Raines, Alexander Starritt, Ariana Neumann, Susan Southard, Christy Lefteri, and Gilbert King. Similarly, I'm thankful for the continued support of friends connected to the University of California Berkeley Graduate School of Journalism, in particular Jennifer Kahn, Elise Craig, Allison P. Davis, Chris Ballard, and the "tiny, terrifying professor" I mentioned in this book's introduction, Lydia Chavez. Big thanks also to members of the Nashville journalistic and literary communities for their encouragement and support, in particular Becca Andrews, Steven Hale, Ben Howard, and Shannon Miller. Thanks as well to the crew at Southern Grist Brewing and Portland Brew East Nashville (RIP) for keeping me hydrated and caffeinated while I wrote so many of these pages.

I'm eternally grateful to the "Bible Study guys" for showing me what vulnerable male friendship looked like all those years ago, and for the ways they've remained cherished friends in the years since. I won't go name by name, because I've been told it's "not cool, man," to out you for your masturbation habits all these years later, but you know who you are.

At every stage of life, from early childhood through early middle age, I've been so lucky to have intimate, reliable, life-sustaining male friendships, and without them, I would not have been capable of writing this book. Special thanks to Beans, Beezy, Stevo, Phil, Oesch, Bradley, Darnay, the Tims, Stephen, Adam, Drew, and the others who've shown me what trust, openness, and love look like.

This book would not exist without the love and support of my family: my parents, Jeff and Anita Conn; my siblings, Elizabeth and Nathan Conn; my in-laws, Allen and Janice Ritter; Dan Ritter (who read and gave notes on an early draft of Ryan's story) and Byron Lu; and Andy Solomon.

No one has shaped the way I think about gender more than my wife, Beth Ritter Conn. Her influence is on every single page of this book. And no one has made me reflect more on my own relationship to masculinity than my son, Noah. You're not allowed to read this until you're at least in high school. But when that day comes, I hope you find some meaning in these pages.